Sicily's Rebellion against King Charles

Sicily's Rebellion against King Charles

The Story of the Sicilian Vespers

Translation and Commentary by

Louis Mendola

Copyright © 2015 Louis A. M. Mendola. All rights reserved.

Published by Trinacria Editions, New York.

This book may not be reproduced by any means whatsoever, either traditionally (print) or electronically (digitally), in whole or in part, including illustrations, photographs and maps, in any form beyond the fair-use copying permitted by the United States Copyright Law (in the first instance) and the Berne Convention, except by scholars in research reports or academic journals, without written permission from the copyright holder. Except for the original Middle Sicilian text of *Lu Rebellamentu* based on the *Spinelli Codex* (a medieval literary work in the public domain) and the poetry in Appendix 1, credit for authorship is claimed by Louis Mendola.

The right of Louis Mendola to be identified as the author of this work has been asserted by him in accordance with the Copyright, Design and Patents Act, 1988 (UK).

Some material contained herein, authored by Louis Mendola, specifically the chronology, several maps, and part of the text ("Prelude") relating to Sicilian history before 1280, was previously published in *The Kingdom of Sicily 1130-1860* © 2015 Louis A. M. Mendola.

Legal Deposit: Library of Congress, British Library (and Bodleian Libraries, Cambridge University Library, Trinity College Library), Italian National Libraries (Rome, Florence).

The title of this book was assigned a Library of Congress Control Number on 10 November 2015, when the ISBN of the first print edition was also registered in the United States of America. Under the effective date 10 November 2015 this book was pre-registered by the United States Copyright Office as number PRE000008355 in the class "Literary Work in Book Form." This book was first printed in 2016 in Italy and in the United States of America.

Illustrations, photographs, maps, genealogical tables, cover design and image editing by the author.

Printed in the United States of America on acid-free paper.

10 9 8 7 6 5 4

ISBN 9781943639038 (print)
ISBN 9781943639045 (ebook)

Library of Congress Control Number 2015957061

A CIP catalogue record for this book is available from the British Library.

IN MEMORIAM

Sir James Cochran Stevenson Runciman

1903 - 2000

Historicus sine pari

ABOUT THE AUTHOR

Louis Mendola is what used to be called a *polymath,* and he makes use of a multidisciplinary approach to decipher history.

His work has appeared in everything from books to academic journals to magazines. He co-authored *The Peoples of Sicily: A Multicultural Legacy* and he wrote a guide to historical research, *Sicilian Genealogy and Heraldry,* which established a new Dewey catalogue subject category in the British Library and the New York Public Library. *The Kingdom of Sicily 1130-1860* is a defining work as the first survey of the entire history of Sicily's monarchy from its foundation by the Normans until its annexation to Italy. *Knighthood and Feudalism in Medieval Sicily* is a point of reference as the first book in English dedicated to its topic. These books are found in the syllabuses of university courses that focus on Sicilian history.

Both scholar and popularizer, Louis Mendola is Sicily's most widely-published chronicler of medieval Sicilian history, standing out as one of just a few Sicilian historians whose work is known beyond Italian borders. Having researched in Italy, Britain, Germany, France, Spain and the Vatican, he has been consulted by the BBC, *The New York Times,* The History

Channel and the *Almanach de Gotha,* and lectured at New York University.

His first article dealing with the conflicts between Guelphs and Ghibellines was published in a scholarly journal in 1985, and his online articles have been read by millions since 1999.

He has been decorated by the Royal House of Savoy, the Royal House of Bourbon of the Two Sicilies, the Sovereign Military Order of Malta and the Imperial House of Ethiopia.

He is descended from a Sicilian knight who fought in the War of the Vespers.

PROLOGUE

"Justice belongs to the subjects who are ruled as well as the kings who rule them."

— Thomas Aquinas

Nobody noticed the gathering clouds.

Today was a holiday, after all, though with none of yesterday's ceremonies or pageantry. This year, 1282, Easter Monday fell on the penultimate day of March, the rainiest time of the year in Sicily, and by late afternoon large, gray clouds meandered across the skies over Palermo.

The revolt began outside the Holy Spirit Church, in a grassy field beyond the city walls when, according to the story's traditional telling, an Angevin soldier harassed a local woman. The woman's husband and some other men present attacked the soldier and his companions, who may have been drunk. Chaos quickly possessed the city on the Tyrrhenian.

"*Moranu li franchiskj!*" screamed one of the men. "Kill the French!"

Whatever spark ignited the violence, the hatred had been

festering for a decade. Any soothsayer worth his salt knew that it would boil to the surface sooner or later.

The mob flooded into the city through two poorly-guarded gates, the Mazara and New Saint Agatha's, which were usually open. The Balarah Souk was next, the angry crowd growing larger with each passing minute.

At this point the uprising was exploited by an embittered, vindictive baronage full of Swabian sympathizers nostalgic for the previous regime. But it didn't take much to goad the overtaxed citizenry into action against the vassals and bureaucrats left in Sicily by nasty Charles of Anjou, the absentee monarch who ruled the island from Naples.

Swords, daggers and long knives appeared as if by magic. Every peasant seemed to be armed. Mass fighting spilled into the vast labyrinth of streets and squares between the high ground of the imposing Norman Palace and the shore.

In Palermo, the streets were the key to everything.

You could gauge a street's importance by the way it was paved, or not. Most of the residential streets were little more than narrow paths that could accommodate nothing wider than a one-horse cart, or perhaps a flock of goats marching four abreast on the way to slaughter. All but untouched by sunlight, many of these streets curved slightly, especially those running along the rivers or the old Punic walls that traced the contours of the city's hills. More than one was a mere alley, ending abruptly with a stone wall.

The majority of the row houses in Palermo had at least two floors, even if the upper one was little more than a loft, and facades and supporting walls made of stone, and no gardens. Like the nameless streets they lined, these humble homes dwelled in shade and shadow.

There were wider commercial streets for metalsmiths, for shoe makers, for potters and bakers. There were streets for glass blowers, for bankers, for notaries, for fruit vendors and money lenders. There were unkempt market streets full of merchants. There were streets for nuns and streets for whores. If there was a need for it, Palermo had a street for it.

Daylight more willingly penetrated the wider stone streets and the paved squares around public buildings like churches. The city's main street was the broad Balat, so named by the Arabs for its marble stones. It followed a straight line from the harbor gate and thence through the center of town, past the cathedral and the ruins of the Roman *urbs* to the Norman Palace, where a square led to another gate, the Fatimids' Riyad, in the outer wall.

Not that much marble could be discerned in the Balat now, for most of the precious pavement stones had been stolen long ago, replaced during the last two centuries by the same gray slabs of the other streets. Said to be one of the longest straight urban streets in Europe, the Balat bisected the city.

In the chaos of today's revolt, destiny was calculated by the length and breadth of city streets. How many angry citizens could chase how many terrified Angevins along them. How much distance a frightened Frenchman could put between himself and the angry mob pursuing him while running through a slippery muck of mud and manure. How likely it was that a door along the street might open to offer refuge. To stumble was to die.

Today every street was a path to Hell.

Never in the Middle Ages had urban street-fighting occurred in anything like these numbers, not even in contested Jerusalem, whose streets bore an uncanny resemblance to Palermo's. It seemed that every Palermitan between sixteen and sixty was stabbing a Frenchman.

If for nothing but its sheer scale, the rioting was astonishing, and it knew no distinction between social classes or even, in many instances, sexes.

Early on, the justiciar, John of Saint Rémy, abandoned the

Norman Palace, fleeing to the countryside. Such French as could regroup put up a valiant fight involving dozens of men-at-arms around his residence near what is now Saint Ann's Convent.

Here the combatants were knights and esquires trained in the best martial tradition. These were elite warriors, men who lived by the sword and were proud to die by it. Ferocity was their stock in trade. In evidence were plenty of swords and a few shields, but there was no time to don armor.

For centuries, since time out of mind, the code of chivalry forbade the killing of knight by knight in a melée after the word of surrender was given. But today *chevalerie* was just another French word.

No prisoners were taken. Hundreds of Angevin defenders were felled. Down to the last man. Knights and esquires and pages. Even heralds, officers who usually enjoyed diplomatic immunity. But they were not the only French here in Italy's largest city.

The carnage continued. United by a singular fury, the frenzied Palermitan mob killed French men and women wherever they could be found. Even monasteries were not immune to the communal rage, and French monks and nuns were murdered in cold blood. There was at least one case of a Sicilian woman pregnant by her Angevin husband being cut open because her unborn child was French.

This was the day that chivalry died.

It was necessary to unmask the French, so the revolutionaries quickly devised a simple linguistic test. Those suspected of being French were ordered to pronounce the Sicilian word *ciciri,* for chickpea. Any Frenchman unable to pronounce it with an acceptably Sicilian accent instantly sealed his fate, and perhaps that of his wife and children.

From their commandery next to the Magione church, the Teutonic Knights, ever sympathetic to the Hohenstaufens who

Charles had defeated years ago, did nothing to discourage the butchery.

At hilltop Monreale Abbey the heart of Saint Louis, elder brother of King Charles, remained undisturbed, yet the stronghold was taken. The towers of its fortified Benedictine monastery afforded the rebels a commanding view of Palermo and its large port.

Just before dusk, the rebels seized control of the stalwart fortress guarding the harbor in the *Kala,* the bay. From this vantage point one could make out the Fatimid cupolas that dotted a cityscape dominated by mountains.

An occasional scream punctuated the constant din of distant church bells as darkness enveloped the seaside districts. The bells of the Martorana's tower continued ringing long beyond the few minutes needed to call the faithful to vespers. This evening the only faithful were priests and nuns, and even *their* faith might have lapsed in view of all the killing.

By nightfall, *vendetta,* that much overused word, had earned its place in the Italian vernacular, its legacy written in blood that flowed like so much water.

The passing hours saw the clouds above Palermo bathed in an ethereal glow. It was as if a giant halo hung over the city. The truth of the spectacle was far less heavenly — fire had been set to the Angevin armada docked in the harbor, along with the customs houses. The flames spread quickly as the winds increased. Care was taken to spare the merchant ships of the Pisans and Genoans, potential allies.

In the larger squares the ringleaders built bonfires fed by wooden boxes full of tax records, the rebels literally fanning the flames of popular discontent.

It wasn't long before wrath gave way to gaiety. There was singing and dancing to the music of minstrels. So much for the Palermitans' Paschal piety.

People were soon roasting hundreds of giant black Nebrodian boar they'd found in some pens near the Zisa palace in the lush Genoard park beyond the city walls. Wine pilfered from the royal cellars was being consumed by the gobletful, some of it from chalices stolen from the Palatine Chapel.

At a domed pavilion on the edge of a woods along the Kemonia River in another part of the park, some peasants freed around two dozen tall dogs that looked like shaggy greyhounds. The canines promptly ran off into the woods. That was the last time the Norman deerhound, the breed Sicilians called the *cerveru,* was ever seen in Sicily.

The only monks who hadn't fled the city were the Benedictines of Saint John of the Hermits, a monastery near the Norman Palace. The Greek clergy of the Martorana church partook of the general merrymaking, along with the rabbi of the nearby synagogue.

But not all were celebrating. In the general confusion, five mounted couriers loyal to King Charles managed to escape the beleaguered metropolis by fording the Oreto River. Their explicit order, uttered as the desperate behest of a dying Angevin knight on behalf of the bishop of Monreale, was to make their way eastward as far and fast as their Arabian steeds could take them, to warn Herbert of Orléans, the king's governor for Sicily, who was in Messina.

La vitesse de dieu. Godspeed.

These were unwed men who in the event of capture would have little to lose, except perhaps their own lives. They rode eastward at full gallop on a trek that would see them into the morrow. Their route would take them along winding roads muddied by the Winter rains, shadowing the rugged coasts, where giant rocks tumbled right into the sea, past the gaze of the snow-capped Madonian, Nebrodian and Peloritan mountains.

They knew well these roads, the slopes and twists and turns. They had travelled them dozens of times. But never in the dark of night.

Incessantly they rode, each armed with little more than his sword and the memory of the bloodbath he had witnessed in Palermo. Of friends now gone forever. Onward into the darkness. Past the church of the lepers, past the pleasure palace of Palermo's last emir, past the Phoenicians' ruined city at Solunto, past the remains of the Greeks' temple at Hymera.

Fleeing the nascent storm that threatened the world they knew, they rode farther and faster than the flashes of lightning in the foreboding clouds to the west. Not a moment was spent glancing back to check for pursuers. Only in alacrity was there a chance of survival.

Could they make it as far as Milazzo or Messina? Even with fresh horses every twenty miles, the journey would take many precious hours. By the time they reached Cefalù, though, it was clear the couriers would cover the distance needed to get word to the Angevins at Messina, the gateway to the peninsular part of the *Regnum,* The Kingdom.

Back in Palermo, amidst an almond orchard dividing the walled Kasr district from the seaside Khalesa, heavy raindrops pelted the red tile roof of the majestic Magione, the last church built by Sicily's Norman kings. Two Teutonic Knights stood guard in full armor at the church's entrance, ordered by their Commander, Nicholas of Tuynto, to keep intruders out.

Next door, in the commandery on the other side of a tiny cloister, three dozen feudal knights and barons met in secrecy in the Great Hall on the second floor, far from the eyes of the drunken populace. Joining them were the jurats James Simonide, Thomas Grillo, John of Lampo, Simon of Farrasio, Godfrey de Rosa and Michael fitz Frederick, members of the city council. The session, *lu parlamentu secretu contra re Carlu d'Angiù,* was expected to last all night.

None of the visitors had ever set foot in this inner sanctum of the secretive knightly order that functioned almost as a state within a state. Hanging on the wall beyond the head of a massive oak table in the middle of the cavernous chamber was a silver shield bearing the black cross of the Teutonic Knights. The legs of the table were fashioned from gray stone pillars removed from a nearby mosque some four decades earlier when Palermo's last Muslims were converted to Catholicism; on one was carved a Koranic verse in Siculo Arabic.

Pressed into service as scribes, four local notaries, one seated at each corner of the table, took copious notes: Frederick of Baldo, Peter fitz Tancred, John of Manso, Luke of Guidayfo.

The noblemen debated every detail, their eclectic Middle Sicilian tongue unlike any language that most of us would recognize today. In the men's faces were all the colors of Sicily. Eyes of blue or green or brown. Complexions light and dark. The blondish and reddish and brown hair of Swabians and Normans and Greeks and Saracens.

They bore names like Nicholas Ebdimonia, Roger Mastrangelo, Henry Baverio, Richard of Fimetta, Simon of Escula, Nicholas Ortoleva, Richard of Podio, Pascal Coppola, Cosmano of Fasano, William Ricici, Bartholomew Banker, William fitz Michael, Oddobono of Bagnola, Matthew Markisano, Richard of Galgano, Nicholas of Caltavuturo, John of Lonfredo, Rainier fitz Martin, Karo Palmer of Licata, Baldo of Salimbeni, Peter Faville, John of Bilé, Robert of Calvello, Walter of Caltagirone, Alaimo of Lentini, Palmer Abbati and William of Calatafimi.

Fueled only by adrenaline, most of the men in this tableau stood the entire time. This way, they need not ungird their long swords.

The younger men, some now still in their twenties, had been raised on tales of Frederick II, *Stupor Mundi,* "the wonder of the world," the monarch who died in 1250. Others, being a generation or two older, still remembered with fondness the most remarkable European ruler of the thirteenth century. Nobody seemed to think about eating or drinking.

As their first order of business, they organized bannerets, fully-armed units of knights, footmen and archers, to take control of the island's demesnial towns, beginning here in the west. Belonging directly to the crown, each of these large localities was defended by a mini-army of knights. Here the element of surprise would be an advantage, nay a necessity. On the other hand, a remote feudal village controlled by a solitary Angevin baron and a few unprepared knights or esquires was unlikely to put up much of a fight. Those tiny manors were a lesser priority.

The attacks would begin the following morning, come rain or shine. That these missions would entail killing was tacitly understood. That's what knights did; those present had done plenty of it this afternoon, and at least two of them were wearing tunics stained with blood.

Maps of the island were unscrolled, scrutinized and re-scrutinized. A few were tacked to the table.

The meeting was surprisingly orderly, so united were the barons in their sense of purpose. Some had waited long for this day. It was whispered that several even planned it.

All concurred that coastal defenses were a high priority. The hours passed. Every once in a while, three pages arrived to change the eight huge torches that illuminated the hall. Around midnight, the same pages served platters of rice balls, baked artichokes and roasted boar sent from the citizens of the Khalesa quarter nearby.

Roger Mastrangelo was elected, along with Ebdimonia, Ortoleva and Baverio, to govern Palermo as a free *commune* like the cities of northern Italy. Yet the Hohenstaufen flag was ordered flown from a staff atop the Pisan Tower of the Norman Palace, the highest point in Palermo, as a sign of allegiance to the heirs of fondly-remembered Frederick II.

It was nearly dawn, and still raining hard, before the most crucial element of the rebellion was discussed.

Now a mission occupied the barons that aimed to make their effort something more than a localized experiment in the creation of mischief. A diplomatic embassy had to be sent to Catalonia to their ally King Peter of Aragon, who was known to be assembling a fleet at Port Fangos that could challenge the large Angevin force Charles was gathering at Messina to attack Constantinople. At least three speedy squadrons should be sent, each equipped with multilingual emissaries. Hopefully, one would survive the voyage to Spain, a tricky undertaking in the choppy seas this time of year. It was imperative that they set sail within hours.

At sunrise, the barons strode across the cloister to the Magione church to hear the end of matins. The rain had stopped, and the city was quiet now. Only a crowing rooster broke the silence.

Before noon, a contingent made for Vicari's castle, set upon a craggy summit in the Sicanian Mountains, to negotiate with the fugitive justiciar. Unlike many of his compatriots, John of Saint Rémy was known for his integrity. He deserved fair treatment despite the sovereign he served.

The next day, Sicilian knights sent by Mastrangelo were reasoning with Saint Rémy, shouting proposals to the tower where he was lodged. According to the terms of the most recent offer, the justiciar was to be permitted safe conduct off the island. Just then, an overzealous archer fired an arrow upward into a loophole and hit Saint Rémy, killing him. So ended the negotiations. Mastrangelo would not be pleased.

The Teutonic Knights were far more disciplined than Sicilian archers. By cultivating serendipity, they could look forward to another two centuries in Sicily, their support rewarded by grateful Spanish kings. For the moment, however, it might be judicious to destroy any written account of the baronial meeting that had taken place in their commandery. The events of the previous day had shown just how suddenly power could change hands, and King Charles, should he ever return to Palermo, was more than adept at manipulating the subtleties of the written word to his own ends. Even for German warriors, discretion sometimes spelled the better part of valor. Knightly or not, official neutrality could be expedient in times like these.

By now, the Teutonic Knights of Sicily were long accustomed to concealing the truth. Upon being given the magnificent Magione church way back in 1194, their very first task was to destroy the tomb of Tancred Hauteville, Sicily's last Norman king, of whom Henry Hohenstaufen, the new sovereign — and the Teutonic Knights' patron — wished to erase every trace.

Whatever one could say about Charles of Anjou, the monarch was nothing if not calculating. But what to make of the populace? The Sicilians might seem like sheep, but the uprising proved that ruling them was like trying to herd cats.

The days passed and more Spring rains fell, nourishing the untamed snapdragons and wild asparagus in the green hills of the countryside. Peasants poached deer and boar in the king's forests. Woodlands like Ficuzza, near Corleone, were left unprotected with the departure of the Angevin justiciars. The town of Corleone itself became one of the first localities to fall to the rebels.

In mainland Italy, hearing reports of the loss of Palermo, Charles was not amused, but his worst nightmare was the forfeiture of the entire island. Sicily was worth a sleepless night or two.

In Catalonia, Peter, whose wife was a granddaughter of Frederick II, contemplated his dynastic right to rule the realm proffered by the Sicilian barons. Further afield, Michael, the Emperor of Constantinople, was happy to learn that Charles would now have to divert his attention, and his military efforts, away from the Byzantine Empire.

Before long, most of the royal garrisons around Sicily had surrendered: Trapani, Sciacca, Marsala, Girgenti, Milazzo, Mazara, Castrogiovanni, Taormina, Catania, Syracuse. Some offered only token resistance. At the large fortress of Caltanissetta, Raoul of Grollay, the castellan, capitulated to a small banneret, which proceeded to loot the premises.

At remote Sperlinga, which initially defied the rebellion by supporting the Angevins, the French garrison was permitted to depart for Messina which, defended by the Angevin fleet, held out for a time. By then, the death toll was believed to have soared into the thousands.

The vice-justiciar for western Sicily, the benevolent William of Porcelet, like Saint Rémy a Provençal, was escorted with his family from Calatafimi to the port of Palermo and permitted to leave. Not many of his countrymen had been as fortunate.

Herbert of Orléans was one of the few. He had taken refuge in Mategriffon, the castle built by Richard Lionheart almost a century earlier, and would be granted safe conduct.

Peter threw down the gauntlet. Charles was game to accept it.

And so began the crafting of legends.

PREFACE

"If history were taught in the form of stories, it would never be forgotten."

— Rudyard Kipling

Barely had the blood dried in the sullen streets of Palermo before the Sicilians were thinking of ways to commemorate their singular victory over odious King Charles of Anjou. It was important to record for posterity the bloody episode that began in the Sicilian capital in 1282.

A few years after the War of the Vespers, John of Procida, one of the revolt's leaders, approached a Sicilian monk to write about the events that led up to the conflict that altered the course of European and Mediterranean history.

Whilst the war itself was over, the political conflict still raged, to culminate formally, if only tenuously, with the Peace of Caltabellotta in 1302. Chronicles, the news media of their day, were being written from every possible point of view.

In mainland Italy, Saba Malaspina sympathized with the Guelphs of the Angevin camp. If the Angevins had any say in the matter, posterity would come to know only one side of the story. The Angevin side.

The onetime physician to Frederick II, John of Procida advocated for the opposing Ghibelline point of view. He had helped plan the revolt to place upon the throne somebody in whose veins coursed the blood of the Hohenstaufen monarch he had so faithfully served.

The monk's chronicle was to be Procida's memoir, and perhaps even his legacy. Unlike Augustine's fourth-century *Confessions,* it would be told in the third person.

Many of the chronicle's passages would imitate the prose style of the Bible. Here was unabashed *protagonismo,* the refined Italian art of placing oneself at the center of attention.

In retrospect, the chronicle may well be an early precursor of the captivating "literary" journalism popularized in the twentieth century by the Americans Gaetano "Gay" Talese and Thomas Wolfe.

In contrast to Malaspina's chronicle which, like most such works, was written in Latin for the benefit of the tiny literate class, Procida's memoir would be written in the spoken vernacular, Middle Sicilian. It was meant to be read, understood and enjoyed by all, bloody tales of violence being just as appealing to the medieval *hoi polloi* as they are to the modern one.

Here is how we read of the massacre of the French on that fateful Easter Monday in 1282 in the Latin of Saba Malaspina in his *Rerum Sicularum Historia* (Book 8, Chapter 5):

Irruunt ergo in gallicos tamquam in parietem inclinatam et impulsam maceriem et quos capere possunt interficiunt universos, sicque pereunt.

The Middle Sicilian of *Lu Rebellamentu di Sichilia contra Re Carlu* (Chapter 47) has a different resonance, something approaching the slightly melodious cadency we recognize in modern Italian:

Et intraru intra la chitati cum grandi rimuri et foru per li plazi, et quanti franchiskj trovavanu tucti li auchidianu.

In its modern telling the War of the Vespers has been portrayed as a taste of Armageddon, parlous as a morsel but fatal when swallowed whole. The chronicler's writing brings us a tale complete with elegiac praise heaped upon the shadowy anti-hero, for the story would be far less dramatic without the invisible hand of John of Procida. His role is what lifts us beyond the amphitheatre of apathy that is the typical medieval chronicle. The intensity, the urgency, are what touch the reader.

It is this timeless dramaturgy that still captures our imagination seven centuries later. Here we find the spy story, the swashbuckler, the wartime saga and the morality play in a work that transcends any single genre.

As a literary form, memoir itself was unusual in the thirteenth century. In the monk's account the protagonist was to be quoted directly in something approximating his actual words. This was a rare practice.

Poetry had been composed in Sicilian since the reign of the emperor Procida had once served, yet nothing like this narrative had ever been written in Sicily. Indeed, so far as we know, this kind of writing had never been attempted in Tuscan or any of the other Italic languages of its time. Dante's use of a new vernacular was decades away.

Occasionally attributed to the apocryphal figure known in recent times as "Athanasius of Iaci," *Lu Rebellamentu di Sichilia contra Re Carlu,* or *Sicily's Rebellion against King Charles,* is the earliest surviving narrative work of prose, as opposed to poetry, written in a language similar to what we now call *Italian.* With the chronicles of Malaspina, Neocastro and a few others, it forms the basis of our knowledge of the Vespers. Like all such chronicles, it is biased and frequently speculative, yet indispensable. With the poetry of Ciullo of Alcamo and Giacomo of

Lentini, it comprises an important element in the *corpus* of the earliest literature written in Sicilian.

Because "Athanasius of Iaci" was identified, or invented, only in the seventeenth century, and only in connection with a work thought to be an outright forgery, most historians consider the authorship of the *Rebellion* to be anonymous. As the work is a memoir, or highly similar to one, the chronicler's role was essentially that of an amanuensis.

Included in this book is the *Contrasto* of Ciullo of Alcamo, the lengthiest, most significant, surviving poem composed in Middle Sicilian as its original language and a symbol of the Sicilian School.

The *Contrasto* and the *Rebellion,* if considered together as the archetypal Middle Sicilian works in their respective categories (poetry and prose), represent opposite sides of the same coin, epitomizing two social elements that have come to define Europe's High Middle Ages in the popular mind, namely romantic chivalry and warring knights.

There are no incunable printings of the *Rebellion,* and not until 1791 was the *editio princeps* published. Yet this remarkable chronicle is the very cornerstone of medieval Sicilian prose literature.

The usefulness of this volume is threefold.

Firstly, on a historical level, the *Rebellion* can now be read and enjoyed by a global readership far greater than the fraction of one percent of the world's population fluent in Italian and the infinitesimal number of people proficient in Middle Sicilian, serving as an invaluable part of our knowledge of an important event while complementing works already published about the War of the Sicilian Vespers. Any student of history proficient in English, the *lingua franca* of our times, can benefit from this translation of the chronicle.

Secondly, on a literary level, the tiny canon of medieval Sicilian literature available in English translation has now grown to include the most important *opus* written in Middle Sicilian, itself an early influence on the Italian language. Unlike the great majority of books in its category, which provide translations only in the "target" language, this volume includes the original medieval texts of both the *Rebellion* and the *Contrasto,* as well as the English. Readers proficient in Spanish, Italian, Portuguese or Latin can probably comprehend at least some Middle Sicilian. The text of the *Rebellion* in Middle Sicilian is that of the *Spinelli Codex,* the oldest known manuscript of the chronicle.

The value of the *Rebellion* transcends the historiographical and literary realms, important as both are. For some of us, *Lu Rebellamentu di Sichilia contra Re Carlu* serves a third purpose. In expressing a tongue spoken in the thirteenth century, it touches the very identity of those of us descended from Italians, and especially Sicilians and Calabrians. Eclipsing any question of the veracity of the events the chronicle describes, reading the language spoken by our medieval ancestors is a personal experience. This is a priceless heritage.

Middle Sicilian is the language that was spoken in Sicily when the crusaders of Saint Louis marched down the streets of Palermo to place their monarch's heart in an urn in Monreale Abbey. It is the language that was spoken in Calabria when a pregnant Queen Isabella of France, the sister of King Peter III of Aragon, fell from her horse while fording a stream outside Cosenza. It was the language of kings and queens, knights and damsels, heralds and clerks, minstrels and troubadours, blacksmiths and farmers. It was the language of a people.

Beyond Sicily and the Italian peninsula, the chronicle's historical significance encompasses northeastern Spain, whose "Crown of Aragon" emerged as an important force in Mediterranean politics during the High Middle Ages. The multicultural medieval societies of Catalonia, Navarre and Aragon were strikingly similar to that of the polyglot Kingdom of Sicily under the Normans and Swabians. Indeed, several of the realm's queens hailed from that Iberian region.

The Crown of Aragon is directly relevant to the study of Sicily's history beginning in 1282. Palermo and Barcelona were essentially "sister cities" in this Mediterranean thalassocracy for the next century.

The chronicle is full of details. In a view echoed by Dante and Boccaccio, people in Messina expressed their esteem for King William II of Sicily a century after the monarch's death. Guy de Montfort and Hugh of Brienne, two of the most colorful knights of their time, led an attack on the coastal town of Milazzo.

The memoir of John of Procida offers us an object lesson in the ever-eclectic writing of medieval history, its vicissitudes and complexities.

Over the years, lengthy analyses based on sophisticated philological and historiographical methods have been published regarding certain Italian medieval chronicles. One that springs to mind is Evelyn Mary Jamison's magisterial *Admiral Eugenius of Sicily,* published in 1957, which considers the disputed authorship of the *Liber de Regno Siciliae,* the pseudonymous chronicle of "Hugh Falcandus," a man thought to be present at the royal court in Palermo during the twelfth century.

Conversely, the *Rebellion* has been all but ignored by scholars writing in English, even as the intricacies of the war it describes embrace wider themes concerning geopolitics, law and religion.

The Vespers re-drew the map of European power while laying the foundation of what later emerged as the Spanish Empire. At the same time, the Aragonese victory saved the Orthodox Church, which subsequently flourished in Greece and Russia, from integration into the Church of Rome. Whilst its immediate focus was Sicily, the conflict had repercussions on all three continents washed by the waters of the Mediterranean. Even the King of England played a role in the rivalry between the two monarchs fighting over Sicily. Aragonese rule reinforced the impetus of Sicily's perduring Latin monoculture.

An oft-overlooked element of the *Rebellion,* one involving a crime little changed since the thirteenth century, is revealed only in the chronicle's penultimate chapter, where we read about a rape that went unpunished despite a personal appeal for justice to an indifferent King Charles. The very last chapter is nothing less than a call for leaders to respect the rights of the people they rule, a principle as timely now as it was then.

It is fortunate indeed that texts like the *Spinelli Codex* have survived to be published, for many medieval manuscripts have long since vanished. In 1943, for example, German troops set fire to the greater number of the numerous, largely untranscribed, royal charters preserved in Naples, ignoring the fact that some of these documents were issued by monarchs of Swabia's Hohenstaufen dynasty, among whom *Kaiser Friedrich der Zweite.*

Somewhere in knowledge lies the key to power. Though romanticized, the *Rebellion* is a unique account by an "insider," a man who knew the principal players. It may not be entirely accurate, but it bequeaths us a contemporary perspective on the events of its era. To ignore it altogether is to imperil our potential for acquiring knowledge about one of the key events of the latter decades of the thirteenth century.

Buona lettura.

ACKNOWLEDGMENTS

"No man was ever wise by chance."

— Lucius Annaeus Seneca

Posthumous thanks are due Sir Steven Runciman, to whom this work is dedicated. We met over two decades ago, in what now seems like another lifetime, and he very kindly corresponded with me occasionally thereafter (this was before email was in wide use). Every ounce of his encouragement was very much appreciated.

It was Sir Steven who wrote *The Sicilian Vespers.* Published before I was born, it stands the test of time as the best overview of the topic ever written in English or indeed in any language, unsurpassed in either its insight or its eloquence. In 1958 it still seemed necessary for Sir Steven, ever the freethinking Cantabrigian, to debunk much of the propagandizing inherent in Michele Amari's book on the Vespers, first published in French over a century earlier.

Worthy of mention are my friend His Eminence Jacques Paul Cardinal Martin (1908-1992), Prefect of the Pontifical

Household, and my *confratello* His Eminence Alfons Maria Cardinal Stickler (1910-2007), onetime Archivist and Librarian of the Holy Roman Church, who made possible my consultation in the Vatican of some of the manuscripts translated here.

Among the living, those deserving of gratitude include Jacqueline Alio, my co-author on *The Peoples of Sicily*, and the staff of the National Library in Palermo, where I was permitted to study the *Spinelli Codex,* the oldest surviving copy of *Lu Rebellamentu di Sichilia contra Re Carlu* and the chief source for this book's translation. Thanks also to the staff of the splendid Aljaferia Palace in Zaragoza, which permitted me special entry to the residence of the Kings of Aragon on a rainy February day.

Any shortcomings which might present themselves in the pages that follow are, of course, solely my responsibility as *auctor et scriptor* of this work.

— L. Mendola

Montefranco, Sicily
November 2015

CONTENTS

INTRODUCTION

"One who is ignorant of what happened before his birth will always be a child."

— Marcus Tullius Cicero

The importance of the *Rebellion* transcends its brevity. Unlike most European chronicles of its era, it represents vernacular literature as well as political history. It is impossible to consider it in the light of one field while ignoring the other. The medieval form of the Sicilian language itself merits our consideration, perhaps even our esteem.

The Sicilian Language

Reigning from 1197 to 1250, Frederick II learned a respect for Sicily's peoples and religions, acquiring a working knowledge of Greek, Latin, German, French, Arabic and the new vernacular, Sicilian, influenced by all these languages. He was probably the first ruler of the island to speak Sicilian, and there exist a few verses of Sicilian poetry attributed to him.

More mellifluous and less guttural than its modern successor, *Middle Sicilian* (the author's term) was strongly influenced by Latin; Modern Sicilian, conversely, sounds rather like Catalan, a language introduced in Sicily with the Vespers. The author himself has noted this similarity during his travels in Catalonia, but not every language similar to Catalan sounds like Sicilian, and here Occitan comes to mind. Like Italy, Spain has a number of minority languages; Navarro-Aragonese went the way of Middle Sicilian, yet Basque has survived. (One of this book's maps identifies the regions and languages of what are now northeastern Spain and southwestern France in the days of the Vespers.)

Middle Sicilian, loosely defined, is the Romance language spoken in Sicily, Calabria (from Cosenza southward) and parts of Apulia until around 1380. By that time, a language was emerging that sounded rather more familiar as the Sicilian spoken during successive centuries. This, of course, is a gross generality, as most languages evolve slowly, over generations, not from one day to the next, and there are too few surviving documents written in Middle Sicilian during the fourteenth century to argue for a precise transitional date.

One that does survive is a Sicilian translation of a lengthy extract from Saba Malaspina's chronicle. *La Conquista di Sichilia fatta per manu di lu Conti Rugeri di Normandia,* or "The Norman Conquest of Sicily," was written in Cefalù in 1358 by Simon of Lentini, a monk reputed to be the confessor of King Frederick "the Simple." Like the *Rebellion,* this is an important contribution to our knowledge of Middle Sicilian, containing passages whose language is rather similar. Unlike the *Rebellion,* it does not offer much in the way of *original* information. Not to be overlooked, another significant text of this period is a Sicilian translation of Virgil's *Aeneid* from Tuscan by Angelo of Capua, of Messina.

Ciullo, or "Cielo," of Alcamo was one of the better known poets of the Sicilian School that found the epitome of its expression at the court of Frederick II. Here the sonnet was born, probably created by the prolific Giacomo of Lentini. It is quite possible that, had Frederick's dynasty (and Sicily's political importance) survived the thirteenth century, the modern Italian language we know today might be based on Sicilian rather than Tuscan.

Writing in 1985, the late Frede Jensen, one of the world's foremost Romance philologists, observed that, "The decisive role of the Sicilians in the development of a refined poetry in an Italian vernacular can hardly be over-emphasized. The Sicilian School is the fountainhead from which a splendid tradition has never ceased to flow." [1]

Ciullo's only complete surviving work is the *Dialogue,* variously known as *Rosa Fresca Aulentissima,* for its first phrase, or *Il Contrasto.* Most likely composed a few years before 1240, his poetry reflects the romantic age of chivalry in Sicily. To the ear, this poem sounds more like Tuscan than Modern Sicilian (see the excerpt in the following section).

While Lentini's voluminous *corpus* of work is far more significant if considered *in toto,* Ciullo's poem is the longest piece of poetry written in Middle Sicilian to find its way into our times. That is why it enjoys pride of place among scholars here in Sicily.

It has been suggested that most of the authors of the Sicilian School were notaries or scribes rather than full-time court poets. Differing from the majority of Sicily's chroniclers, most of whom were monks or courtiers, they took their inspiration from the itinerant troubadours.

The importance of the Sicilian School is recognized by Dante in his *De Vulgari Eloquentia* ("On Eloquence in the Vernacular") written early in the fourteenth century, where he quotes a line from Ciullo's poem:

Et dicimus quod, si vulgare sicilianum accipere volumus secundum quod prodit a terrigenis mediocribus, ex ore quorum iudicium eliciendum videtur, prelationis honore minime dignum est, quia non sine quodam tempore profertur, ut puta ibi: *Tragemi de'ste focora, se t'este a boluntate.*

By then, the prominence of the Sicilian language had vanished along with the polyglot kingdom that gave birth to it, even though works were still being composed in this tongue.

What vestiges of Middle Sicilian and its influences have come down to us? While linguists debate precise etymologies, at least a few hundred seem to be on solid ground. Here are a few examples.

A number of Sicilian words derive from Norman French: *buatta* (jar, from *boîte*), *custureri* (tailor, from *coustrier*), *largasia* (largesse), *racìna* (grape), *vuccèri* (butcher, from *boucher*), *accattari* (to buy, from *acater,* modern *acheter*).

And from Medieval Greek: *carusu* (boy, from *kouros*), *cona* (icon, from *eikona*), *crastu* (ram, from *krastos*), *pistiari* (to eat, from *apestiein*), *naca* (cradle, from *nake*), *bucali* (pitcher, from *baukalion*), *grasta* (a terracotta vase, from the classical *gastra*).

Among words from Middle High German we find: *arbitrari* (to work, from *arbeit*), *vardari* (to wait or watch, from *warten*), *sparagnari* (to save money, from *sparen*), *guastari* and *vastari* (to waste, from *wastjan*).

Provençal has made a few contributions, notably: *lascu* (thin or sparse, from *lasc*), *addumari* (to light, from *allumar*), *aggrifari* (to kidnap, from *grifar*).

Some words come directly from Arabic: *babbaluci* (also the Greek *boubalàkion*) for *lumache* (snails), *fatùk* and *fastùk* for pistachio, *saia* (from *saqiya*) for "canal," *gébbia* for "reservoir" and *azzizata* ("beautified") from a*ziz*. Other words rooted in Arabic: *favara* (a well), *mischinu* (an unfortunate person), *zagara* (orange blossom), *zammù* (anise), *balata* (stone), *cafìsu* (a liquid measure, from *qafiz*), *tarì* (a coin). The Italian *carciofo*, like the English *artichoke*, derives from the Arabic *kharshuff*, but the Sicilian word is *cacocciolu*.

Most words in common use in the days of the Vespers evolved over time, so the medieval *ipsu* and *illu* (he) have given way to *iddu* and sometimes even *iddru*. In Middle Sicilian young children were not *piciriddi* but *pichulilli*, and *casteddu* (castle) was *castellu*.

One or two words have found their way into our modern English vernacular; the Middle Sicilian *vindicta* which appears in the *Rebellion* arrived in the guise of the modern *vendetta*.

Legion are the words borrowed from Catalan after 1282, for example *sùsu* (upper) and *jusu* (lower). We also find a number of proper nouns; the Catalan *Boqueria*, akin to the Old French *bochier* (butcher), gave rise to the Sicilian *Vucceria*, the street market in Palermo where the church dedicated to Saint Eulalia, Barcelona's patron, is still the property of the Spanish Crown.

Apropos Catalonian influences, there are vestiges of Catalan Gothic architecture in Sicily, most notably the portico of Palermo Cathedral, whose lines trace those of Barcelona's magnificent Basilica of Santa Maria del Mar.

This is not the place for a sociological treatise. For the sake of historical context, however, it should be mentioned that until the middle of the thirteenth century most Sicilians were literate and many were multilingual. In multicultural Sicily there were speakers of Byzantine Greek, Siculo Arabic (similar to Maltese), Judeo Arabic, Norman French and Middle German, with Latin clerics (as opposed to those of the Byzantine tradition) fluent in Latin. Inroads were being made by the new Romance tongue, Middle Sicilian, that grew out of all these traditions.

Here we should seek to avoid the fallacies advanced by rabidly "Sicilianist" contrarians who claim a greater antiquity for

Middle Sicilian, as if it derived *directly* from Latin following the fall of the Roman Empire; conversely, contemporary chronicles inform us that when the Normans arrived in 1061 they encountered speakers of Greek (the liturgical language of the island's Christians) and Arabic (a dialect of which was also spoken by the Jews). That makes sense in view of Sicily's Fatimid and Byzantine heritage. Until around 1100 most Sicilians were described simply as "Arabs" or "Greeks." It was the Normans and the Church of Rome that latinized the language of the Sicilians during the twelfth century. Composed in Palermo around 1140 in Greek, Latin and Arabic, the Harley Trilingual Psalter in the British Library collection (Harley MS 5786) suggests the nature of the shift in language and the mechanism of the conversions of Sicily's Muslim Arabs to Catholicism.

A tenuous analogy might be made to Plantagenet England, where the Norman French tongue gradually introduced vernacular words of Latin origin into the spoken language. This is still obvious in blazon, the arcane language of heraldry; witness *argent two bars gules in chief three mullets gules,* the coat of arms of the Washington family of County Durham and later Virginia.

By 1800, most Italians were illiterate and most official records around Italy, not only in Tuscany or Sicily, were being recorded in Italian. Civil vital statistics records were instituted (in Italian) in Sicily in 1820. Rarely written, Modern Sicilian was the language of the common folk, even though aristocrats necessarily spoke it to communicate with people on the street and those who worked their estates.

Although our focus is Middle Sicilian, a few passing observations about Modern Sicilian follow in the next section.

The Translation

It is to be noted that the translation of the chronicle presented in this volume was effected *ex novo* by the author from the original Middle Sicilian, not from an intermediary text in a modern language (although Pasquale Castorina's Italian translation was consulted). A few passages may differ slightly from those translated by other authors, that being normal in this kind of work.

No effort has been spared to achieve accuracy. As regards language and historical context, special reference was made to the commentary and notes provided by several specialist scholars whose work is mentioned in the Sources.

In this type of *opus,* one hopes (and hope springs eternal) to avoid the pedantic and the semantic. Nevertheless, there will be those who gleefully take issue with the English translation of certain phrases. In the interest of clarity, the author has sought to avoid a literal translation of every word while respecting the literary quality of the original work. Even in today's Italian, certain words, such as *intanto* (most literally "meanwhile"), must be translated carefully, with an eye — and an ear — to context.

Ubiquitous are the inexorable idiosyncrasies of "canonical" English translations; to Russians the title of Ivan Turgenev's *Fathers and Sons* is understood as *Fathers and Children,* and the Italian *figli* likewise refers either to sons or to children generally regardless of gender.

As a historical chronicle, the narrative *per forza* had to be approached with profound respect for historical accuracy and social context. As an important literary work which must be understandable to the reader, it required more than a simple (literal) translation. In any case, it would have served little purpose to refer to the European region of the Byzantine Empire as the *Rumania* of the original text, and in this instance a simple note suffices in explanation.

Narrative prose is not poetry, but three distinct interpretations of Ciullo's poem (mentioned above and published in this volume) attest to the potential for individuality of expression, invariably influenced to a great degree by the era in which a work is being translated. In centuries past translators sought to maintain a poem's prosody and rhyme.

The original Sicilian:

Rosa fresca aulentissima chi apparj inver la state, le donne ti disirano pulzelle et maritate; trajimi di 'ste focora, si de'ste a boluntate; per te non aviu abbento notte e dia, penzando pur di vuy, madonna mia.

A close translation by the author in 2002:

"Rose fragrant and fresh that blooms in summer, maids and maidens envy you; deliver me from this raging flame. For you I have only restless days and nights, thinking always of you, my lady."

By Dante Gabriel Rossetti in 1861:

"Thou sweetly-smelling fresh red rose, that near thy summer art; of whom each damsel and each dame would fain be counterpart. Oh! from this fire to draw me forth, be it in thy good heart, for night or day there is no rest with me, thinking of none, my lady, but of thee."

By Lorna Lancaster de'Lucchi in 1922:

"Oh fragrant rose, born on a summer's day; thou dost both damsels and dames with envy sway. Out of this furnace flame, sweet, rescue me, I pray; from thoughts of thee madonna, I ne'er cease; and day and night I am bereft of peace!"

The precise (or intended) meaning and use of certain Sicilian words known during the Middle Ages eludes academic consensus, sparking spirited debate. Middle Sicilian differs from Latin, whose diction is more or less universal; true, scholars debate the meaning of words like *servus* ("slave" or "serf," depending on context), but rarely is an entire passage from, for example, the work of Peter of Eboli or "Hugh Falcandus" disputed *ad nauseam.* Possible errors in transcription from the earliest manuscripts are also problematical, and (unlike Tuscan) thirteenth-century Sicilian, with its dearth of contemporary writings for comparison, offers very few orthographical samples to consult. So few are the manuscripts that survive in Middle Sicilian that they almost seem to reflect a *sui generis* "secret code," and that was more than sufficient reason to publish a translation of the *Rebellion.*

Offering a glimpse of Middle Sicilian, this book's concise Glossary provides translations based on the context in which certain words are used in the chronicle.

A central challenge is the fundamental difference between Middle Sicilian, which is not entirely dissimilar to Tuscan, and the "bastardized" Modern Sicilian (with its localized and Catalan influences) spoken today. This, as stated earlier, need not concern us at length, but the reader should know that it enters into discussions among Sicilians in Italy, partly because, with few exceptions (such as Giuseppe Pitrè) scholarly study of this largely-unwritten language was rare until the twentieth century.

Tuscan already held sway by 1400, even if we find Sicilian words *passim* in various records (such as notarial acts and *riveli,* the rolls of the *donativo* tax) into the seventeenth century. Francis of Assisi composed a prayer in an early Italian, but it was only during the twentieth century that the Vatican approved languages other than Latin for use in Catholic liturgy.

The unification of Italy in 1861 was a further impetus in officially discouraging the use of what had become regional languages, the theory being that a single Italian language (based on Tuscan) would unite the Italians; more about this later.

Philological debate continued. Examples of this phenomenon are myriad, but here is one from our time.

In the Sicilian text *misser* appears for *lord* or sometimes "my lord." This obviously derives from French, be it via the Normans or the Angevins, witness *monsieur* and the more medieval *mon seigneur,* as well as the English *sire* and *sir.* But it is not altogether unusual, in the streets of Palermo, for a Palermitan to seek one's attention by shouting out a word that sounds like *misser.* Nowadays, this has been corrupted to the English *mister,* a word popularized in Italy a few decades ago when the coaches of many football (soccer) teams were British, and thus addressed in this way. Beyond the Italian obsession with football, *mister* has gained currency as an occasional substitute for the Italian *signore,* at least in casual parlance. More formally "my lord" is the more modern, but no less obsolete, *vossìa,* short for *vostra signoria,* literally "your lordship."

In Modern Sicilian we find hundreds of similar examples in everyday use. Imagine the bewilderment of the non-Sicilian from Piedmont or Tuscany who seeks to interpret the nuance of a spoken word as simple as *piciriddi* (boys, children), or a mundane phrase like *lu pisciottu dabànni*, "the young man over there." Some words, like *maniscalco* (blacksmith), for which the Italian is *ferraro,* are now rare. Then there are common words like *parrinu* (priest) and, until recent decades, *fuitina* (a kind of elopement).

Some words are readily understandable in context; *figghiu* is *figlio* (son), *beddu* is *bello* (beautiful), *vastasu* is *sgarbato* (rude), *chistu* is *questo* (this), *nuddu* is *nessuno* (nobody), *joviri* is *giovedì* (Thursday), *cona* is *icona* (icon). However, words like *camurrusu* (annoying), from which *cammuria,* and *cajordu* (vile and dirty) have no direct cognates or translations in Italian. To this day, Sicilian has no universal spelling or pronunciation, nor a true future tense, and localized dialects of the language are spoken (albeit to an ever diminishing degree) in Palermo, Catania, Trapani, Caltanissetta, Agrigento and Syracuse. Even localities like Mussomeli and Caltagirone have some of their own words and phrases, and the very meaning of certain words varies from town to town.

Returning to the complexities raised by Sicily's medieval language, it is obvious that a vernacular tongue lacking a standard orthography or spelling presents challenges even in simple transcription, apart from the question of one scribe or another mistranscribing items which may be unclear in the original manuscript. In the *Rebellion* we find the same word spelled differently in various passages, so *chi* is sometimes *ki* (more about this below). We find distinct spellings preferred by various scribes and scholars, such as the more Sicilian *lictri* instead of the more Tuscan *littiri* (letters). Indeed, we find linguistic disagreements among nineteenth-century philologists.

Orthography constitutes a field in itself. In Sicilian a classic usage is the writing of *x* for the digraph *sc,* similar to the English *sh*, hence *Xacca* for Sciacca (a city in Sicily). In the *Rebellion* we find *inbaxata* for what in Italian is now *ambasciata* (embassy) and *nixunu* rather than *nissunu* or, in modern Italian, *nessuno* (nobody).

In practice, pronunciation (and spelling) in the Italian languages is almost purely phonetic; words are spelled as they are pronounced. It was through pronunciation that the male definite article *lu* of Middle Sicilian became *lo* in the languages of central and northern Italy.

Paleography is still another field of study relevant to this work. The Middle Sicilian text in this volume makes use of the original medieval spelling and (so far as typesetting permits) diacritical marks, which are particularly evident in the *Spinelli Codex* consulted by the translator, rather than the slightly "italianized" orthography of later manuscripts, and so we find frequent use of the letters *h, j, k* and *y.*

Except for Ciullo's *Contrasto,* the translations in this volume are original, and even the existing translations of the *Contrasto* were edited for clarity for this publication. A point to be reiterated is that, unlike the work of Dante or Boccaccio (or the Bible or the Koran), there really are no standard, "quasi-canonical" English translations of Middle Sicilian texts, Ciullo's poem arguably being the nearest thing to such a paradigm.

As stated earlier, the translation of the *Rebellion* in this book is based on the *Spinelli Codex,* which is the oldest text known to us and makes use of the original Middle Sicilian spelling, orthography and diacritical marks. The division of the *Rebellion* into chapters follows Pasquale Castorina's transcription and translation of the "Catania Codex" published in 1882, thus permitting the reader a basis for comparing the Middle Sicilian text to a modern Italian one.

The texts of the various codices are not without their differences, most due to simple mistranscription errors centuries ago. In Chapter 26, for example, the *Spinelli Codex* uses the phrase *alcunu modu* ("some way") while the "Catania Codex" uses the wording *a lu mundu* ("to the world"), the latter propagated in Castorina's Italian translation. Another mundane difference occurs in Chapter 45, where the Spinelli text refers, accurately, to *Munti Flascunj,* the town of Montefiascone near Viterbo, while the Catania text gives us *Munti Falcuni* ("Mount Falcon"). The other manuscripts also contain errors of this kind (see note 41), and this is one of the factors that argues for the prior antiquity of the source of the Spinelli text.

In practice, there was never any question but that the *Spinelli Codex,* of which the Catania text is nothing more than a modern copy, should be the basis of the first English translation to be published. Filippo Evola's verbatim transcription of the *Spinelli Codex* is accompanied by eighty-four end notes explaining every detail, including the manuscript's occasional inconsistencies in grammar, and this was the basis for Enrico Sicardi's transcription a few decades later. Nevertheless, Castorina's fine Italian translation, which is generally accurate, served as a good "control sample" in translating the Middle Sicilian text.

Within the manuscript there is frequent variation in spelling. We find "Catalonia" spelled *Cathalogna* and *Catalogna.* We encounter "John" spelled *Iohanni* but sometimes *Iohannj,* and we likewise encounter *chi* and *ki* as well as *kj,* and *mari* as well as *marj.* In Chapter 38 we see "emperor" spelled *inperaturi* and then, just a few words later, *imperadurj.* In this book's transcription of the Sicilian text, most of these idiosyncrasies have been retained so that what the reader sees is faithful to the earliest known manuscript; that includes *Missina* (Messina) occasionally spelled *mMissina* and *loru* (they) sometimes spelled *lloru,* as well as both *ligatu* and *legatu* (legate).

Some similar words, such as *dananti* and *davanti,* have subtly distinct meanings which are largely insignificant in translation. A few verbs seem to have been conjugated incorrectly by the narrator; Enrico Sicardi suggested that in the first paragraph of Chapter 55 the verb form *putirinj* identifies the chronicler as a Sicilian, perhaps even a Messinian, through use of the first-person plural.

The manuscript provides us with no punctuation to indicate quotations of dialogue (this has been added), but spoken words are very clear from the context of each passage. Moreover, in the Sicilian text of this volume entire words are written where the manuscript abbreviates these through the use of diacritical marks; this necessitates a fundamental knowledge of paleography. For example, *Cãlu* is understood to be *Carlu.* Orthography of some words is less obvious; the first two characters in the word *xpranissimu* (literally "most Christian") come from the traditional XP monogram of Christ, based on the first two letters of the Greek *Cristos.* We see something rather similar with the word *cristianitati,* "Christendom," written in the manuscript as *xanitati.*

Et cussì fu factu. "And so was it done." The prose style of the *Rebellion* is quasi-biblical by intent; readers should not presume that speakers of Middle Sicilian spoke that way most of the time. The prose is sometimes inconsistent grammatically; hence we find the singular, familiar *tu* appearing alongside the plural, formal, *vui* or *vuy* (the *voi* of Italian) in the same sentence when addressing the same person as "you."

Neither of these stylistic characteristics so obvious in the Middle Sicilian text are very evident in the English translation, where some subtle elements are absent.

This volume presents a verbatim transcription of the entire text of the *Spinelli Codex* featuring clear orthography (distinguishing between the letters *v* and *u* and other characters), and quotation marks indicating dialogue. Some of the other published transcriptions corrupt (or "correct") the spelling or insert various passages extracted from other manuscripts.

The Sources describe the various texts and analyses consulted in the preparation of this work. In the interest of accuracy, this book, like others written by the author, relies principally on "primary" (contemporary) sources rather than those published later, which in some cases, like the chronicle attributed to "Athanasius of Iaci," may be apocryphal.

In the English text most spellings are American, albeit with some nuanced exceptions, so *honor* is a verb while *honour* and *favour* are nouns. The British sovereign, after all, bestows *honours,* not *honors.*

The History

In its original form, the *Rebellion* was probably authored in Sicily between 1286 and 1294. Little is known of its chronicler except that, based on his writing style, he was probably a monk. This would not be exceptional; most medieval chroniclers and scribes were clerics, from which the term *clerk.*

It would be surprising if the chronicler had not written other material besides the *Rebellion,* but his anonymity, and the scarcity of Middle Sicilian texts, both preclude investigation into this.

An apocryphal work that survives only in modern copies is sometimes attributed to the author of the *Rebellion.* The succinct *La Vinuta di lu Re Iapicu in Catania* ("The Arrival of King James in Catania"), reputedly penned around 1295, recounts the arrival of young King James of Sicily in that city in 1287. A "reconstructed" text of the *Arrival of King James* thought to be faithful to the Middle Sicilian prose of a putative (as yet undiscovered) original was published in Chapter 2 of Pasquale Castorina's *Catania e Dante Alighieri* in 1883. It is here, in citing the supposed similarity between this text (as he believed it probably existed in a medieval form rather than its modern incarnations) and the style of the *Rebellion,* that Castorina affirms a certain "Athanasius of Iaci" as the author of *both* chronicles.

But was that, in fact, the name of the author who wrote the *Rebellion,* or indeed *any* chronicle of proven medieval provenance? Did a monk named "Athanasius of Iaci" even exist during the thirteenth century?

First adduced publicly by Vincenzo De Gaetano in 1898, a hypothesis which is now generally accepted in scholarly circles (both historic and philological) posits that the earliest known copy of the *Arrival of King James* is, in reality, an *ex nihilo* forgery composed by Pietro Carrera (a priest, poet and chess master) around 1638. Obviously, this calls into question the existence of a person named "Athanasius of Iaci," first identified by Carrera as the author of the *Arrival of King James.* In theory, the *Arrival of King James* could well be *inspired* by a medieval codex, now lost, but only the discovery of such a manuscript would resolve this contentious question. Until then, the authenticity of the text known as the *Arrival of King James* can be accepted (if at all) only with the greatest equivocation, and for that reason it is not included in this book.

Whilst the question of the historicity of pseudo-Athanasius must be considered *pro forma* in historiographical discussions such as this one, it is not relevant to the authorship of the chronicle published in these pages because, even were pseudo-Athanasius identified conclusively as an actual historical figure, that would not, in itself, establish him as the author of the *Rebellion* as Castorina propounded.

At the end of the day, the name of the chronicler of the *Rebellion* is not extremely important. He was most likely a Sicilian monk resident in Sicily after 1282 who knew John of Procida or one of his sons. Here we find an enigma rather similar to the controversy surrounding the identity of the chronicler known as "Hugh Falcandus," author of the *Liber de Regno Siciliae.*

A rose by any other name.

The autograph of the *Rebellion,* the manuscript written by the chronicler himself, is not known to exist.

Two Tuscan manuscripts of the *Rebellion* were written after the *Spinelli Codex,* namely the "synoptic" *Liber Jani di Procida et Palialoco* and the *Leggenda di Messer Gianni di Procida.* A total of nine manuscripts survive (in Italy, Spain and the Vatican), the *Spinelli Codex* most likely having been copied from the autograph written by the hand of the chronicler known to John of Procida; here the language is the least adulterated.

It should be noted that others besides Saba Malaspina wrote contemporary chronicles that describe the Vespers at some length. Bartolomeo of Neocastro and Niccolò Speciale were Sicilian, and the former, a judge present at Messina in 1282, lived through the war. Tolomeo of Lucca lived farther away from the action, and Giovanni Villani was still a child in 1282. In his detailed chronicle, the Catalan Bernat d'Esclot (Desclot) wrote an excellent contemporary account, with a focus on the role of King Peter, although the work of his eloquent countryman Ramon Muntaner was written later. Dante, it should be remembered, was a Guelph apologist, and this colored his views about everybody from Frederick II to contemporary Pontiffs.

Dino Compagni, like Dante a Guelph, was one of the first writers to advocate for an Italian vernacular in chronicles as well as poetry. His *Cronica delle Cose Occorrenti ne' Tempi Suoi* is nearly contemporary to the *Rebellion.*

Significantly, both Boccaccio and Petrarch, each born just a generation following the Vespers, accepted the *Rebellion* as essentially accurate and authentic. Its influence on Italian poets is perhaps comparable to that of the texts in the Auchinleck Manuscript on the English writers of Chaucer's generation. Indeed, it is quite possible that Geoffrey Chaucer, himself an early influence on the English vernacular tradition, met one of these two Italian poets; at the very least, he knew their work.

However, whereas William Caxton was publishing Chaucer's work by 1478, the first printing of the *Rebellion* was, as we have seen, long in coming.

Among publishers, the importance of the *Rebellion* was recognized in the sixteenth century, when Tommaso Fazello, "the father of modern Sicilian history," wrote his monumental *De Rebus Siculis.* This is significant because a handful of revisionists writing after 1800 (most notably Michele Amari who we shall meet shortly) would have us believe that "reliable" general histories of the War of the Vespers, such as their own books, appeared only in more recent times.

In his *magnum opus,* Fazello describes in some detail the uprising and the involvement of John of Procida. We read, at the outset, of the physician's presence in Sicily based on information drawn from the very first paragraphs of *Lu Rebellamentu.* In Fazello's words: *Erat eo tempore in Sicilia Ioannes Prochytae.* Indeed, Fazello's colorful narrative is the source of most descriptions of the War of the Vespers published today. Despite the contestations of a few later historians who cast unwarranted aspersions upon Fazello's work, these few pages are just as tenable in our time as they were centuries ago.[2]

Historiography evolves over time. If the history of the War of the Vespers as a signal event engenders eclectic opinions, so does the *Rebellion* as a historical work. Everything from the provenance of the earliest surviving manuscript, a copy dating from around 1330 if not somewhat earlier, to the style of the writing has been hotly debated.

Vehement Michele Amari, whose opinions were parroted abroad by the likes of the Earl of Ellesmere (Francis Egerton), petulantly declared the *Rebellion* to be unreliable as a chronicle. That position, which held sway in Italy for decades following Amari's death in 1889, was greatly influenced by the Risorgimentalist views espoused by Amari and his partisans, who sought in the War of the Vespers a facile metaphor for the Italian unification movement of their own era. The hypothesis that the uprising of 1282 might have involved even a modicum of prior organization detracted greatly from the credibility of the image of a spontaneous "popular" revolt favored by Amari and his ilk. In the event, a certain degree of planning and international intrigue, some of it seeded by Amari himself, facilitated Garibaldi's invasion of 1860 just as it did King Peter's 578 years earlier; to claim otherwise is disingenuous.

In the wake of this wave of criticism, the prestige of the *Rebellion* was tainted by the sordid revisionism (or "historical denialism") that reigned in the Kingdom of Italy into the twentieth century. The young nation's segue to Fascism formed the framework of a rabidly nationalist, "Italianist" view of history that was the very antithesis of cosmopolitan historiography. In this bizarre milieu Amari's history of the Vespers was enshrined as an immutable truth. Unfortunately, this kind of apologia still characterizes much Italian historiography, where "confirmation bias" is the order of the day.[3]

Every now and then, an outspoken historian summoned the courage to express his own view. One of these rare birds was Enrico Sicardi. Writing in 1917, he accepted the *Rebellion* to be essentially factual, and contemporary to the era it describes, yet even Sicardi repeated the popular misconception, supported by Amari, that the *Arrival of King James* (mentioned above), with its pseudo-medieval language and its bizarre version of history, was a genuine piece of medieval literature.

As part of Italy's nationalist trend, languages like Sicilian were disparaged as "dialects" of Tuscan Italian. This belied reality because regional languages, far from being esoteric, were part of everyday life in Italy long after unification. Vittorio Emanuele III (1869-1947), the penultimate King of Italy, whose parents were both Savoys born in Turin, was fluent in Piedmontese, yet Italian officialdom feared regional languages as a threat to Italy's fragile national unity rather than part of an adiaphorous heritage. Times change, and several of Italy's regional languages are now recognized by UNESCO as an important cultural patrimony.

The vestigial effects of Italy's blind nationalism poisoned the academic sphere long after the establishment of the Italian Republic in 1946, if only because many tenured professors educated, and indoctrinated, under Fascism were still teaching history and literature until around 2000. By then, of course, the advent of the internet had begun to make a mockery of censorship. (See Appendix 4 for observations regarding pseudohistory and censorship in Italy into recent decades.)

No wonder it was a foreigner educated *outside* Italy, erudite Steven Runciman, who stood among the first to accord the *Rebellion* serious consideration as more than a work of literature. Not that he was alone; for a score of years following the end of the Second World War, the Siculophiles writing most cogently about the island's Norman and Swabian dynasties were foreign scholars like Evelyn Jamison (1877-1972).

Indeed, the more zealous detractors have seized upon rare inaccuracies in the *Rebellion* as "proof" of its unreliability. Sir Steven sagely conceded that it had value despite the kind of flaws regarding names, dates and details that appear in many a medieval manuscript. He correctly notes that John of Procida was in Barcelona witnessing documents issued by the King of Aragon when, according to the *Rebellion,* he was elsewhere.

At all events, virtually every significant fact reported in the *Rebellion* is confirmed by the documentary record, and many reflect details that could have been known only by somebody at court. One example among many is the betrothal of a child of Emperor Michael of Constantinople to a child of King Peter of Aragon. Mentioned in Chapter 32 of the *Rebellion,* this is the subject of a letter issued by King Peter in Palermo on 20 September 1282.

Whatever one thinks of it, the *Rebellion* keenly reflects the spirit of its times, the sentiments and geopolitics that led to what some have described as "the 'world war' of the thirteenth century." A glance at this book's map showing the patchwork of alliances and territories in southern Europe in 1282 will suffice to support such a characterization. This is not to suggest that the Vespers revolt was merely a pretext for the Aragonese invasion, but the Angevins and Aragonese (along with the Byzantines, Arabs, Genoans, Venetians and Pisans) were vying for control of the contested Mediterranean long before 1282.

In these pages the Kingdom of Sicily (which existed into the nineteenth century), the *Rebellion* and Middle Sicilian are not defined "dialectically" in relation to the unitary Italian state established in 1861 and the Italian (Tuscan) language. All three existed in Sicily independently of those developments.

It is not the purpose of this book to offer an exhaustive analysis of the various chronicles of the War of the Vespers or to take sides in prolix debates running to many thousands of pages, but rather, in removing the boundary of language, to provide a resource for scholars along with a concise syllabus which may serve as a springboard for further study. *Lu Rebellamentu* is an invaluable contemporary historical source for the War of the Vespers, to be considered in tandem with others, such as the chronicles of Malaspina, Neocastro and, regarding the period more generally, Salimbene di Adam. As the first narrative work of prose (rather than poetry) written in an Italian language that has been handed down to us, it would have great literary value even if it were nothing more than historical fiction. It stands on its own merits. We need not be overly concerned with what was written about it generations after the death of John of Procida.

"His friends will be your friends, and his enemies will be your enemies." That line by John of Procida (from Chapter 31) is one of several which might have made their way into our modern canon of quotations had the entire text of the *Rebellion* been translated before the twenty-first century.

A few words about its protagonist are in order.

John of Procida

Born in Salerno around 1210, John of Procida was educated at that city's medical school. His family, which had held the island of Procida as a fief since Norman times, had large estates around Salerno and Naples. John was granted still more lands. His blood was the bluest blue, but as an intellectual his fame was deserved.

He became the chief teacher at the medical school, which was then one of the finest in Europe. One of his patients was Cardinal John Orsini, the future Pope Nicholas III.

For a number of years, John of Procida was the personal physician to Emperor Frederick II, travelling with him extensively and becoming one of the most important diplomats in his service. Indeed, much of Frederick's achievement as a great ruler must be recognized in the brilliance and pragmatism of people like Procida.

He became an advisor to the monarch, being entrusted with the education of his son, Manfred, who as king made him his chancellor.[4]

Procida is thought to have been with Manfred Hohenstaufen at the Battle of Benevento in 1266, which saw Manfred's defeat and death. The same year, he betrothed one of his daughters to the son of a prominent Neapolitan Guelph (Angevin supporter), even though John himself was devoted to the Ghibelline (Hohenstaufen) cause.

Longstanding tradition has it that John was present in the crowd at Naples when Conradin Hohenstaufen was executed following the decisive Battle of Tagliacozzo. Afterward, John found refuge in Venice. King Charles divested him of his lands, and one account tells us that John's wife and daughter were raped by the Angevin knights sent to evict them, who also murdered one of his sons.

The episode recounted in the *Rebellion* differs slightly. Here, in a passage devoid of linguistic nuance, we learn that John sought justice from King Charles for a daughter who was violently raped by an important baron. The plea fell on deaf royal ears. This touches upon a social issue that is important for all time, whatever language we speak. In 1231, the Constitutions of Melfi made rape a serious felony; this law eventually fell into disuse, and Italy made rape a felonious form of personal assault only in 1996 (sic).

To the modern reader, this detail about the suffering of a rape victim is one of the most relevant aspects of the chronicle, whose very last chapter admonishes those who govern to defend personal liberties. Historians have tended to focus on the general policies advocated by Charles I, yet this poignant point transcends the subtleties of medieval geopolitics.

The years 1269 and 1270 found John of Procida in the Imperial lands seeking support for an insurrection against King Charles. Here he encouraged Frederick of Thuringia, a grandson of Frederick II (through his daughter Margaret), to claim the Kingdom of Sicily by right of the Hohenstaufen patrimony and invade Italy. Unsuccessful in persuading Frederick of Thuringia to embark upon such a campaign, John sought out Hohenstaufen descendants further afield.

By 1279, according to the *Rebellion,* the only chronicle that offers much insight into the planning of the uprising, John was in Sicily encouraging dissent among the disgruntled nobility. This is where the chronicle picks up the story of one of the most remarkable men of this time.

However, there remains great doubt regarding the extent of John's travels from 1279 until 1282. It is quite possible that one of his sons, either Thomas or Francis, undertook at least part of the mission at John's behest. John's younger brother, Andrew, also figures in the story of the War of the Vespers.

In 1283, Peter of Aragon made John his chancellor, leaving him on the island as its *de facto* viceroy. King Charles II restored John's feudal lands in 1295. Three years later, just before his death, John of Procida seems to have been pardoned by the Papacy.

Having travelled around Italy and the Mediterranean and having served at three courts, John was one of the key "power players" of his age. Modern historiography has recognized him as one of the first *diplomats* or *politicians* as we understand those words today.

Much legend surrounds his life. His legacy was colored, perhaps tarnished, by the politics of the thirteenth century. To Guelphs he was a traitor, to Ghibellines he was a hero. Even the Italian unificationists of the nineteenth century besmirched the reputation of John of Procida. Few are the men whose very names can sow the seeds of disquietude in the hearts of those living half a millennium later. Unlike Julius Caesar and Genghis Khan, John of Procida wielded his greatest influence behind the scenes; his was an *invisible* threat, but no less real for being unseen.

In our times the sophistry of the loosely-woven, paranoic *conspiracy theory,* divorced as it is from sound epistemology, warrants a generous dose of skepticism. Yet, from America to Russia, some of the world's most significant revolutions were the outcome of keen planning by the likes of men as ideologically diverse as Samuel Adams and Leon Trotsky.

From its first chapters, the *Rebellion* overstates the power of King Charles, with descriptions of him as "the most powerful monarch in Europe." True, this may represent the perception that prevailed in 1282, but it is not unlike the kind of exaggeration used elsewhere in medieval literature, and the practice has ancient precedents. Julius Caesar's *Bellum Gallicum* probably overstated the Gauls' military might to make Rome's enemies seem more formidable, thus rendering the effect of Caesar's victories greater in the court of public opinion. In the *Rebellion,* John of Procida, or his heirs, may have used the same technique.

Given its literary nature, the *Rebellion* contains much fanciful language, such as John's rousing speech to the Sicilian barons in Chapter 11. This doesn't detract from the possibility that certain of the events recounted in the chronicle may indeed have taken place in some form, however colorful their description by the chronicler.

John of Procida had no monopoly on hyperbolic use of the concept of servitude, which irascible General George Patton exploited to great effect on the eve of a later struggle for Sicily, one every bit as acrimonious as the conflicts between Guelphs and Ghibellines, Angevins and Aragonese:

"Many of you have in your veins German and Italian blood. But remember that those ancestors of yours so loved freedom that they gave up home and country to cross the ocean in search of liberty. The ancestors of the people we shall kill lacked the courage to make such a sacrifice, and remained slaves."

Old metaphors, like old soldiers, never die. The Allied invasion represents the only time since the Vespers that Sicily played a pivotal role on the world stage. Whilst few were then cognizant of what developments the future might hold, the Allies' liberation of the island from the clutches of Fascism in 1943 was destined to bring about the establishment of Sicily's regional autonomy three years later.

Metaphors aside, we should be prudent in comparing modern wars to medieval ones. Yet the Italians' retreat across the Strait of Messina in 1943 bore uncanny similarities to the Angevin withdrawal of 1282. It could be argued, for example, that both operations were rooted in a mentality that found the island of Sicily "expendable" in the minds of leaders based on the peninsula, considering that (if each were judged by the standards of its own time) the Angevin force of knights, archers and foot men was far more competent than the mediocre army of Fascist Italy. It could also be argued that each invasion, once accomplished, came to be viewed by the great majority of the Sicilian populace as liberation from a despotic regime.

A treatise on national independence, be its focus Sicily, Scotland or Catalonia, would be a lengthy one, but it is clear that John of Procida was passionate about the issue.

If Sicily were still a sovereign state, it might be a nation comparable to Portugal, founded as a kingdom during the same period; Sicily's capital city, Palermo, may well have become a small Barcelona (itself the seat of an autonomous region since 1979). History, of course, is based on what happens, not what *might* have happened. Nevertheless, Italy and Spain, among other countries, have come to recognize the cultural significance of "regions" which were once kingdoms complete with their own languages.

Were the Vespers part of a conspiracy, as some have suggested? At this distance of time, certainty lies beyond our grasp. But if any man could have devised and executed such a plot, it was John of Procida.

MAPS
&
IMPRINTS

TYRRHENIAN SEA
SICILIAN CHANNEL
IONIAN SEA
Trapani
Marsala
Mazara
Erice
Segesta
Calatafimi
Alcamo
Monreale
Palermo
Piana
Vicari
Corleone
Caltabellotta
Bivona
Caccamo
Sciacca
Agrigento
(Girgenti)
Licata
Caltanissetta
Cefalù
Enna
(Kasr'Janni)
Piazza
Armerina
Gela
Caltagirone
Sperlinga
Nicosia
Troina
San Marco
d'Aluzio
Paternò
Palagonia
Vizzini
Ragusa
Modica
Noto
Lentini
Catania
Augusta
Siracusa
Pachino
Iaci
(Acireale)
Taormina
Messina
Rocca
Amatore
Milazzo
Lipari
VAL DI MAZARA
VAL DI NOTO
VAL DEMONE
VAL ETNA
SICANIAN MTS.
MADONIAN MTS.
EREAN MTS.
NEBRODIAN MTS.
PELORITAN MTS.
HYBLAEAN MTS.
N

Kingdom of Sicily 1130-1282

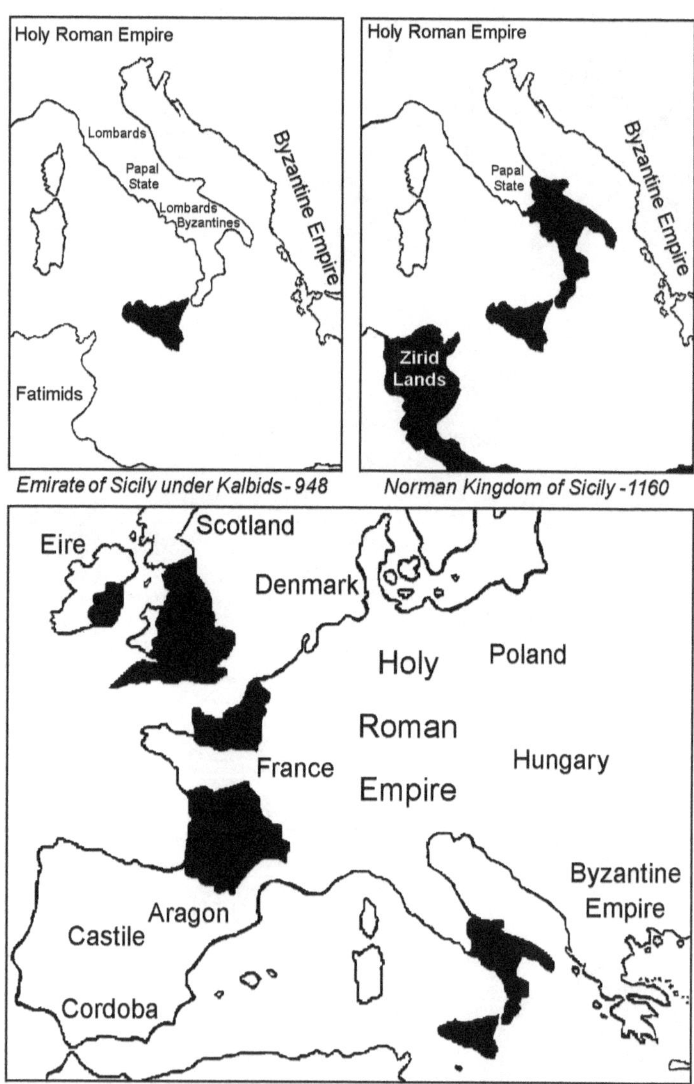

Emirate of Sicily under Kalbids - 948

Norman Kingdom of Sicily - 1160

Norman control in 1180: Normandy, Sicily, England, Ireland, Aquitaine, Malta

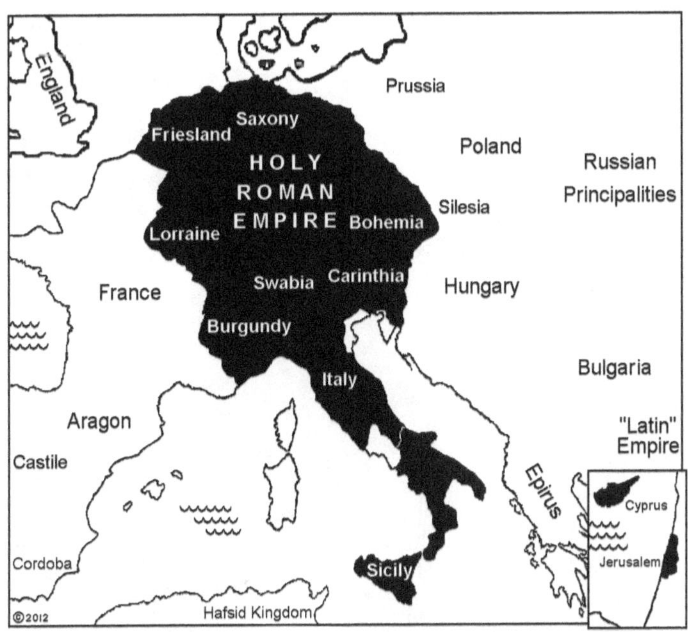

Greatest extent of Hohenstaufen dominion under Frederick II - 1230

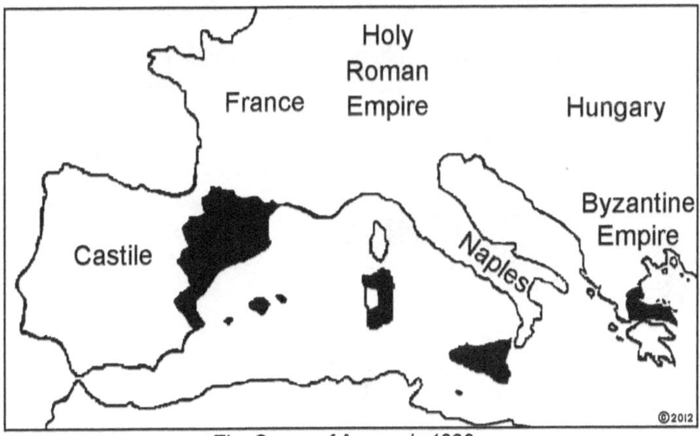

The Crown of Aragon in 1330

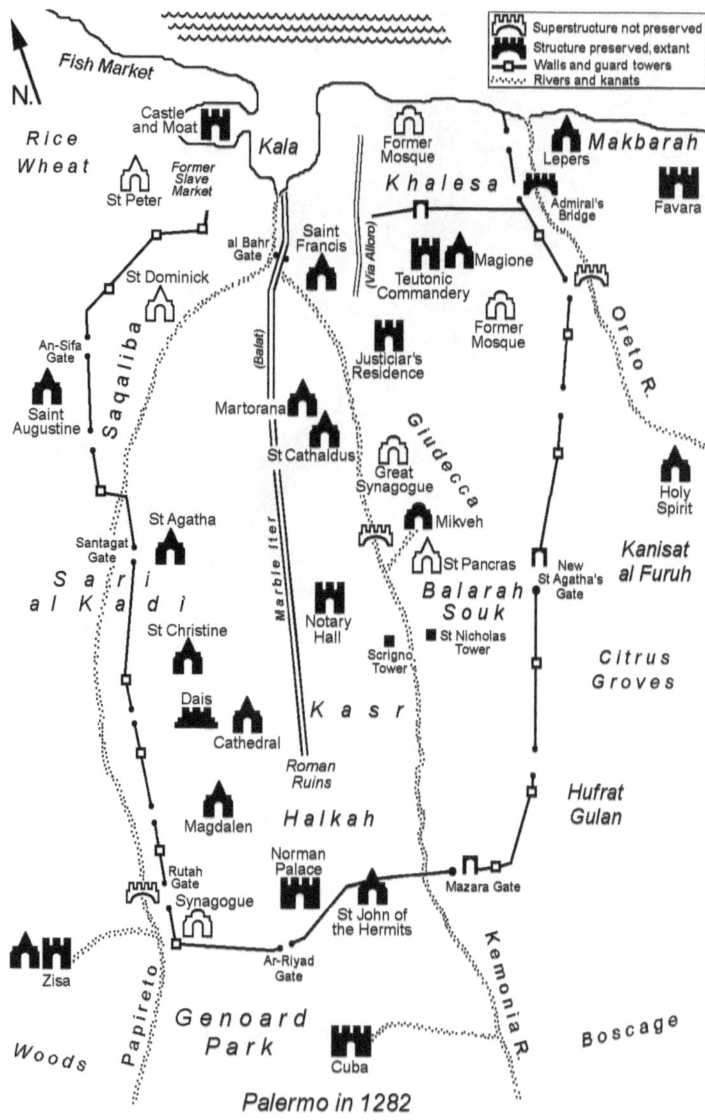
Superstructure not preserved
Structure preserved, extant
Walls and guard towers
Rivers and kanats
N.
Fish Market
Castle and Moat
Kala
Rice Wheat
St Peter
Former Slave Market
Former Mosque
Khalesa
Makbarah
Lepers
Admiral's Bridge
Favara
al Bahr Gate
Saint Francis
(Via Alloro)
Teutonic Commandery
Magione
St Dominick
Former Mosque
Oreto R.
An-Sifa Gate
Saqaliba
(Balat)
Justiciar's Residence
Saint Augustine
Martorana
St Cathaldus
Giudecca
Great Synagogue
Holy Spirit
St Agatha
Mikveh
Santagat Gate
Sari al Kadi
Marble Iter
St Pancras
New St Agatha's Gate
Kanisat al Furuh
Balarah Souk
Notary Hall
St Nicholas Tower
St Christine
Scrigno Tower
Citrus Groves
Dais
Cathedral
Kasr
Roman Ruins
Hufrat Gulan
Magdalen
Halkah
Norman Palace
Rutah Gate
Synagogue
St John of the Hermits
Mazara Gate
Zisa
Ar-Riyad Gate
Kemonia R.
Papireto
Genoard Park
Cuba
Boscage
Woods
Palermo in 1282

Europe and the Mediterranean in 1280

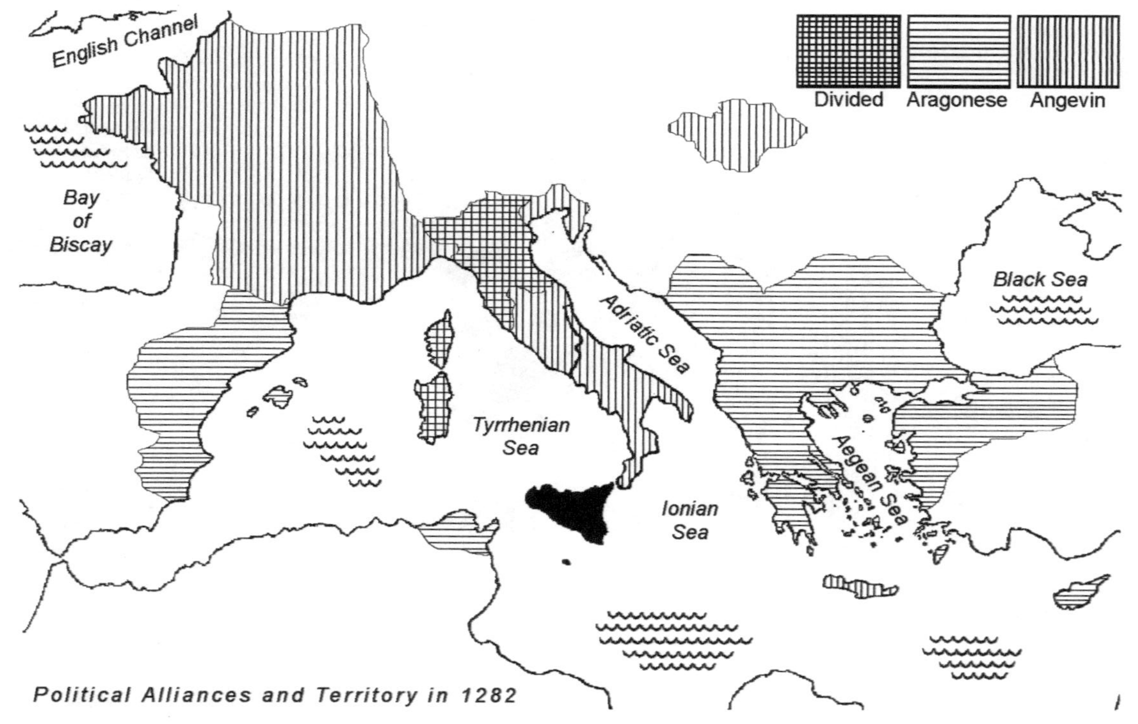

Political Alliances and Territory in 1282

REGIONS *and* **LANGUAGES** *of northeastern Spain and southwestern France in 1282*

English Channel
HOLY ROMAN EMPIRE
Paris
MAINE
ANJOU
Tonnerre
Angers
FRANCE
Bay of Biscay
Bordeaux
AQUITAINE
SAVOY
PROVENCE
Aix
Arles
Toulouse
Marseilles
Pamplona
LEON
NAVARRE
Perpignan
ARAGON
Zaragoza
CATALONIA
CASTILE
Barcelona
VALENCIA
Port Fangos
Minorca
Majorca
Valencia
Ibiza
MURCIA
Kings and Countries
Peter of Aragon
Charles of Anjou
Edward of England

Palermo map of 1570 showing some medieval streets

Chief Jewish Communities of Sicily in 1282

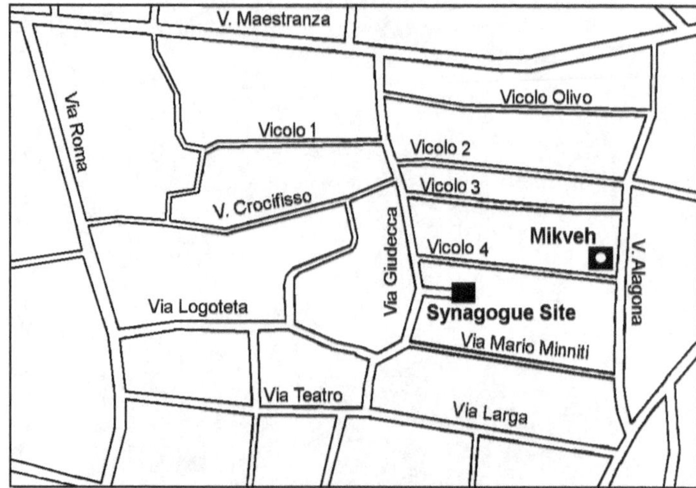

Giudecca (Jewish Quarter) in Ortygia, Siracusa
Great synagogue site is St John's Church. Mikveh at Via Alagona 52.

Palermo's Jewish Quarter, Souk (now Ballarò Market) and Kemonia Spring
Great synagogue site is San Nicolò da Tolentino Church. Mikveh under Jesuit cloister.

Medieval Sicilian languages in a Norman tombstone dated 1148 (Latin, Hebrew, Greek, Arabic) displayed in the Zisa Palace (Palermo): the polyglot linguistic heritage of Sicily under the Normans and Swabians

F. THOMÆ FAZELLI SICVLI OR. PRÆDICATORVM

DE REBVS SICVLIS DECADES DVAE, NVNC PRIMVM IN LVCEM EDITAE.

HIS ACCESSIT TOTIVS OPERIS INDEX LOCVPLETISSIMVS.

CAVTVM EST PHILIPPI ANGLIAE, HISPANIAE,
Sicilieq; Regis, Pauli. IIII. Pont. Max. ac Venetæ Reip. priuilegio, ne
cui has Decades de Siculis rebus ad decennium in eorum di-
tione vel imprimere, vel alibi impressas venales
habere, neue in sermonē Italicū iniuſ-
ſu authoris vertere ſub mul-
cta liceat.

Published in 1560, Fazello's book was one of the first histories to feature details from the Rebellion

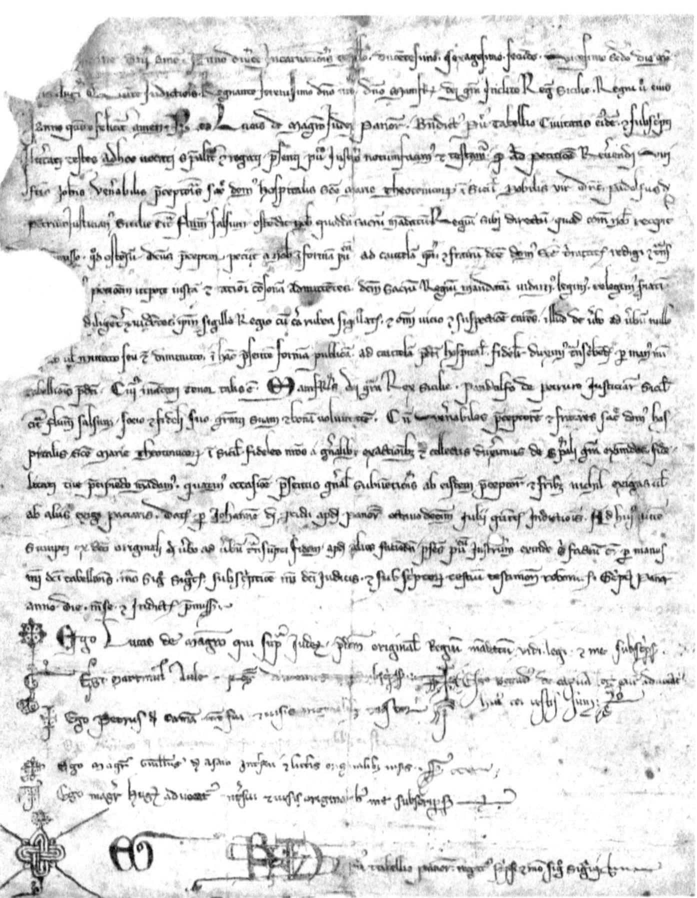

Contemporary copy of a charter issued by King Manfred in 1262, when John of Procida was Chancellor; it orders the Justiciar Pandolfo of Petruro to refrain from extracting a newly-instituted tax from John of Walkorn, the Preceptor of the Teutonic Order's Commandery of the Magione in Palermo. It is typical of the austere documents of its era.

Chapter 63 from the Spinelli Codex, earliest extant manuscript of Lu Rebellamentu, showing typical spelling and orthography of 13th-century Middle Sicilian (see also the following page).

Most of the Spinelli Codex is more legible than this first leaf.

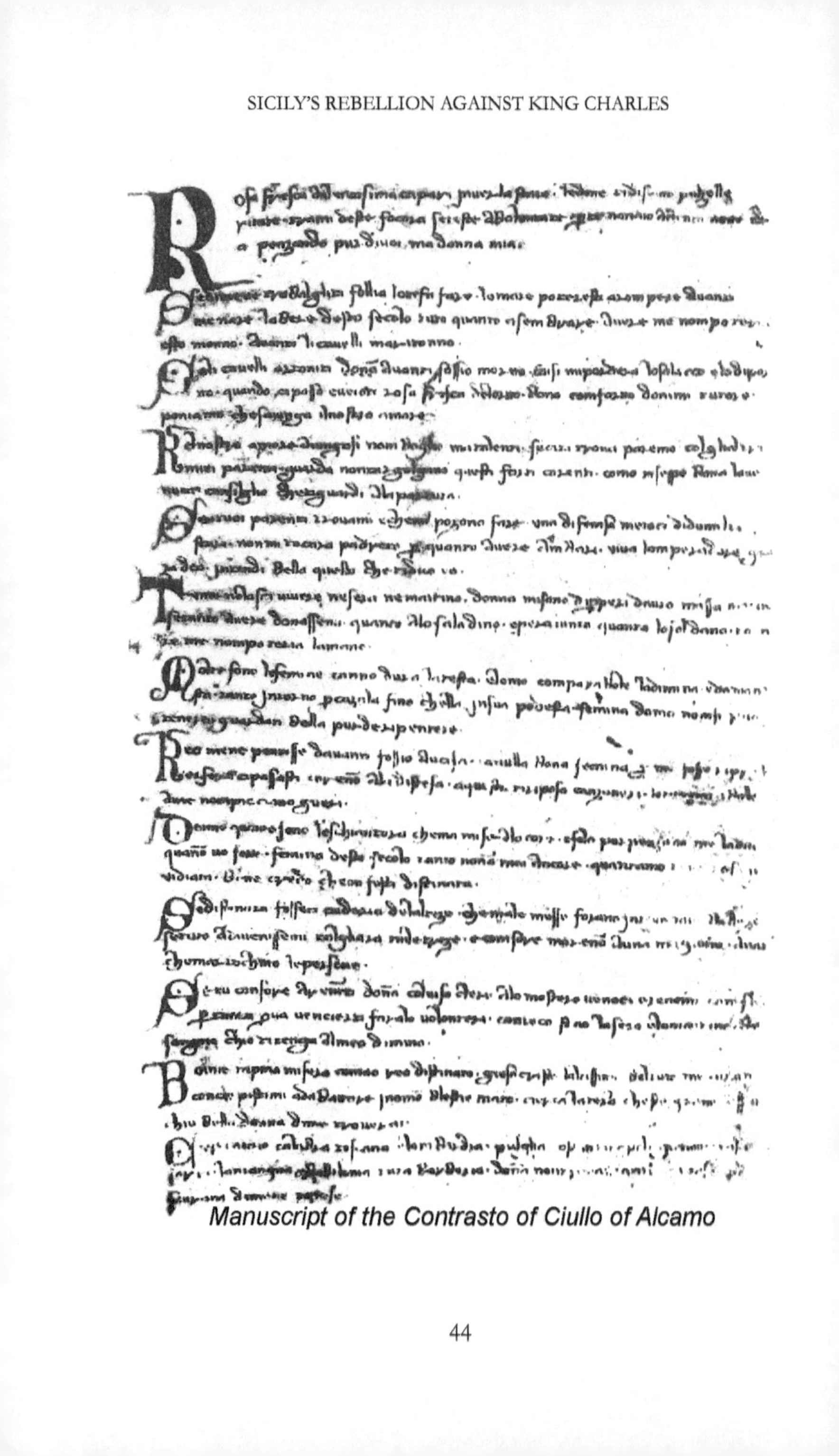

Manuscript of the Contrasto of Ciullo of Alcamo

PHOTOGRAPHS

Effigy of a Teutonic Knight in Palermo

Teutonic Knights' Commandery of the Magione, Palermo

The Magione church, now a minor basilica

Martorana tower and Saint Cathaldus

Saint Cathaldus nave and apse

Pisan Tower of the Norman Palace

Cloister of Saint John of the Hermits, a Benedictine monastery

A high tower of Monreale Abbey viewed from the cloister

Bell tower of the Martorana church, Palermo

Church of the Holy Spirit today

Saint Ann's Convent in Piazza Croce dei Vespri, where the justiciar's residence stood in 1282, its site marked by the plaque visible near the column at the corner of the building

Apse and cupola of the Palatine Chapel

The Cubola, *one of the few Norman-Arab pavilions standing in 1282 that survives in what was once the* Genoard *network of gardens extending from Palermo's city walls southward to the royal hunting grounds (this part is now an orchard)*

Church of Saint Francis of Assisi, Palermo

New Saint Agatha's Gate (top) and Mazara Gate (above)

Views of the Zisa's facade, muqarnas and mosaics

Cefalù Cathedral viewed from the fortress where the son of King Charles was imprisoned during the War of the Sicilian Vespers

Zaragoza's Mudéjar Aljaferia Palace (shown), residence of the Kings of Aragon. Peter III spent more time in coastal Barcelona (in Catalonia) or visiting his foreign dominions.

Peter III was crowned King of Aragon in Zaragoza Cathedral (top) but only the apse remains from that era. A small part of the city wall is preserved in the same district.

Very little remains of King Peter's palace in Barcelona

Barcelona's Basilica of Santa Maria del Mar is the supreme example of the Catalan Gothic architecture introduced by King Peter's dynasty in Sicily, where the portico of Palermo Cathedral is typical of this style.

The splendid Catalan Gothic facade of the Basilica of Santa Maria del Mar in Barcelona

Top: Palermo Cathedral much as it appeared when Peter of Aragon was crowned King of Sicily, centuries before the unsightly cupola was added. Above:Portico in the Catalan Gothic style,added in the 15th century.

Barcelona's Sant Pau de Camp, a typical church of rural Catalonia during the rule of King Peter III

Constructed beginning in 1298, Barcelona Cathedral is dedicated to Saint Eulalia. Palermo's Church of Saint Eulalia of the Catalans (still owned by Spain) is located in the Vucceria market, named for Barcelona's Boqueria.

Canterbury Cathedral: Geoffrey Chaucer was influenced by the writings of Petrarch and Boccaccio, and it is quite possible that he met one or both of them during his travels in Italy.

Mushrooms and snails at Barcelona's Boqueria market, inspiration for the name of the Vucceria in Palermo

Apses of Palermo Cathedral, where Peter was crowned King of Sicily. This part of the exterior has not been altered in subsequent centuries.

Cloister of Monreale Abbey: An Arab fountain amongst Norman arches supported by Byzantine columns

Chapel of the Chiaramontes' castle at Mussomeli in the Gothic style that flourished in Sicily after 1282

The Bourbon dynasty of Francis II, who ruled the Kingdom of Naples and Sicily (the Two Sicilies) until 1861, shared the Capetian lineage of Charles of Anjou

PRELUDE

"When acquiring lands in a place where there are differences in language, customs and laws, great luck and effort are needed to hold them."

— Niccolò Machiavelli

The Kingdom of Sicily was founded by a Norman dynasty, the House of Hauteville, in 1130. It included most of Italy south of Rome and it was ruled initially from Palermo, its largest city. Such was its territory until the war of 1282 described in the *Rebellion*. This was the Kingdom of Sicily ruled from Naples by Charles of Anjou.

This concise overview shall take us from the advent of Norman rule in the middle of the eleventh century to the time when the chronicle about John of Procida begins. Our journey, though brief, will not be uneventful.

The Polyglot Island

Until the arrival of the Normans at the Battle of Messina

in 1061, the island of Sicily was part of the Fatimid Empire ruled for over a century as a unified emirate by the Kalbid dynasty. It was squabbles among the Kalbids' heirs, leading to the establishment of several rival emirates around the island, that made the Norman conquest of Sicily possible, but a long decade would pass before Bal'harm (Palermo), the capital, fell following an invasion by land and sea. This was led by Robert "Guiscard" Hauteville, accompanied by several younger brothers, including Roger.

By then, another band of Normans had conquered Saxon England. Indeed, some Norman knights fought in both England and Italy.

Polyglot Sicily boasted a prosperous, multicultural society. The Byzantines, or "Greeks," were the "native" *corpus* of Sicilians whose ancestors had dwelled on the island since time immemorial, descended from Sicanians, Elymians, Sikels, Phoenicians, Greeks, Romans, Vandals and Ostrogoths. They were Christians. The great influx of Arabs arrived beginning during the ninth century, when the Aghlabids of Tunisia seized Sicily from the Byzantine Empire. These colonizers were Muslims. The Jews had been in Sicily since the days of the Roman Empire, forming part of what has come to be known as the *Diaspora.*

Bilingualism was the norm. It was not unusual to meet a Sicilian fluent in both Greek and Arabic, and perhaps a bit of the Latin vulgate. The Jews' vernacular was the Judeo Arabic spoken in Tunisia.

Following the Great Schism of 1054, the island's Christians fell under the ecclesial jurisdiction of Constantinople rather than Rome. The Papacy had encouraged the Norman conquest of Sicily in order to convert these "schismatics" as well as the Muslims. This the Normans did, but very slowly.

Despite Sicily's ethnic and religious diversity, or perhaps because of it, we find in the latter decades of the eleventh century the first seeds of Sicilian national identity, with Roger Hauteville as the Great Count of Sicily.

In 1130, another Roger, son of the Count Roger who arrived in 1061, was crowned Sicily's first king. He is known to us as Roger II.

Often referred to simply as the *Regnum,* the Kingdom of Sicily was one of the wealthiest states of Europe and the Mediterranean. The assets in Palermo's treasury eclipsed those of the entire Kingdom of England, and the city's splendor rivalled that of Baghdad. Smaller cities like Syracuse, Messina, Bari and Salerno also prospered; Naples had yet to emerge as the great metropolis it was to become.

Certain Fatimid institutions were retained. Here the most obvious example is the royal *diwan,* the treasury. Even the architecture was a syncretic Norman-Arab style with strong Byzantine influences, something very obviously epitomized in the Palatine Chapel, Palermo's Martorana church, and the cathedrals of Monreale and Cefalù. On the site of Saint John of the Hermits in Palermo once stood a mosque, and before that a church. Jewish communities were found across the island; in Sicily are Europe's two oldest surviving mikvehs, in Syracuse and Palermo.

Yet the Normans gradually latinized Sicily in every way, principally through introduction of Latin clergy and liturgy, and by the time their rule ended the island was predominantly Roman Catholic, although there were still some Muslims and Jews. The peninsular part of the Kingdom of Sicily, where the principal cities were Bari and Salerno, never had a substantial Muslim population, and in Sicily there were conversions of Muslims to Catholicism. This was less the case of the Jews, with whom the Papacy maintained a tenuous accommodation. Feudalism was introduced.

There was enlightened rule. The court of Roger II was full of great thinkers like the geographer Idrisi. Roger himself is

Roger II, depicted as a Byzantine basileus, crowned by Christ in engraving based on mosaic in Palermo's Martorana church

rightfully regarded by historians as one of the most brilliant rulers of his age.

Until Roger's reign, Sicilians were each judged by their own law, be it Maliki law, Halakha law or Canon law. In 1140 or shortly thereafter (historians debate the precise date) a uniform legal code, the Assizes of Ariano, was formulated and applied to all subjects living in the Kingdom of Sicily.

When Roger died in 1154, his wife, Beatrice, was with child. A daughter, Constance, was born a few months later. Much has been written about Roger's reign, most of it good. King Roger II of Sicily found a county, and founded a country.

Roger II was succeeded by his son, William I, in turn succeeded by another William. Lacking surviving sons, William II was succeeded by a cousin, Tancred, in 1189. Tancred was the last Hauteville king to reign, but he was not the last Hauteville.

That was Constance. Following Tancred's death in 1194, the Sicilian Throne passed to this red-haired daughter of Roger II. Although she bore the title of *Queen Regnant,* it was her husband, the Holy Roman Emperor Henry VI, son of intrepid Frederick "Barbarossa" Hohenstaufen, who ruled the *Regnum* by *jure uxoris,* marital right. At Henry's death a few years later, Constance's son, Frederick II, inherited the Kingdom of Sicily and the right to succeed his father as Holy Roman Emperor, though he would have to fight to enforce his authority in the parts of his European empire beyond the island of Sicily, especially in the regions north of the Alps.

Stupor Mundi

Ruling regions from Saxony to Sicily, Frederick emerged as Europe's most powerful monarch. Like his Norman grandfather Roger, he was an exceptionally intelligent man. His scientific treatise on falconry is the lengthiest literary work authored by a medieval European king.

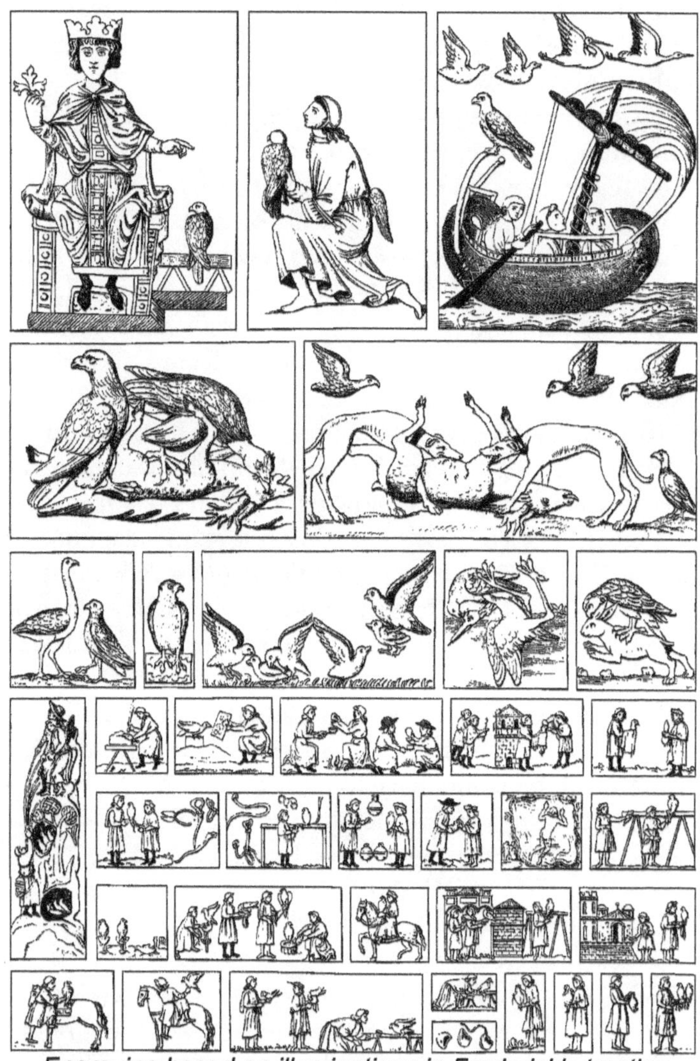

Engraving based on illuminations in Frederick's treatise on falconry (Frederick is shown at top left)

In Palermo, Frederick heard from sailors and merchants of foreign lands and customs. He absorbed much knowledge from scholars, philosophers, historians, artisans, chroniclers and sundry scientists. The names of a few are known to us. Michael Scot, the court astronomer, mathematician and science advisor, translated *On the Sphere* by the Arab astronomer Al-Bitruji, or Alpetragius, who died circa 1204. He also translated Aristotle's *De Animalibus* from the existing Arabic translation of ibn Sina (Avicenna). Scot was a mentor to the young Leonardo Pisano Bigollo, or Fibonacci, the mathematician who introduced Hindi-Arabic numerals in northern Italy and other parts of Christian Europe. (These were already used in Sicily, while Spain's *Codex Vigilanus,* compiled in 881, features such numerals.)

Frederick's political *modus vivendi* was more complicated than his intellectual life. Undertaking a crusade, he reached Jerusalem, which he claimed by right of his young wife, only to establish a peace with the Muslims who claimed it.

The Pope was not happy about a crusade without bloodshed, nor with the fact that Frederick ruled all of Italy except for the Papal lands in the peninsula's central region. Frederick often found himself excommunicated, but the fact did not seem to bother him greatly.

Like his Norman grandfather, he established a legal code based on traditional law, the Constitutions of Melfi of 1231, drafted in Latin with a translation into Greek; no Arabic text is known to us. There were still Muslims in Sicily, but Frederick resettled some of the more rebellious among them to Lucera in Apulia.

By now, a genuinely Sicilian language was heard. It was a Latin tongue with numerous borrowings from Greek, Arabic, Norman-French and even German. Giacomo of Lentini, Ciullo of Alcamo and other poets at Frederick's court wrote in this new vernacular.

Frederick died in 1250.

It was with simple eloquence that Matthew Paris recorded: "Frederick, peerless wonder of the world, died in Apulia on Saint Lucy's Day." *Obiit insuper stupor mundi Fretherícus, die Sanctae Luciae, in Apulia.* It is here, immediately after his death, that Frederick was attributed the enduring appellation *Stupor Mundi,* "Wonder of the World."

Composing a profile of Frederick's personal character has proven elusive. He rarely displayed hubris. On the other hand, he fathered numerous children outside his marriages, and his treatment of his later wives left much to be desired, even by the standards of the times. His personal religious beliefs were ambiguous at best. He was not especially devout, yet he zealously enforced Catholic law.

The fiercest modern criticisms of Frederick's personality reflect a conventional view of him as taciturn, obstinate, even sardonic. Such inferences are drawn from just a few contemporary accounts, yet they led the medievalist Morris Bishop to comment that Frederick was "enlightened, but he was not really a very nice man."

Frederick's death signalled the end of Sicily's great multicultural experiment, a decline that before long would culminate in a Sicilian "monoculture."

The Last Hohenstaufens

Who would rule the Kingdom of Sicily? Frederick was succeeded by Conrad, his son by Yolanda of Brienne, but he had several other sons, legitimate and otherwise. Most prominent among them was Manfred, who we shall meet shortly.

In 1246 Conrad had married Elizabeth Wittelsbach of Bavaria, who in 1252 bore him a son, also Conrad ("Conradin"), who was to figure in the history of the *Regnum.* In the event, although Conrad's reign was not a long one, he seems to have been willing to exercise more latitude than his father in domestic affairs. The Franciscans, who had been suppressed by Frederick, were permitted to return; their greatest church in Sicily is Saint Francis of Assisi in Palermo.

Amidst Papal intrigues and challenges to his royal authority in Germany, Conrad died of malaria in Basilicata in 1254, having been excommunicated the same year. He was succeeded by his young son, the Bavarian-born Conradin, whose regent was Conrad's half-brother Manfred, Frederick's natural son born in 1232 of Bianca Lancia, a noblewoman the Emperor was said to have wed when she was on her deathbed. Certain it is that Frederick cultivated an affinity for Manfred at least equal to that of his other sons, having bestowed upon him the lucrative principality of Taranto. That Conrad found Manfred overly ambitious was now a moot point with the former dead. Conrad's death had wide implications, as it brought about an interregnum in Germany that ended only two decades later.

In Italy there emerged two political factions. The *Guelphs* supported the Angevins and the Papacy, while the opposing *Ghibellines* supported the Hohenstaufens. These movements were especially felt in Papal circles and in northern Italy's communes. Sicily was more firmly in the Hohenstaufen camp. Some cities were divided.

One thing was clear: Rome did not want a Hohenstaufen on the throne.

Pope Innocent IV offered Sicily, which he viewed as a fief in his gift, to young Edmund "Crouchback," second son of King Henry III of England. His successor, Pope Alexander IV, confirmed this. Henry's taxation of his barons to defray the cost of ousting Manfred rekindled English memories of the fiscal policies of his father, King John, whose unbridled military spending added to the baronial indignation that led to the *Magna Carta.* This "Sicilian business" became a contributing factor, if only a peripheral one, in the Second Barons' War.

Manfred had himself crowned at Palermo in 1258 based on unfounded rumors that young Conradin (dynastically Conrad II) was dead.

When Pope Alexander IV died in 1261, he was succeeded by a Frenchman who took the name Urban IV. This coincided with the loss of Constantinople by the "Latin" kings who had ruled it since the shameful Fourth Crusade. The Byzantine Empire was thus restored to Greek control. One of Urban's first acts as Pontiff was an unsuccessful attempt to initiate a crusade to reclaim Constantinople.

The Pope was the common thread running through most of these events. Faith, expressed through the Church, was a *sine qua non* of everyday life, but the Papacy was the most unsettling, conniving, debilitating political force in Europe during the High Middle Ages, its tendrils reaching into the Baltics, the Balkans and the Byzantine lands. It was a state within every state.

Most Popes were obsessed with power; that was part of the job. Rare was the humble man who was elected to the See of Peter. Pity the king who found himself targeted by the Vicar of Christ. Pity still more the Waldensians and Cathars, and the Jews. Even the Orthodox Christians of the east were not safe from the clutches of Rome. Rarely was Papal politics rooted in true Christianity; most of the time Christianity had nothing to do with it. The medieval Papacy made it possible for bad Christians to be good Catholics. The worthy work of Francis of Assisi was condoned by the Papacy; that is because it posed no obvious risk to the Church as an institution. *Res Publica Christiana,* a phrase sometimes attributed to Frederick II, attempted to express the concept, vaguely similar to "Christendom," of one Europe under one Church. That wasn't enough. The Papacy wanted the world — this one and the next.

Whatever one thought of Manfred, he enjoyed a certain amount of support, even esteem, among the Sicilian baronage.

Never lacking in self-confidence, he betrothed his daughter, Constance, to Peter III of Aragon in 1262.

Meanwhile, as English support for the "Sicilian business" evaporated, other candidates were sought. Surely, if *Pontifex Maximus* could decide who was to be crowned king, he might just as easily cast aside one designee in favour of another. Urban formally annulled the offer of the Kingdom of Sicily that had been tendered to Edmund of England. His new candidate was a fellow Frenchman, Charles of Anjou, younger brother of the ever-crusading King Louis IX.

Louis himself was initially unconvinced. Having supported Conrad as Frederick's legitimate heir, he subsequently endorsed the Papal choice of Edmund. Now, despite his antipathy for Manfred, he saw no immediate justification for an Angevin to be crowned King of Sicily. Yet he eventually consented to it in spite of these reservations.

In 1263, the ambitious Charles accepted a Papal offer weighed down by cumbersome conditions. Papal control of his Italian realm would be burdensome indeed. Legatine powers were to be abolished, and armies were to be provided the Pope whenever requested. A substantial annual tribute was to be paid to Rome. Naturally, there were to be no claims made by Charles on the Holy Roman Empire or any of its territories.

Here Urban was the quintessential Pontiff as Kingmaker. No wonder some historians have come to regard Charles as a Papal puppet.

The Crown itself was a more than sufficient incentive, but Charles may have accepted these outrageous terms partly due to his wife's endless prodding. Behind every ambitious man there is a woman, and Beatrice of Provence was nothing if not ambitious. Her sisters were already the queen consorts of England, France and Germany, and it irked her to be accorded lesser precedence than them.

As Manfred's army made its way up the peninsula in 1264, Pope Urban IV, in flight from the Hohenstaufen, died in Perugia. The next Pope, Clement IV, also a Frenchman, was elected the following year. He had once been an advisor to the Angevins and strongly supported Charles.

As Charles made his way across Savoy and Piedmont into northern Italy, he negotiated cooperation from most of the cities and sovereigns in the region, Ghibelline as well as Guelph. He reached Rome in May 1265 and the next month he was proclaimed King of Sicily by the Pope. Charles was crowned on the Epiphany, 6 January 1266. Beatrice was finally a queen. Now a direct confrontation between Manfred and Charles was inevitable. The wait would not be a long one.

In late January there were some skirmishes around Capua, where Charles occupied several castles. San Germano (Cassino) was captured in early February. The adversaries knew where to find each other.

On the morning of 26 February, Manfred's army attacked Charles' forces outside the Papal city of Benevento. What followed was one of the major battles of the thirteenth century. Here, along rapid streams and rugged hills, two large armies of some three thousand knights each met head-on. Manfred's Saracen archers, recruited from the Muslim community at Lucera, also participated.

The battle was noteworthy for its technology. Some of the Swabian knights were outfitted with the newest innovation, plate armor, which seemed impenetrable until some of the Angevin knights realized that in raising their arms to strike, Manfred's knights exposed their armpits, a vulnerable area to stab.

Their faces concealed, it was the knights' shields and surcoats that distinguished them. Here heraldry was a useful science. (See the chart in Appendix 3 showing Guelph and Ghibelline insignia.)

Most battles have their tactical "turning points." In this one it seems to have been a bottleneck formed by Manfred's cavalry while trying to cross a bridge over the Calore River in a charge against the Angevins. To his credit, Manfred was leading the attack that led to his demise.

By the end of the day, Manfred was dead and Charles was victorious. The Hohenstaufens were at an end, almost.

They still had their supporters. In September 1267, a fleet led by Frederick of Castile landed at Sciacca to support a rebellion that had been fomented in Sicily against the Angevins. This Frederick, a brother of King Alfonso X of Castile, had fought alongside Manfred at Benevento. Another brother, Henry, supported Charles but had grown disillusioned with him for not being repaid a loan. While they initially found themselves on opposite sides in the dispute between Charles and Manfred, Frederick and Henry shared a mutual hatred of their older brother, King Alfonso, who had deprived them of their estates in Spain, thereby forcing them to seek their fortunes abroad. In the tangled web of dynastic genealogies, the brothers were related to both Charles and Manfred.

Frederick of Castile was based at Tunis, where he held a position in the service of Sultan al Mustansir. Although Palermo and Messina refused to join him, the rebellion spread to Calabria and Apulia. Undeterred by excommunication, he won a naval victory over a flotilla launched by Charles.

While Charles attempted to consolidate his power in the *Regnum*, the enmities between Guelphs and Ghibellines simmered to the surface, as they were wont to do every so often. So long as a Hohenstaufen heir lived, the Ghibellines would have a rallying point. Young Conradin responded to their pleas, leaving his Duchy of Swabia to reach Verona, a Ghibelline city, in October 1267. In July 1268, he was received by the crowds of Rome with unbridled enthusiasm.

Meanwhile Charles was laying siege to Lucera, trying to

convince the Muslims to surrender to his authority. Learning of Conradin's approach, he lifted the siege and made his way up the peninsula.

On 23 August, the two armies did battle near Tagliacozzo in western Abruzzi. This time, Henry of Castile fought against Charles. Like Manfred, Conradin had the support of Muslim troops from Lucera, infantry as well as archers. Here too the battle was decided by factors fortuitous to Charles, who was all but defeated until one of his corps, having hidden itself, ambushed Conradin, who in the confusion managed to escape.

Conradin and his faithful supporter Frederick of Baden tried to make their way to Genoa, perhaps with the intention of sailing to Sicily; had they achieved this they might well have changed the course of history. Unfortunately, they were captured and tried. The trial itself was ridiculous, branding them as "traitors" and "murderers," but it suited Charles' purpose. Along with several military companions, they were beheaded in October 1268 in Naples, which by then Charles had made into his official capital. Conradin was sixteen.

The Hohenstaufen kings were gone. They would not be forgotten.

King Charles

For now, Charles I Anjou "of Naples," King of Sicily, was free of dynastic challenges to his position. His socially ambitious wife was an uncontested queen. Charles had several children, including a son, also Charles, said to be exceptionally intelligent.

But his realm was not free of problems. Lucera, which for its Muslim Arab community was referred to in charters as *Lucaera Saracenorum*, revolted against his authority, and so did much of Sicily. In August 1269, walled Lucera surrendered following a long siege. Most of the Muslims were dispersed around the region and forced to convert; the Christian rebels were executed. Indeed, execution was becoming Charles' *modus operandi* in dealing with opponents. Yet the city was not destroyed, and some residents remained.

Further afield, he tried to court the Guelphic element in Lombardy while containing, even eliminating, the Ghibellines. This met with mixed results.

At home, Charles increased taxation around the *Regnum*, from Abruzzo to Malta. He divested a number of vassals by means of legalistic logic, his habitual facade. Here he simply demanded proof that barons had held their lands before Frederick's excommunication and "deposition," reasoning that after that time Frederick and his heirs, not being "legitimate" kings recognized by the Pope, lacked the royal sovereignty to enfeoff anybody. Even many vassals who could meet this standard could not produce the required documentation and risked feudal divestiture, the loss of their lands. Charles gave many of these estates to Frenchmen.

If one seeks to find the origin of the crippling bureaucracy, contorted legal system and generally mediocre government that infect Italy to this day, the rule of Charles of Anjou offers as good an explanation as any. Under his Hohenstaufen predecessors, there was, after a fashion, a method to the madness. Taxation was kept in check and the justiciars meted out some semblance of equal justice. However, to be fair, it must be said that Charles was an able administrator, or at least an efficient one.

Now Charles and the Papacy colluded to impose their will throughout Italy, but achieving such objectives could take years.

More immediately, the transfer of royal power to Naples effectively toppled Palermo from its privileged perch as the capital of the Kingdom of Sicily, at least during the Angevin period. It educed the Sicilians' perception of their island's rule by "foreigners." While it was often misplaced, for Sicily occasionally boasted rule during successive periods by kings resident on the island, this idea became something of a cliché and also a convenient "crutch," a ready excuse to explain or justify every social ill.

Charles sent numerous French administrators to Sicily, but it was their actions, not their ethnicity, that fostered resentment initially. The ethnic bigotry, if it was ever even so widespread as some modern historians would have us believe, was an outgrowth of this.

In Naples, Charles erected grandiose castles and churches. Whereas this city, until now, had been surpassed in size and splendor by Salerno and Bari, Angevin rule saw it blossom into a magnificent metropolis.

The Angevin Kingdom

In 1270, Charles made one of his rare trips through Sicily *en route* to join his brother, Louis IX of France, in Tunis for the Eighth (or "Tunisian") Crusade. Here his motives transcended religious piety, as Sultan al Mustansir, obligated by longstanding treaty to pay tribute to the King of Sicily, had ceased his remittances. Charles reached Tunisia in late August, only to find that Louis had fallen ill and died. In the event, he negotiated a treaty before departing.

The first church funeral for Louis, who was almost immediately venerated, was held in Sicily. His remains, which are thought to have been preserved according to the *Mos Teutonicus,* were brought in a procession from the harbor of Palermo to Monreale Abbey along what is now Corso Calatafimi. Here his heart rests in an urn.

This may have been a way for Charles to placate the restless Sicilians with a lasting gesture that clearly reflected his dynasty's goodness. An Angevin heart in the same church as the tomb of King William I conveyed the subtle message that a French monarch could be as much a part of Sicilian religious culture and dynastic continuity as a Norman. Here Monreale seemed a more suitable choice than Palermo's cathedral, where a Hohenstaufen tomb or two was located. Present at the funeral was the son of Louis, succeeding him as King Philip III of France, who was beginning to fall under the spell of his uncle Charles.

It is difficult to discern in Charles' policy a specific philosophy, yet his was an age of philosophies. Thomas Aquinas (Tommaso d'Aquino), a Dominican or "Black Friar," was a leading proponent of Natural Theology, which brought science and classical philosophy to Catholicism. Composed in the decade immediately prior to his death in 1274, the *Summa Theologica* advanced a reasoned basis for many Catholic beliefs. In retrospect, the writings of Thomas Aquinas, providential as they were, drove yet another wedge between the Christians of East and West, separated since the Great Schism in 1054.

Constantinople, which had been occupied by Catholic "Franks" during the infamous Fourth Crusade but reclaimed by Byzantine Greeks from Baldwin II of Courtenay in 1261, was a jewel the Papacy wanted in its ecclesiastical crown. Charles lusted after its political and economic value, much as a thief covets an antique pearl necklace for its monetary price "on the street" rather than its intrinsic artistic quality. Indeed, he had been plotting a "crusade" against the "schismatic" Greek Orthodox of the re-established Byzantine Empire for years before the Tunisian Crusade side-tracked him. Finally, in 1271, a military expedition left most of Albania in Angevin hands, and Charles proclaimed himself its king, but his rule of this Balkan territory would prove ephemeral.

To justify his claims, the ever-legalistic Charles betrothed his daughter, Beatrice, to Philip, Baldwin's son, who was titular "Latin" Emperor of Constantinople. Beatrice died at Naples shortly after the wedding in late 1275, but not before bearing a daughter, Catherine. If needs be, Charles could use his young granddaughter as his "anchor" to claim the Byzantine Throne.

In an effort to establish alliances in the regions that extended toward the western frontier of the Byzantine Empire, Charles had already married a son and daughter to children of the King of Hungary.

Constantinople maintained close links with the Italian mercantile cities, and particularly the Genoans. Emperor Michael VIII Palaeologue was funding the Ghibellines of northern Italy against Charles, and he was in contact with King Alfonso of Castile. His interests were also theological. At the Second Council of Lyon, the Papacy made serious efforts to heal the rift of the Great Schism. Had its principles been implemented over the long term, they probably would have required the submission of the Patriarch of Constantinople to the authority of Rome; the conditions of the Council, though never accepted by most Orthodox Christians, were later repudiated by Michael's successor.

One of the Ghibelline proponents was a wealthy nobleman, John of Procida, at one time a leading professor at Salerno's medical school and a close counselor of Frederick II. He became Manfred's tutor. After the Hohenstaufen defeat at Tagliacozzo, his estates confiscated by the Angevins, he fled to Venice. He was friendly with newly-elected Pope Nicholas III, a member of the Orsini family lacking trust in King Charles and his motives. John of Procida maintained contact with Michael VIII as well as King Peter III of Aragon, who was married to Manfred Hohenstaufen's daughter, Constance.

Rare was the native baron who didn't have an axe to grind with King Charles. Around 1280, John (or one of his sons) seems to have surreptitiously visited Sicily, meeting with some of the island's malcontent nobles, bringing to them the message of Pope Nicholas that they should trust in Peter of

Aragon to free them from the Angevin yoke.

In 1281, Charles lost most of his Balkan and Greek territory to a Byzantine army, but this defeat was not serious enough to discourage his ambitions. Hoping to seize the entire Byzantine Empire as far as its capital, he had already begun to prepare a full-scale invasion of Constantinople despite the Papacy's ostensibly peaceful overtures to Emperor Michael. The greater part of the fleet was being assembled at Messina. It was difficult to keep this activity secret. The local barons knew about it and, in all likelihood, so did Michael and John. Even if they were not privy to every detail of the invasion plan, it wasn't difficult for them to surmise Charles' intentions.

One glance at a map of the Mediterranean is more than sufficient to elucidate the vulnerability of Sicily and the southern third of the Apennine peninsula to an invasion by sea. In directing their attentions toward the east, Charles' military advisors underestimated potential threats from the west and the south, or from within.

If Charles knew that John of Procida was convincing ever more Ghibellines to ally themselves with his enemies, he seemed unconcerned about it. His faithful nephew, Philip III of France, advised him that a large Aragonese fleet was being readied for a military expedition to Africa, where Aragonese hegemony was supplanting Angevin influence. Charles' own fleet was scheduled to depart Messina for the eastern Mediterranean in April 1282 if all went according to plan.

John of Procida would do everything in his power to ensure that it did not.

THE REBELLION OF SICILY

This is the account of the Rebellion of Sicily that Lord John of Procida commanded us to record.[5]

1

In the Year of Our Lord Jesus Christ one thousand two hundred and seventy-nine, King Charles Anjou of Sicily undertook a great war against the Emperor Michael Palaeologue of Constantinople. To that end, he constructed many large ships and galleys in order that he could attack Constantinople in great force.[6] To achieve this, he recruited many able men from France, from Provence and from Italy in a united army intended to conquer the entire Byzantine Empire.

In Sicily, Lord John of Procida contemplated a way to prevent this expedition against the Byzantines from embarking, and how he might defeat and kill King Charles by inciting the Sicilians to rebel and attack the monarch's troops amassing there.[7] He decided to go to the Byzantine Empire to speak with Emperor Michael and to warn him what King Charles was planning.

Wasting no time, Lord John left Sicily for Constantinople to meet the Emperor. When he arrived at the court of Constantinople, John met two disillusioned, rebellious knights of King Charles who had fled Italy. He spoke with them secretly, explaining why he had come to Constantinople.

"I have been expelled from my feudal lands and from Sicily," he said, "and I have come in search of my destiny. I ask that you might deign to present me to the Emperor as an ally, and tell him that I am a person of importance, and that I can be very useful to him, and that my sage advice could be of much help to him and his interests."

Hearing this, the knights were very satisfied and responded that they would be most willing to help John in his mission. They went to the Emperor.

"My Lord," they said, "we bring you good news from the Kingdom of Sicily. One of the greatest physicians in the world has travelled here to be at your court, and we assure you that he would be a good advisor.[8] Having recently been exiled from his own country, he knows a great deal about the activities of King Charles and his power, and also of the military potential of his baronage."

2

The Emperor was very content to learn of the scope of the visitor's mission. He immediately summoned John of Procida, who the knights promptly brought before him. The physician approached reverently in accordance with the respect to be shown the imperial person.[9]

The Emperor, in his turn, graciously reciprocated this courtesy, appointing John as his master physician. And so Lord John enjoyed a place at court for three months, earning the respect of Greeks and Latins alike.

3

One day John queried the Emperor.

"Sire," he said, "I should most humbly like to ask you, might we speak privately in a place where nobody can overhear our conversation?"

Taken aback by such a request, the Emperor asked, "Of what should you wish to speak so secretly?"

"Of the greatest need that you have in this world," John replied.

The two immediately made their way to one of the highest watch towers of the palace, where they were all alone. There was nobody within earshot.

4

"I assure you that this place is absolutely secret," said the Emperor.

"Sire," said John, "it is clear that everybody who knows you considers you as wise as you are brave, but I wish to speak to you of one most vile, most irrational, like a beast that lies in wait, that can be killed only when stabbed swiftly and forcefully. In these three months at your court, I've heard rumors that your reign is at risk, that death threatens you. Do you think it foolish or unreasonable to prepare a defense against the force that threatens you? King Charles plans to come to seize your crown, and to kill you and your entire family. He is supported by the Emperor Baldwin, who covets the Imperial crown.[10] Charles plans to attack with all the crusaders he can muster. He is preparing a hundred armed galleons and twenty large ships to transport ten thousand well-armed knights, along with forty counts and their companies, to attack your realm."

5

Hearing these words, the Emperor began to sob. He said,

"Oh, Lord John, do you want me to live as a man without hope, knowing that I've tried so many times to negotiate with King Charles without success? That I've tried to treat with the Holy Church of Rome and its cardinals, and with the King of France, the King of England, the King of Spain[11] and the King of Aragon? And that none of them even responds to the letters I send? It is said that somebody is more willing to die than to speak when in the face of the great power of King Charles. So as a man I have no place to seek refuge, only faith that God will come to my aid, seeing as my fellow Christians offer me neither help nor real advice!"

6

"In view of all this fury and the likelihood of a terrible death," Lord John asked, "you don't think yourself deserving of the smallest hope?"

"Of course I deserve it," the Emperor replied, "and I would do all I could to obtain it. But who else would be bold enough, and willing enough, to be my ally in a war against the formidable power of King Charles?"

7

"I'm here to offer you what you are hoping to find," responded Lord John. "I'll destroy King Charles by bringing together your help and my advice. I'll explain what you have to do, and how to do it, with me and some other Sicilian rebels who've been injured by King Charles. You'll have what you seek. God willing, your worst enemy will be unable even to harm you, let alone defeat you."

8

"How do you plan to do this?" the Emperor asked.

"I will tell you if you promise me a hundred thousand gold ounces. Be assured that I can bring to bear the power of somebody who will seize the land of Sicily so quickly that King Charles will barely know what hit him."

"Lord John," said the Emperor, visibly pleased to hear this affirmation, "take all the money from my treasury you need and spend it as you must. Do whatever can be done."

9

Lord John's reply was simple.

"Sire, if you give me your word and issue me a letter under your seal guaranteeing what you have agreed to, I shall depart directly and achieve what I have promised, as soon as it can be done."

10

With this, the Emperor granted leave to Lord John to depart his presence and descend from the tower. But first there was a detail to consider.

"My Lord," said John of Procida, "if it pleases you, I would like to leave your city in a way that discourages any suspicion about our secret, by you announcing before everybody, but especially my Latin friends, that I am a traitor. For my part, I will say that I insulted you and that I am fleeing your realm for that reason."

Emperor Michael agreed to this pact. Of course, both men left the tower happily and serenely.

11

That same year, Lord John of Procida left Constantinople and returned to Sicily, traveling disguised as a Franciscan friar. There he spoke to Lord Palmeri Abbati, Lord Alaimo of Lentini and some other Sicilian barons.

"You miserable men," he said to the nobles, "sold like so many mistreated dogs, has your courage been petrified? If you don't act now, you'll always be slaves, but will you always have regrets and shame thinking that you could have been lords?"

At this, the barons began to complain.

"Lord John," one asked, "how can we do otherwise, finding ourselves under the power of one of the world's most powerful monarchs? It seems to us impossible to free ourselves from this servitude."

"I can free you," responded Lord John, "so long as you and your friends follow my advice, and believe in what I tell you to do."

"We're ready to follow you to the death!" came the reply.

12

"You shall all have to arrange for the common people to rebel on a date to be decided," explained Lord John. "It will be on the day of a religious feast."

"How can it be planned as you are saying?" demanded Lord Walter of Caltagirone. "Don't forget that our king is the most powerful monarch in the Christian world. Your words and your plan strike me as nothing more than vanity."

13

Understanding the sentiments of these noblemen, Lord John responded without hesitation,

"Do you believe that I would have committed myself to so great an undertaking if I hadn't first thought about how to do it? You need only have confidence that within a year your efforts will bear fruit."

With this, the barons gave their consent and swore credence to John's proposal, each man sealing a letter[13] stating the following:

14

To the magnificent, great and powerful lord the King of Aragon, Count of Barcelona, in all your exalted power, to which we commend ourselves for your royal favour.

First among us, Count Alaimo of Lentini, Lord Palmeri Abbati and Lord Walter of Caltagirone, joined by all the brethren barons of the island of Sicily. We greet you with every reverence. Ruled by our present sovereign, we have come to view ourselves as men who have been sold, subjugated as beasts. We wish to submit our fealty to your authority and that of your consort, our Lady, to whom we dutifully convey our homage, praying that you may deign to free us of our enemies just as Moses delivered his people from the hands of the Pharaoh, so that we may ensure our children's future, secure from the deceitful, devouring wolves. We shall write to you every day, or otherwise credit to you Lord John our secretary.[14]

15

Once the letter was sealed, the noblemen prevailed upon Lord John to keep his part of the agreement, as they would keep theirs. At that point, John showed the nobles the letters from the Emperor Michael Palaeologue committing that monarch's faith in him and in this undertaking. This having been done, Lord John departed with the letters and the confidence of lords Alaimo, Palmeri and Walter.

16

In those times the Holy See of Rome was occupied and ruled by Pope Nicholas III, the former Cardinal John Gaetan Orsini, of a distinguished Roman family. He lived in a castle called Soriano, and Lord John of Procida went to find him there.[15]

"Holy Father," he asked, "I should ask to speak to you in private audience."

"Of course," replied Pope Nicholas, who graciously received him.

17

"Holy Father," said Lord John, "you who enjoy the support of the world, which you would rule in peace, are displeased at the fate of those miserable wretches cast out of the Kingdom of Sicily and Apulia, who find nobody to rule them or to keep them, as if they were lepers! I hope it would please you to give them back their homes, like everybody else on this earth, for they are good and decent Christians!"

18

"How can I go against King Charles, my spiritual son, who protects the integrity and the honour of the Church of Rome?" the Pope asked.

"I happen to know that King Charles almost never obeys your orders," Lord John replied.

"How has he not obeyed me? What are you saying?"

"Holy Father, you would do well to remember the time you tried to get him to marry a woman of your family, and not only did he refuse but he disdainfully tore your letter to shreds."

The Pope was without words, perhaps astounded that details of the incident were so widely known.

"Why are you surprised?" John asked. "For years it has been spoken of throughout Sicily and around the Kingdom. Everybody talks about how Charles didn't want to be related to you and how nowadays he just ignores your orders."

19

"What you say is true," the Pope said, clearly irritated. "I wouldn't mind making him regret a few of the things he's done."

"Nobody in the world is in a better position than you are to do it."

"How, pray tell?"

"If you might consider my suggestion," John responded, "if I were you I'd take back Sicily and the rest of the Kingdom."

"By saying that they belong to the Church?"

"I'd let somebody else do it," John explained. "The pretext would be that this other person is loyal to the Church, and acting with your consent, at least implicitly. That he is the kind of man who, if the occasion presented itself, would willingly be related by marriage to you and your family. It'll put all of us in our proper place."

"Who would this man be that could do what you suggest, and risk placing himself against King Charles? Who do you have in mind that would be willing to undertake this kind of thing?"

"If you trust me with your very soul," responded John, "I shall tell you, and I'll show you how all of this plan can come to be."

"I swear on my faith, and I promise to keep it a secret between us."

20

"Holy Father," replied John, "the man in question is none other than Peter, the King of Aragon, and he would act together with Michael Palaeologue, if you so approved. The Sicilian barons would help, and they've already sworn as a group to do so, with me as their representative."

21

"Do as you will, but without our letter," said Pope Nicholas.

"It cannot be that way," said Lord John. "Instead, if you give me a letter, I will take it with me, along with the other two. You shall have my full assurance that it will be kept secret."

22

"I shall have it done as you wish," said the Pope. With this, he had the letters written. When it came time to seal them, he did so not with the Papal lead seal, as was customary for diplomatic correspondence, but with his personal wax seal.[16]

With this, a very satisfied John of Procida, letters in hand, left the Papal presence.

This is what the letters said:

23

To Our Most Christian Son, King Peter of Aragon, Pope Nicholas III sends his blessing.

Knowing that our faithful children in Sicily under the rule of King Charles find themselves ill-treated, we pray and command you to take under your authority, acting on our behalf, the island of Sicily and its Sicilians, ruling them under us as a conquering son of Holy Mother Roman Church. What is more, we ask that you believe the words of Lord John of Procida, our trusted representative, and keep secret these details, which thus far are known to nobody else. Know that if it pleases you to assume this task, you shall do so without fear of reprisals.[17]

24

With the Pope's sealed correspondence in hand, Lord John began a voyage to Catalonia. Once he arrived, he immediately went before the King of Aragon.[18] The king rendered full honours to John, receiving him happily at court.

John was King Peter's guest for some time, not as a stranger but as a friend. Then he accompanied the monarch to the island of Majorca. There Lord John broached the subject of the malcontent Sicilian baronage.

"Sire," said John, "I would like to speak to you privately of a matter that has been entrusted to me, something that best be heard by our ears only, and those of God Himself."

"Tell me whatever you wish," the king replied. "It shall remain between us."

"Anything I tell you must be kept in the strictest secrecy. I must ask you to swear to it."

"You have my word," said Peter.

"Sire," said John, "please know that what I shall tell you is something I know firsthand, whether by what I've seen or what I've been told. On the fate of you and your dynasty, I stand by my words."

"So shall it be," said Peter, slightly startled. "Lord John, what do you wish to tell me?"

"It is a matter involving work that I have already undertaken, and if you grant me your credibility and trust, it is something that could make you an even greater king than you already are."

"John, I place in you my belief and my trust, shall it please God."

25

"Sire, do you wish to be redressed for the injustices perpetrated against you in times past? Things that have disgraced you as a king but also as a Christian? As you already know, King Manfred left the Kingdom of Sicily to his daughter, your wife, yet you, acting as would behove a lesser man, a weakling, a coward, do not want to come forth to assert your rights. I would remind you, once again, of your grandfather, who the French killed so vilely at Muret in Toulouse.[19] Now you can avenge him, and make up for the damage inflicted upon you for so long. You need only be decisive and show some courage."

The king's reply was not long in coming.

26

"Have you taken leave of your senses, John? How could I achieve what you want me to do? Don't you know that the House of Anjou has half the world under its control? Especially King Charles? How can a monarch of limited power, like me, challenge him?" The king thought for a long moment. Then he continued, "But if you were to show me some way to do it, I might be willing to try."

"If I were to give you the entire country without the need to draw a sword, wouldn't you take it? What is more, I'll give you a hundred thousand gold ounces to cover every expense and the land itself."

27

"Since it is you who would pursue this undertaking," ventured

King Peter, "and I honestly have my doubts about the outcome, can you reassure me in some way?"

With this, Lord John arranged to show King Peter the letters from the Pope, the Emperor Michael and the Sicilian barons. Upon reading these, the king's mood changed for the better as he began to consider the potential success of the plan.

"Well, you're a faithful friend," said the king, "which is why I've sought your advice. And I'll trust in God too, if the Holy Father wills it. Your news is comforting, and if the Pope supports me then I could do no less. I affirm my trust in you and your abilities. But I must still remind you to ensure that this task is completed. For my part, I will do everything in my power to make that possible."

28

"Sire," said Lord John, "for now I must return in secret to meet with the Pope, with the Emperor Michael, and with the Sicilian barons. When I come back to meet with you again, I will bring more than enough money to defray the cost of this project, and we can discuss in detail how you have come to be entrusted with this responsibility. But for no reason, as a question of life or death, should you discuss this with anybody. To do so would be far too risky."

29

Having spoken of many things, John of Procida and the King of Aragon sailed together from Barcelona to Majorca. There they took leave of each other, agreeing to keep the proposed plan to themselves until John could return to Catalonia after meeting with Pope Nicholas, Emperor Michael and the Sicilians. For now, King Peter remained in Barcelona.

Lord John returned by sea to Italy, his first stop, arriving at Pisa and riding secretly to Viterbo, where he found the Pope, who was happy to see him.

"How did the King of Aragon receive your proposal?" Pope Nicholas asked.

"Holy Father," Lord John responded, "I have completed the mission with success. The King of Aragon has accepted your command and agreed in principle to the plan. He sends greetings and commends himself to your holy blessing. He has sent you a secret letter offering his cooperation, hoping that everything goes as you wish."

"How did the King of Aragon seem to you?" the Pontiff asked.

"Consider that he is one of the wisest men in the world, and the bravest knight in Christendom today."

"Those are the kind of men I like, and the kind we need. But we also need the Sicilians. So go to Sicily and tell them of my part and Michael's. Tell them that it won't be long before they are free of King Charles and his domination, that they have my word that I will help them behind the scenes. And tell them that they will finally have a good and decent king, if it pleases God to grant them one."

30

With that, Lord John left the Pope and made his way to the port of the town of Tarquinia, north of Rome. There he boarded a Pisan merchant ship bound for Trapani, where he met Lord Palmeri Abbati, who summoned the allied Sicilian barons to that western Sicilian city.

John recounted to the assembled nobles how the Pope had ceded the rule of Sicily to King Peter of Aragon, and how King Peter had happily and willingly accepted it, and how he swore the death of the barons' enemies.

"You must keep the fact secret until you see me again," John explained. "I must go to the court of Emperor Michael, to whom I shall explain the details, including the question of funds to cover the expense of the war. We will need a great military force, and we shall execute everything well, God willing. I ask you in God's name to keep this plan secret. The time has finally come for you to be freed from servitude and from the power of your enemies. We shall avenge the mistreatment and misery we have endured."

Lord John then took leave of Palmeri Abbati. From Trapani he took a Venetian galley to the Byzantine lands, to Negropont. From there he travelled to Constantinople, disguised as a Franciscan friar to avoid being recognized.

31

When John arrived in Constantinople he hastened to meet with the Emperor Michael secretly.

"Be cheerful," John told the Emperor. "What you wished to see done has finally been done. The Pope has agreed to the death and destruction of King Charles. We'll have the support of the Sicilian barons and our friends. Our most important ally, who will lead the battle, is King Peter of Aragon. He has sworn alliance to us in life and in death. His friends will be your friends, and his enemies will be your enemies." At this point John pulled several scrolls from a leather bag before continuing. "I can show you that what I am saying is so. Here are letters from the Pope and from the Sicilian barons. Everything is in motion. During 1282 Sicily will rebel against King Charles and the French there will be killed. We'll seize his galleys, his merchant ships and every other vessel he has, along with their cargo. Everything he was planning to attack you with. His plans will be thwarted. King Charles will be so busy contending with his problems over there that he won't be able to make any trouble over here."

32

When the Emperor saw the sealed letters, he said,

"I feel compelled to tell you to do whatever you wish, seeing as you have achieved something that no other man in the world could have. It seems that God Himself gave you the will to do it."

John wasted no time in responding. "Sire, give me thirty thousand gold ounces to raise an army and a fleet, and to recruit knights. I ask that you send with me to Catalonia your delegate and your best friend to consign the money personally to King Peter."

"Listen John," said the Emperor. "I'd like to establish more than a military alliance. I'd like to welcome King Peter into my family by betrothing one of my daughters to one of his sons. That will show the courage of my conviction."

33

"That seems to me like a good idea," said Lord John, "and I believe the King of Aragon will gladly consent to it. For now, I ask you to take care of what I have requested, as I cannot stay here too long. Also, I'll need to be escorted by somebody you can trust."

The Emperor immediately had the gold weighed and placed in the Genoan galley on which Lord John was to set sail for Barcelona. John was accompanied by a valiant, wise, prudent knight named Accardo Latino, a native of the Lombard Plains of northern Italy.

34

Further along in his travels, Lord John boarded a Pisan ship. He asked the crew of news from Italy. They responded that

Pope Nicholas had died recently, but they knew nothing more.[20]

"Godspeed," said Lord John, pretending not to give credence to gossip — at least not while Accardo was present. Whatever had happened in Italy, the Summer seas were tranquil, and John tried to enjoy the rest of his voyage to Sicily.

As soon as he landed at Trapani, he met with Palmeri Abbati and the other barons, who had to go to a meeting on the island of Malta. Lord John went with them.

When they were all assembled there, the Sicilians gave a great feast for Accardo, the ambassador of Emperor Michael.

"Well," said Lord John, "since the Emperor of Constantinople has sworn solemn alliance with the King of Aragon and with you barons of Sicily, he has sent me with more than enough money to undertake the war, so victory is now within our reach."

Then Alaimo of Lentini stood up and spoke. "Lord John, we heartily thank Emperor Michael for all he has done, working day and night to tear us from the servitude our enemies have kept us in. But know that recently we have reached a crossroads that could change our predicament. With Pope Nicholas, who was at the head of all this planning, anything could be achieved, but he is now dead. And because he is now gone, I don't agree with the idea of proceeding with this plan, but we should keep secret what we've done so far. I fear that God may not be on our side, seeing as He has seen fit to strike down the Pope. I take that as a sign of God's will. Let's all wait to see who becomes Pope. The next one might even, per chance, be friendly to King Peter. In that case, he'd be our friend, and then we could decide whether to act. I believe this to be the best counsel for now."

The barons nodded and murmured their unanimous agreement. Disturbed by the fact of the Pope's death, many seemed doubtful, even intimidated. Withdrawing from the plan seemed reasonable.

35

One glance at John's face was enough to see his annoyance growing as he listened to these words. He did not long hold his tongue.

"My lords," he railed, "I am utterly amazed at what you are saying. It's true enough that the Pope is dead, but should that be anything to alter our plan? We mustn't abandon such a great undertaking. If the new Pope is friendly to us, so much the better, for the Church of Rome forgives all sinners. If, on the other hand, the new Pope is less than friendly to us, we'll take the country by force despite him and the Church of Rome. So long as you are loyal and strong, we'd be following in the footsteps of Emperor Frederick II, who wielded power far greater than King Charles. I appeal to you to remain loyal to the king in whom you have placed your trust, and that you go ahead with the plan we have discussed, wholeheartedly and without reservations."

Hearing John's words roused the barons' courage, but they still insisted on hearing the opinion of the King of Aragon.

"I would like to go to him," John responded, "and Lord Accardo personally wants to deliver the money provided by the Emperor to pay for the fleet and soldiers we need to carry out our plan."

36

John and Accardo soon embarked for Catalonia incognito, dressed as Franciscans. The seas were still summery, and before long the pair stood before the King of Aragon in the royal palace next to Barcelona's cathedral.

King Peter was happy to see John, who he took by the arm and led into a private chamber. Here the sovereign expressed his sorrow at the passing of Pope Nicholas.

"I'm afraid this puts an end to our scheme. After all, we relied greatly on the Pope for support. There seems to be no point in talking about the plan, much less going ahead with it."

37

"Sire," replied John, "you best not tempt fate with such words. We must have faith that the next Pontiff will be a good one sympathetic to our cause. But there is nothing to fear. You have already considered this plan carefully, and our friends in Sicily know as much. They and I are as steadfast as ever in our conviction, regardless of the Pope's death. The man who has travelled here with me is a knight sent by the Emperor Michael. His name is Accardo Latino and he is very wise. I ask that you receive him with full honours and listen to what he has to say. Please know that we have brought with us thirty thousand gold ounces to arm the forces that are needed."

38

The King was encouraged by these words. "Well, I see it is God's will, as well as your own, for this plan to go ahead."

"Sire," said John, "the nobleman who I wish to present to you is a trusted knight of the Emperor of Constantinople, and also serves as his ambassador." With this, John and King Peter left the private chamber and stepped into the throne room. Lord Accardo stepped forward, bowed slightly, and was announced.

After conveying the Emperor's greetings, Accardo explained to King Peter that, "my lord the Emperor has expressed the greatest wish to welcome into his family you and your son." Two footmen brought forth a small but heavy chest full of the gold coins, placed this before the throne, opened it and left the room, leaving only the three men to speak with each other about the plan to be undertaken the next year.[21]

Within weeks, there arrived a message from the Court of Rome. A cardinal had been elevated to the Holy See. This was none other than Simon of Tours, a Frenchman, who had taken the name Martin III.[22]

When they heard this news, they agreed that, "there is much to say and much to think about, considering that the new Pope is a close friend of King Charles. As Pontiff, Simon could create grave obstacles to our plans."

39

At this point King Peter said to Lord John, "Good God, let's think carefully about what we are going to do."

"The best friend of King Charles' court is this Pope," said John. "For now, let's prepare ourselves, and then we'll see how to obtain success. We'll find a way. Let's be careful, and let us not overlook any details."

Together they began working to raise the forces necessary. The weeks passed.

In April an ambassador of the King of France called at the Aragonese court. The visit was an exercise in formality, yet amicable.

"The King of France commands me to convey greetings to his fellow sovereign," the ambassador began. After pausing for a moment, he continued, "My lord King Philip has been given to understand that you are preparing a great army and armada to attack the Saracens.[23] He wishes to offer to you every assistance. He should like to know if you might send to him, with one of your messengers, a letter setting forth details of your route and the specific Saracens you shall attack. Should you need monies to equip your fleet, you need only tell him and he will provide as much as you require."

40

Formality seemed to be the order of this day, but so was candor.

"I heartily thank your lord the King of France for all that he has offered," replied Peter, "and for his kindness, but I already have all the funds sufficient to my needs. There is no purpose in speaking of letters. As you know, your sovereign lord was my brother-in-law.[24] So, in speaking to him through you, as if speaking to a knight, I place my trust in the honour of your word. Here is mine. Tell the King of France, on my behalf, that the truth is that I have a fine army with which to attack the Saracens, but I would never divulge to anybody the route I shall take or the place I shall attack. Still, I believe that all will soon be known, and the world will speak of what has come to be."

41

With this proposal the ambassador departed Barcelona and returned to his lord the King of France. Seeing and hearing the message from his brother-in-law the King of Aragon, King Philip immediately sent word to his treasury in Paris, ordering that forty thousand tornesels be sent to the King of Aragon, and this was done.[25] He also dispatched an ambassador to his uncle King Charles with news of Peter's planned campaign against the Saracens, noting that he knew not where it might take place, "and therefore I suggest that you guard your territory[26] and your realm, and that you advise the Holy Father to do the same."

42

The French ambassador undertook to go to Apulia.[27] Finding King Charles at Viterbo with newly-elected Pope Martin, he conveyed the message sent from the King of France.

Upon hearing these words, King Charles hastened to the Pope's residence on the other side of town, where he explained, "Holy Father, an ambassador has come to me from the King of France with news from Barcelona. The King of Aragon is building a great fleet and does not wish to say where he will take it. He is a felon prone to treachery.[28] So I ask that you send him a letter asking where he plans to go, offering him great assistance if he attacks the Saracens. But if he attacks Christians, I would ask you to order him, on pain of the earthly punishment you hold in your hands, not to go against the faithful of the Church of Rome or damage their property."[29]

43

Hearing Charles speak these words, the Pope commented, "My son, what you wish will be done."

He immediately summoned to the Papal presence Brother James, a Dominican.

"Listen," said Pope Martin to the friar, "I order you to go to the King of Aragon on my behalf and explain to him that I have come to understand that 'you are preparing a great armada to attack the Saracens.' Those are the precise words you are to use. Tell him that, if such be true, he is to go ahead with God's will, that God shall bestow upon him every honour and victory. Tell him that I shall willingly help him if there be such a need. Ask him, on my behalf, to advise me where he plans to go, be it Egypt, Granada or the Berber lands.[30] Wherever he is planning to go, I want to know. But should his enterprise touch the Church of Rome, he must not act without my command. What is more, he has a standing order, on pain of the earthly punishment I exercise, to refrain from making war on any Christian. And tell him, in no uncertain terms, that I await a plain and honest reply."

44

James, the Dominican friar, travelled to Aragon with one of his confreres. Received by King Peter, the cleric explained the purpose of his mission, reciting the Pontiff's own words.

The monarch summoned John of Procida, saying, "Listen to the message sent to me by Pope Martin."

Then king and counselor immediately met privately, and in the same place and on the same day King Peter issued a response for Brother James to take to the Pope:

"Please tell Pope Martin that we thank him, as if he were our own father, for offering to aid our enterprise and for the paternal love he has shown us. Tell him that if we should ever need his help we shall not hesitate to ask it of him, naturally turning to him as if he were our earthly father. Tell him that, as to the matter of knowing where we shall attack the Saracens, by no means can he be told. We would cut off our own hand if it revealed such a secret. Therefore, we ask the Pope to pardon us on this occasion, because no other course is imaginable, but if it pleases God I shall go visit the Holy Father and his brother cardinals, who will not be disappointed. For which, I hope it will please him to pray for us and our undertaking."

45

Upon receiving King Peter's reply to the Pope, Brother James immediately departed for Italy, where he found both Pope Martin and King Charles at Montefiascone.[31]

Hearing the friar's report, the Pope was astounded to the point of speechlessness.

That was rarely the case of King Charles, who remarked acidly, "Well, Holy Father, I told you that the King of Aragon is a felon.[32] Just listen to the beautiful riposte he has sent you!" Charles could never resist a sarcasm. "But let him do as God pleases," the monarch continued, "and as long as he wages war on the Saracens, you and the Papal court should be satisfied enough."

The Pope was still silent as he mentally tallied the sum value of Charles' comments with the response received from Peter, as if the words of one king could nullify those of the other. But he finally spoke.

"Take care to protect the lands you rule," the Pontiff warned his friend. "for I've heard it said that Peter of Aragon is adept at prosecuting a military campaign like no other king alive."

"Holy Father," Charles said, "we'll have to wait and see what he does."

46

Meanwhile, back in Catalonia, John of Procida explained to King Peter, "I wish to go to Sicily to arrange that this year it rebel against King Charles."

King Peter reminded him to treat the matter with the utmost secrecy, so as to ensure its success. With this, John of Procida and Accardo Latino took leave of the Aragonese court.

Upon arriving at Trapani in January, Lord John sent for Palmeri Abbati, Alaimo of Lentini and Walter of Caltagirone, along with the other Sicilian barons who were to participate in the plan.[33]

Standing before the assembled baronage, Lord John set forth something of the strategy.

"Distinguished lords," he began, "know that the King of Aragon has put together the greatest armada in the world, to be manned most competently. Its admiral, the most loyal, most courageous man to sail the sea, is Lord Roger of Lauria, who is from Calabria but has served the King of Aragon for many years. He is the greatest warrior and military planner one could find, and a sworn enemy of the French, who killed his father at the Battle of Benevento. So just imagine how this will shake the very ground upon which King Charles stands. And never could it be done better than now, with King Charles at the Papal court and his son the hereditary prince in Provence. But I am telling you these things much in advance, so that you can best prepare your lands and manors across Sicily."

All present agreed to Lord John's clarion call to cut the ground from under King Charles' feet and break his hold on them once and for all.[34]

47

These are the events that came about on the first Tuesday of April (sic) immediately following Easter Sunday in the year one thousand two hundred and eighty-two.[35]

Palmeri Abbati, Alaimo of Lentini, Walter of Caltagirone and the barons in league with them were in Palermo to incite the rebellion as they had secretly planned.

Feasting was customary on the days following Easter. This year, as usual, such a feast took place outside the city walls in the fields of the rural district called "the Holy Spirit."

It was during this merrymaking that a Frenchman grabbed hold of a local woman, groping her zealously. This kind of molestation had occurred in the past with other women.

But today the woman being touched let out a loud scream, and several enraged local men came to her aid. In the violent riot that ensued, some of the barons incited the crowd against all the French. There, in the noise and confusion, the few French soldiers present tried to defend themselves with daggers and swords. The Palermitans responded with similar weapons, and began to hurl stones at the outnumbered soldiers, shouting, "Kill the French!"

Before long, the angry crowd was within the city walls. Making their way along streets and into squares, they killed every Frenchman they came upon.

In the confusion the captain, a local man who had sworn fealty to King Charles, confronted the mob but he and his men were immediately beaten into retreat. They sought refuge in his tower.[36]

The Palermitans, meanwhile, hastily organized themselves into squads. They went through the city streets, killing as many French as they encountered.

Then several squads made for the captain's tower. The captain agreed to surrender on certain conditions, and with this the men descended from the tower. At that point, finding themselves with absolute power in their hands, the rioters broke their word, killing the captain and his company.

Next, the mob went to the monasteries of the Franciscans and Dominicans, where all the French-speaking friars were killed in their churches.

Seeing all this, the barons returned to their lands and followed the mob's example across Sicily. The exception was Messina, which held out for a while.

In Palermo alone three thousand French were killed.[37]

48

King Charles was at the Papal court when a messenger brought him news of the rebellion from the archbishop of Monreale.[38]

The archbishop's letter recounted to King Charles how all the monarch's French compatriots were killed, and how the revolt had spread from Palermo across Sicily. The archbishop did not know why they were killed, nor how the massacre had come about, "so do reflect upon this matter and the best course of action to be taken."

49

Naturally, King Charles was profoundly disturbed at the messenger's news. The King of Sicily went immediately to the Pope, to whom he said,

"Holy Father, I bring terrible news of my affairs, brought to me by a messenger sent by the archbishop of Monreale. His letter tells of how the Sicilians have rebelled against me and killed all of my people. I do not know why they did this. I ask for your best advice, if it pleases you to offer me any. After all, if my kingdom suffers, so does the Church of Rome."

"My son," the Pope replied, "fear not but that I shall offer you every help and advice that is in my power to give. Return to your kingdom, equip an army and go to Sicily to take back the realm that is yours. Do so without violence if you can. Take with you my delegate and my letter, and tell the Sicilians, on my behalf, that their island belongs to the Holy See, that it is in the Papal gift, and that they must return it to you."

With this encouragement, King Charles took leave of the Pope.

50

That very same day, Charles met in council with all the cardinals and all his friends in the Papal court, asking, in the name of God, that they advise him how to confront the Sicilians, who had massacred his people. A cardinal stood up to speak. It was James Savelli.[39]

"King Charles, know that the entire Court of Rome wishes to advise and assist you, and that we have every reason to do so, seeing that you have done much to honor the Church of Rome in her mission. For that reason I wish that, before anything else is done, you send to Sicily a cardinal legate to negotiate. He should pursue everything that can be said and done so that your realm can be reclaimed, through peace and diplomacy if possible, and through war only if that fails."

All present were in agreement with his wise words. The Pope was pleased too, and he immediately summoned Gerard Bianchi, a cardinal, to undertake the mission to Sicily on behalf of the Holy See and King Charles.[40]

51

Meanwhile, King Charles sent messages to other courts describing recent events, and to his son Prince Charles as well as his nephew King Philip of France.

To King Philip he explained that he knew not the reason for the rebellion or why the Sicilians killed the French, asking his nephew, "if the King of France can offer any words of counsel," at his earliest convenience. The reply was not long in coming.

Indeed, hearing the news, the King of France became very irritated, saying to Prince Charles,

"My kinsman, I truly fear that this might be the work of the King of Aragon, who you may recall did not wish to tell me where his expedition was going even though I contributed forty thousand tornesels to it. I have great suspicions about his motives. May the crown be snatched from my head shall I not make him regret his actions if it be he who has instigated this affront to our house!" King Philip paused to think about the impact of his words, then continued, "Take this message to your father. He should go to Apulia and order our kinsmen Robert of Artois and Peter of Alençon, along with our vassal John of Dammartin and as many barons and knights as he can find, to prepare for a campaign. They should be told what has happened in Sicily, and that they must stand ready to support their king."

52

Now in that same year, 1282, King Charles left Brindisi with a large fleet. His army then made its way by land into Calabria to the city of Reggio, the force composed of troops from France, Provence, Lombardy, Tuscany and the environs of Rome. After crossing the strait into Sicily, the army, accompanied by Gerard Bianchi, encamped at Santa Maria of Rocca Amatori.[41]

The large invasion brought dread to the Messinians, many of whom feared being put to death. They hastened to send envoys to beg for mercy from King Charles and Cardinal Gerard, who had come to retake control of the island in the name of its lawful temporal and ecclesiastical lords.

The Messinians reasoned that Charles would be content enough just to have Sicily back under his control, and that he would make no further demands upon them.

They were sorely mistaken. The monarch flatly rejected their pleas, telling the envoys that traitors to his royal authority could expect no promise that their lives would be spared. Indeed, death awaited them and their children. So great was the offense perpetrated against the Church of Rome and the House of France that the only forgiveness the rebels could expect was death itself, which would serve them right. "And do not come before me again," he added dryly.

With that, a messenger returned to Messina to convey the response of King Charles. The leaders of the Messinians spent four days in council debating whether to defend themselves or to consign themselves for execution.

53

One day Guy of Montfort arrived with Hugh of Brienne and a large contingent of knights and foot soldiers and headed westward along the Tyrrhenian coast to a town called Milazzo, laying waste to everything they encountered.[42] The local residents came out of the city thinking they might defend themselves, only to be slain by the French. When the news of this massacre reached Messina, that city's leaders sent for the Papal legate, Cardinal Gerard, who was already headed there to meet King Charles.

This ugly incident occurred in June, when the legate entered Messina and presented the Pope's letter to the city informing the residents of the actions that were being taken against them. To keep the peace, they offered the key to their city to King Charles, as their lawful sovereign, who held in his hands the power of life and death. The Pope's letter expressed Rome's sentiments in these unequivocal words:

54

To the treacherous 'Jews' of the island of Sicily, Pope Martin III sends the kind of greetings one sends to those who break the peace, kill Christians and spill the blood of our faithful.

We command you, immediately upon reading our letter, to return the dominion you have usurped to our spiritual son, namely Charles, King of Jerusalem and Sicily by authority of the Holy Church of Rome.[43] You are ordered to obey him, Charles, as your legitimate ruler. In the event that you do not obey him, we will declare you to be under excommunication and interdict, this to be confirmed according to the customary legal means.

55

Once they understood the letter and its orders, the Messinians were gravely fearful. They elected from among the populace a delegation of thirty men to consider how the city should come to an agreement with King Charles and the Papal legate. After having met and considered their choices, they went to the legate, saying, "We have come to you to explain what must be done."

"Tell me what you would like to do," responded the legate.

"Here is the agreement we wish to make with King Charles," the chief delegate said. "We will return his dominion to him and render to him the taxes to which he is entitled, just as we paid them in the time of King William long ago.[44] But we do not want to be ruled by lords other than Latins, which is to say that we want to be governed by our own officials, not by Frenchmen or Provençals.[45] We wish to be pardoned the offense we and our sons have committed against his knights and his people. If he grants this, he shall have our goodwill and our fealty."

Hearing this, the legate said, "We will send this proposal to King Charles' encampment and we shall await his reply. We'll make every effort to achieve a good result, if it pleases God."

Cardinal Gerard immediately called his chamberlain, commanding the man to deliver to King Charles a letter setting forth the proposal and its conditions. As legate, he added his personal recommendation that the sovereign accept the proposal and pardon the Sicilians, so that God, in turn, might forgive he who sat upon the throne.

56

Hearing the Messinians' demands, a very irritated King Charles exclaimed,

"Those who deserve death are demanding terms! Not only do they seek to deprive me of my dominions, they have the audacity to invoke the ancient laws of King William, who lacked lands and revenues of his own![46] Tell them that I have not the slightest intention of meeting their terms, but to keep peace with the Pope's legate I will suspend their death sentences. Having said that, I expect them to submit to my authority and will. They shall accord me all the rights to which I am entitled as their lord, paying taxes as tradition and law dictate. Whether they like it or not, they have to accept my terms. Otherwise, they'd better be prepared to defend themselves."

With that, the legate's chamberlain returned to Messina carrying the royal response. When the thirty Messinian delegates heard it, they brought together the townsfolk to hear King Charles' terms. In a single voice the populace replied,

"We'll fight for our rights before bowing to vendetta. Better to die defending our city than to be punished at the hands of our enemy!"

The citizenry's reaction was recounted to the legate. Infuriated, he told the leaders,

"As you don't wish to agree to this accord with me as the Papal legate and with King Charles as your lord, I, acting on behalf of the Holy Father and the Church of Rome, declare all in your city excommunicated and interdicted."

Without further comment, an angry Cardinal Gerard left Messina, but first he ordered all the local clergy to depart from the city immediately, remaining outside its walls for three full days. He then commanded the Messinian leaders, under pain of grave penalty from the Church of Rome, to present themselves to the Pope within forty days to hear the formal decree of excommunication and interdict.

57

When King Charles met with the legate and heard the Messinians' response, he called a council of his counts to decide what to do. The barons advised him to prepare for battle, in order that he take back his dominion by force.[47]

King Charles spent a day and a night meeting with his most trusted advisors. The following morning he sent for his barons and said,

"Lords, I disagree with you, with the council I have called. If I were to attack directly, as you advise me, I would lay waste to the land I rule. What is more, I do not wish to kill children, for they are not at fault. Instead, I'd rather lay siege to the city, leaving to its leaders the choice of starving to death. Instead of anybody dying, we'll have back our land and with it our authority. Our tactics and our war machines will be more than enough to frighten the citizens into complying."

And so the strategy was set in motion.

One day, planning to do battle, the Messinian men, the women both aristocratic and humble, and even their children, constructed a wall around a high quarter of the city.[48] In this way they defended themselves. They elected a captain and a regent, and withstood the siege for two months without excessive sacrifice.

58

Meanwhile, it was said that King Peter of Aragon was about to launch his military expedition to Tunisia. There, in northern Africa, his forces occupied a territory called Alcoyll. Following a brief battle, he stayed there for a fortnight in August. John of Procida and the other Sicilian ambassadors went by sea to Catalonia (sic) to meet Peter, who above all else wanted to take the island of Sicily.[49]

The emissaries were John of Procida, a certain William of Messina and two other representatives from elsewhere in Sicily. Upon reaching the place where the King of Aragon was staying, the four were received with great honour.

John of Procida informed King Peter that King Charles

was at Messina, where he was laying siege to the city with a large army.

"What do you advise me to do about it?" King Peter asked.

"Act decisively, without doubting yourself," came the reply. "Go to Sicily, and send a message to King Charles to withdraw from the island that the Holy Father Pope Nicholas bestowed upon you, seeing as the realm belongs by right to your wife. Then wait for his response. Know that William, this gentleman who has accompanied me here, is an ambassador sent from Messina. The other two gentlemen with us are also representatives from Sicily. Sire, please listen to what they have come to say."

59

But first John of Procida, acting as ambassador of the Sicilian barons, spoke.

"Sire, all of us greatly wish for you to go to Sicily, to rid us of King Charles and his army. You are our only hope. For the love of God, we hope it pleases you to consider our request. If you do not decide to come to our aid, then please forgive us for submitting to the authority of King Charles and the Church of Rome."

Following his plea, the other representatives and ambassadors expressed similar sentiments to the King of Aragon.

60

"I shall willingly go to the island of Sicily," King Peter replied, "to aid those who have shown such great faith in me. Go tell everybody there, in every locality, that I will arrive soon. Tell them to take heart, that I'll soon be there to help them."

With this reassurance, the delegates left the royal presence and returned to their island.

61

King Peter immediately left Alcoyll and set sail for Sicily. Before long, he was at Trapani with Palmeri Abbati and the other Sicilian barons opposed to King Charles. His first act was to call a council to plan what to do next.

John of Procida rose to say, "Sire, if you wish to know what we think you should do, it seems to us that you must go first to Palermo. There, in the capital, it will be easiest to learn what King Charles is doing presently, and what he has done to Messina and to the country. Then, God willing, the situation itself will dictate what we must do."

And so it was done.

62

In the month of August in the Year of Our Lord Jesus Christ one thousand two hundred and eighty-two, the King of Aragon rode from Trapani to Palermo.

The Palermitans celebrated his arrival as do men liberated from the shadow of death. Six thousand welcomed him in a great revelry: dames and damsels, men and women, counts and barons.

The archbishop of Palermo, who should have crowned him, was recently deceased. There being an episcopal vacancy in Palermo, the archbishop of Monreale, not wishing to be the one to crown Peter, fled Sicily to go warn the Pope of the turn of events. And so Peter was crowned by the assent of the people.[50]

A few days later, he convened a great council with the Sicilian barons in Palermo.

63

There Palmeri Abbati rose to speak.

"Sire," he said, "God be praised that you and John of Procida, in your goodness, have acceded to our request for assistance. We hope that this enterprise proceeds and then ends as well as it has begun. But I wish that you had brought a larger army. King Charles can call upon as many as fifteen thousand mounted men if he launches a full attack against Sicily. It will be all we can do just to meet him on the field of battle. So it seems to me that we will need more men, I know not from where. Anyway, I believe Messina to be lost, being besieged nearly to the point of starvation."

64

Hearing these comments about the potentially great battlefield strength of King Charles raised grave doubts in King Peter's mind. Considering that his opponent might be emboldened enough to march on Palermo, Peter sent couriers around the island to keep watch on the situation.

That night, a notary arrived who was acting as an emissary on the part of the city of Messina. He told King Peter how that city had victuals enough for eight days and no more, saying that, "you must help and succor us by sending men and food, for there is no way we can continue to resist against King Charles. Otherwise we'll have no choice but to surrender."

65

After listening to these words, the King of Aragon convened a meeting of the Sicilian barons and explained this dire predicament to them. Then Walter of Caltagirone rose and said,

"Sire, as I see it, you should lead your knights to Milazzo, which is not far from Messina. It seems to me that as soon as King Charles knows you are nearby, he'll lift his siege and withdraw his army. On the other hand, if we lose Messina then we will have lost everything."

John of Procida suggested a slightly different course of action, saying,

"My opinion is that we do it another way, because King Charles is not a man who frightens easily and then flees. So let's do this. Let us send a letter to King Charles from King Peter stating that Pope Nicholas ceded this island to the King of Aragon, and therefore King Charles must depart. If he chooses not to release Sicily and not to leave, then you, Sire, defend it as your own. When King Charles contests your claim, as he will, send your admiral and galleys to Messina with the order that every vessel in those waters transporting food and arms to Charles' army be commandeered. At that point it will be expedient for Charles to lift the siege and Messina will be saved. What is more, you and your new subjects will be vindicated by refusing to bend to the will of any other ruler in the world. When Charles leaves, we'll see where he goes, whether it's on the island or in Calabria or someplace else in the Kingdom."

66

When King Peter and the assembled barons heard this, they all immediately agreed. Two Catalan knights, Sir William and Sir Almingo, were dispatched to King Charles' encampment with a letter from King Peter. This is what the letter said:

67

Peter of Aragon, King of Sicily, sends greetings to you, Charles, King of Jerusalem and Count of Provence.

We wish to make known our arrival on the island of Sicily, judged our realm by the authority of the Holy Church of

Rome in the person of the Successor of the Apostles, Pope Nicholas III. We command you, upon reading this, our letter, to leave the island of Sicily with all your people. Know that if you do not do so, the knights under our command will see fit to bring harm to yours.[51]

68

When he read this letter, King Charles called a meeting of his barons. The letter's contents astounded the nobles in its unabashed effrontery toward the monarch and his knights.

Count Guy of Montfort rose to say that it seemed strange to him that a king having so little power in his hands would have the audacity to confront one of the best and greatest kings on earth.

King Charles then announced that he was willing to entertain suggestions from anybody present willing to offer one.

At this, Count Hugh of Brienne[52] rose to declare that it seemed appropriate to respond to the King of Aragon with a letter accusing him of perpetrating great deception and betrayal, which were both grossly inappropriate, all the more so because Charles had never acted that way toward Peter. Furthermore, the letter should say that Peter's claim to Sicily was not, by any means, based on the authority of the Church of Rome or the Pope. Rather, the King of Aragon claimed it dishonestly, by treachery.

"Sire," Count Hugh continued, "you should send him an explicit order to remove himself from your dominion, that you will make him regret his treachery, that no noble lord should go against another without justification, and that he had dishonestly said that he was going to fight the Saracens but instead now places himself against fellow Christians and the Church of Rome, 'and against me, and I speak as well for the barons, who have voiced their agreement with me.'"

Whereupon King Charles had a letter drafted, to be delivered by King Peter's emissaries. This was the tenor of the letter:

69

Charles, by the Grace of God King of Jerusalem and Sicily, Count of Provence and Forcalquier, Prince of Capua to Piedimonte, sends greetings to Peter, King of Aragon and Count of Barcelona.[53]

We are amazed at the means you have used to enter the island of Sicily, judged ours by the authority of the Church of Rome. We order you, immediately, upon reading this letter, to depart the realm of Sicily, insofar as you are an evil traitor. Presently you shall witness my advance, along with my knights, who very much wish to encounter you and your forces.

70

The messengers departed as per Charles' command, soon reaching Palermo, where they presented the letter to King Peter, who hastily met with the barons in council. Here John of Procida rose to say,

"In God's name, send your admiral to Messina with a fleet right now. Order him to commandeer all of Charles' cargo ships, and to inflict every possible damage upon the enemy. I tell you this is something within our capacity to achieve. We can imprison Charles and leave him to starve to death. He'll be so miserable that he will welcome that fate."

Without hesitation, King Peter summoned his admiral, Lord Roger of Lauria, ordering him to undertake this mission. Arriving in the waters around Messina, the Aragonese fleet began to seize or destroy every Angevin cargo ship it encountered.

Meanwhile, an agent of Henry of Mari, Charles' Genoan admiral, had been spying in Palermo. As soon as he learned of the departure of Roger of Lauria with the Aragonese fleet, the spy made his way, as quickly as he could, to Charles' fleet near Messina to warn Henry.

Admiral Henry of Mari wasted no time going to warn Charles of the impending arrival of Peter's formidable fleet.

"Sire," said the admiral, "you should cross the strait over to Calabria. A spy has returned from Palermo to tell us that King Peter's admiral is heading toward Messina with his entire armada. He has enough strength to take the city. There is no question that we'll be defeated without so much as a land battle if he manages to intercept our supply route from the mainland. We'll run out of food within three days. If that isn't reason enough for you to decide as I advise, it'll soon be Winter, and you don't have a suitable port to harbor your cargo ships, which will be damaged in the rough seas. You best get back to the peninsula, where you can't be cut off from the resources of the rest of your realm."

This angered Charles no end. He convened a meeting of his barons and told them what Lord Henry of Mari had said. The barons were profoundly disturbed by this.

"This pains us all greatly," said one among them. "We wanted nothing more than to take Messina, whether by negotiation or by conquest, and now we shall not have it one way or the other. But there's nothing more to be done. We'll leave Sicily if that be the will of God."

And all the barons agreed this was the only course of action left them.

72

Hearing this comment, Charles was beside himself with rage, but he finally spoke after letting out a sigh of resignation.

"I'm as good as dead," he muttered, speaking more to himself than to anybody present, "so great has my failure been. Half of my kingdom is lost, taken by a man to whom I never committed the slightest offense. It pains me that I won't be able to take back Messina, but if that is the reality then we'll cross over to Calabria. When I manage to strike back, he who attacked me with this treachery, and whoever helped him do it, shall suffer so greatly that they will beg for death."

So ended his words to the barons. This was in September, when the army lifted the siege of Messina and began to withdraw to Calabria.

73

The next day, Queen Margaret[54] crossed the strait to Calabria with her suite, followed the day after by King Charles and most of his army. They ensured that the Messinians saw this evacuation, for Charles had one last plan. Leaving behind two captains commanding two thousand knights, he said,

"Stay beyond sight of their sentinels.[55] But when the Messinians leave the city to take what's left of our equipment, attack them. If you can get into the city, let me know and I'll return."

That was his order, but a spy told the Messinians what Charles had in mind, and nobody came out of the city. Seeing that Messina's gates remained closed, its walls ever impregnable, the knights abandoned their plan and embarked, crossing the strait and joining King Charles in Calabria.

"Sire," one of the captains reported, "we could not act on your plan because none of the Messinians left the city."

74

Hearing this irritated King Charles still more, moving him to say,

"From here, we'll watch to see what happens to them, as well as the King of Aragon and his army."

The next day, Admiral Roger of Lauria, acting on his lord's order, reached the harbor of Messina in great commotion escorted by a flotilla of ten galleys. He attacked what remained there of King Charles' fleet, either seizing or burning galleys and cargo ships. Five Pisan vessels were commandeered, and then docked in Messina. Roger hoped to capture King Charles at sea.

Learning what transpired at Messina pained King Charles so much that he wished he were dead. At the city of Reggio, in Calabria, he discharged from service all manner of men-at-arms, mercenaries as well as regular soldiers, except for those holding feudal tenure.[56]

This was during the month of October.

75

It was during the same month that King Peter arrived at Messina accompanied by John of Procida. They were received with great gaiety along a wide street by knights, ladies, damsels and all the aristocrats of the city in a feast fit for princes and kings and their lords and ladies.

And this is the end of our account.

76

It was a personal reason that compelled Lord John of Procida to plan this rebellion.

After one of his daughters was raped by an important

baron, John went before King Charles to seek justice. But King Charles refused to render the justice John sought.

This led Lord John to think, in the depth of his heart, of how he might destroy King Charles and vindicate the grave injury that had been suffered. That is why he planned the events about which we all have come to know.

77

May all those lords of kingdoms, cities, lands and castles, and those in every other position of authority, heed this example, ever avoiding the use of humiliation and injury against their vassals and their serfs. Those in power should never condone the perpetration of an atrocity. Rather, they should seek to ensure justice.

POSTLUDE

"Kings may be judges of the earth, but wise men are the judges of kings."

— Solomon ibn Gabirol

Emperor Michael of Constantinople died in December 1282, secure in the knowledge that the mass invasion planned by King Charles had been stymied. In April 1283, Queen Constance arrived at Messina with her children and John of Procida, who Peter named chancellor for Sicily, effectively a viceroy *pro tempore.*

In one of the war's memorable episodes, Charles and Peter were to meet for a duel to decide the fate of Sicily, each accompanied by a hundred fighting knights. This was to take place in June at Bordeaux, capital of the neutral French territories of Edward, King of England. Each warring king agreed to appear with his suite but it was tacitly understood that each would arrive at a different time. Then each sovereign claimed that the other was a coward. Most of the military engagements were more serious than this charade.

In a significant incident, King Charles' son and heir, Charles "the Lame," was taken prisoner by Roger of Lauria during a naval battle near Naples in June 1284 and held in the citadel of Cefalù.

By the time King Charles died early the next year, Angevin influence in Sicily had all but evaporated. The new king of Naples, his son (now Charles II), was still a prisoner, and the Papacy was at first reluctant to recognize him as the late monarch's heir. In the event, Pope Martin himself died a few months after Charles I.

In a gesture of alliance with his Angevin cousins, Philip III of France attacked Aragon, but his army was quickly defeated — as much by malaria as by force of arms. So ended the Aragonese Crusade.

In fact, all the key players were dead by the end of 1285: Charles of Naples, Philip of France, Peter of Aragon, Simon de Brion (Pope Martin).

The conditions of Peter's will dictated that his eldest son, Alfonso, would succeed him as King of Aragon, with James as King of Sicily. According to these terms, neither son was to ever rule both realms at the same time.

Although the fighting was finished for the time being, the end of the political conflict was nowhere in sight. The very name of the kingdom was disputed. As there were now rival claimants to the *Regnum,* there were two "Sicilies," the island ruled from Palermo by the Aragonese and the mainland ruled from Naples by the Angevins.

The war's bloodshed was real. Yet destiny, be it expressed through public will or Papal resolve, had shown itself to be a palimpsest that could be rewritten. It was politics that delivered Sicily into the hands of the Angevins, and it was politics that took it away.

The War of the Vespers re-drew the map of Europe, in the process saving the Eastern Orthodox Church from the dire fate (and likely extinction) that awaited her in the event of an Angevin conquest of Constantinople. Owing to its wide political impact, spanning the Mediterranean and a chunk of Europe, the conflict is referred to by a few modern historians as "the 'world war' of the thirteenth century."

In Sicily, paradoxically, the Vespers would serve as the impetus for centuries of rule from abroad, which was one of the things that the Sicilians ostensibly resented about the ousted French. Thus began Sicily's long "Spanish" period, even if Spain itself would not be unified for another two centuries. In the event, Sicily became a cornerstone in Aragon's Mediterranean thalassocracy, part of what later became the Spanish Empire.

Considering its effects on Mediterranean history, the resonance of the Vespers is more than justified. The revolt was certainly atypical of its era, yet very unlike the modern revolutions to which it is sometimes compared.

Was it, as the *Rebellion* states, part of a grand conspiracy to divert Charles' invasion away from Constantinople, or was that merely an unintended consequence? Here certainty is elusive, but the known facts suggest a plot as a distinct possibility, with John of Procida sowing the seeds of dissent and the Genoans, occasional allies of the Byzantines, as covert supporters and obvious beneficiaries.

The swiftness, efficiency and ruthlessness of the Vespers quickly became known to monarchs across Europe, but its clarion call went unheeded, for what was its overt message except that common people in large cities could take up arms?

The Angevin presence in Sicily is a phase noted but rarely celebrated. James, the second son of Peter of Aragon, was crowned King of Sicily in 1286 at the age of nineteen. With coronation came excommunication. No matter. Young James was acclaimed by the Sicilian nobility.

It was impossible to denigrate the position of King James

on purely dynastic or juridical grounds. His mother, as a Hohenstaufen, was the last heiress of her house. His father's line had been Kings of Aragon for centuries. His elder brother had recently succeeded to the "Crown of Aragon," a burgeoning mini-empire, as Alfonso III. His young sister was married to the King of Portugal. Last but not least was the undeniable fact that James actually ruled Sicily.

What is more, the peninsular kingdom ruled by Charles II was for the moment in disarray, its *de jure,* if uncrowned, monarch now languishing in a Catalonian citadel, where he was detained to avoid any possibility of his liberation in Sicily by Angevin forces.

Apart from the excommunication of James, the new Pontiff sought to put affairs in order. His predecessor had placed Sicily under interdict. Pope Honorius IV, conversely, wished to address the underlying problems that led to the war. In 1285, before the contested coronation, he had issued his *Constitutio Super Ordinatione Regni Siciliae,* a set of principles sympathetic to the Sicilians, which were to take effect in the event of an Angevin restoration in Sicily.

Pope Nicholas IV, who succeeded him three years later, was less amenable to reason. He ordered an attack on Sicily, which failed.

It was King Edward I of England, not the Pope, who mediated a tenuous peace in 1288. Charles II was released on condition that he renounce his claim to the island of Sicily. When the freed monarch reached Italy, Pope Nicholas absolved him of his vow to abide by the conditions he had agreed in Catalonia. In short, the treaty Charles had negotiated with the Aragonese was annulled.

The following year, after recognizing the Pope as his feudal suzerain, Charles was crowned "King of Sicily."

Gazing upon the record of the next few decades, we see the Aragonese of Sicily and Spain pitted against the Angevins of Italy and France, with one Pope after another acting as judge, jury and excommunicator. An endless series of pacts were formulated, a few agreed to, and all broken. Several attempts were made to invade Sicily. All failed miserably.

In early 1291, Alfonso III signed a peace treaty with Charles II of Naples and with Philip IV of France. Pope Nicholas was dead by the end of the next year.

In Sicily, James and his government were displeased with a treaty that left them excluded and politically isolated, unable to call upon Aragon for assistance in the case of an Angevin attack on the island.

Two years later, Pope Boniface VIII forced upon King James the infamous Treaty of Anagni. According to its terms, James wed, as his second wife, Bianca, a daughter of Charles II. He was required to rule Sardinia and Corsica and cede Sicily to Angevin control. Instead, the following year James succeeded his elder brother, Alfonso, as King of Aragon. His younger brother, Frederick, became his regent, or "viceroy," in Sicily, which James — acting against the provisions of his father's will — refused to relinquish.

Sicily was becoming an Aragonese colony in everything but name. Catalan merchants supplanted many northern Italians in commerce, while Catalan nobles were given estates. (In Sicilian historiography, the gentilic *Aragonese* refers generically to the society of Catalonia as well as Aragon.)

The baronage preferred their monarch to rule from their island, not from Aragon. Here their concerns were more financial than sentimental, as direct rule from faraway Barcelona (or even Zaragoza) meant higher taxes to defray the cost of Aragon's military power. To this end, in late 1295, they elected Frederick King of Sicily. This sparked a war with James which the Angevins exploited.

As a condition of his election, Frederick conceded to the barons a charter of liberties. According to this, he was not to leave Sicily or declare war without their consent. It was not the *Magna Carta,* but it might have led to similar developments in Sicily as occurred in England. Unfortunately, that was not to be the case.

A series of intrigues and battles continued until 1302, ending with a treaty known as the "Peace of Caltabellotta" (for the town where it was signed) and the marriage of King Frederick of Sicily to Eleanor, another daughter of Charles II. As a condition of this accord, Frederick was to be known officially as "King of Trinacria" while Charles in Naples would continue to be styled "King of Sicily."

Pope Boniface died the next year following a protracted feud with Philip IV of France. Dante put Boniface in Hell. More importantly, the poet's treatise *De Monarchia* was a riposte to the zealous Pontiff's claims to political supremacy.

By now Sicilian rule and government were thoroughly Aragonese. The island would find herself in the Spanish orbit for the next four centuries.

EPILOGUE

"It is a wonderful place, built in the Cordoba style, entirely from cut limestone. A river divides the town, and four springs gush in its suburbs. The Christian women of this city follow the fashion of Muslim women, are fluent of speech, wrap their cloaks about them, and are veiled."

— bin Jubayr

It is cold enough to snow, and the wee hours of a blustery January morning find me walking through the older districts of the city described by the medieval visitor.

Only at night is Palermo without chaos, without secrets, and in the historic center of the city walking is the only efficient way to get from point to point.

In Palermo the streets are the key to everything.

I have made my way past the Norman-Arab Cuba palace, along Corso Calatafimi in what was once the royal Genoard park. Passing a Phoenician wall near Piazza Indipendenza, I walk through Porta Nuova, where the Riyad Gate used to stand. I stroll past the imposing Pisan Tower of the Norman

Palace, then across the Roman archeological site in Piazza Vittoria, past the cathedral along the Cassaro, now Via Vittorio Emanuele, the erstwhile Balat, the "marble street" known to the Fatimids and Normans.

The once-golden limestone of the city's medieval landmarks is faded by weathering and smog. A fractured facade on Via Protonotaro, the High Notary's Street, with its Fatimid loopholes, Norman arches and Swabian two-light windows, is an unabashed declaration of multicultural architecture.

Undisturbed in the dead of night, I reach a more significant square where two twelfth-century churches, San Cataldo and the Martorana, still stand guard on high ground. The Martorana's splendid bell tower was one of the wonders praised by the Muslim visitor bin Jubayr when he visited in 1184.

Via Discesa dei Giudici, as its name implies, descends in a gentle slope. After walking past another exposed Punic wall supporting Saint Catherine's Convent near what used to be the confluence of the Kemonia and Papyrus rivers, I cross Via Roma, one of the city's main avenues, near Via Giovanni da Procida and the old Jewish quarter. Striding along the lower part of the Discesa, I arrive at Piazza Croce dei Vespri, where Saint Ann's Convent is now the city's modern art museum. A plaque commemorates the fighting that took place here in 1282 when part of the edifice was the residence of John of Saint Rémy, the justiciar for Val di Mazara.

Onward down Via Alloro, whose name comes from *all'oro,* "to the gold," for the mint once housed in Palazzo Cefalà. Farther along this street is stately Palazzo Abbatellis, with its arches and crenels. Of vaguely Catalan Gothic style in the mold of Barcelona's splendid Basilica de Santa Maria del Mar, it is one of the few buildings in Sicily to boast gargoyles.

My watch tells me that I've just traversed some twenty-six centuries in about twenty-nine minutes. No time traveller could have done better.

The world's most conquered city, unkempt Palermo is a diamond in the rough, or an old bronze artefact. One scratches the surface of its patina to find still another crusty layer. But something is always lurking there. It need only be discovered. In this part of the city history reaches its hand out to us at every corner. Here the streets talk. They speak the language of diversitude, of Sicanians, Phoenicians, Carthaginians, Greeks, Romans, Jews, Vandals, Ostrogoths, Aghlabids, Fatimids, Kalbids, Normans, Swabians, Angevins and Catalans.

No other city in Europe boasts the number of medieval churches, castles and palaces one finds in Palermo, many hidden from view except along narrow streets or lonely squares. It is a city that the Hautevilles, the Hohenstaufens, the Angevins and Aragonese would still recognize, if only they could ever return.

Perhaps they never really left.

CHRONOLOGY

"The stream of time, irresistible, ever moving, carries off and bears away all things that come to birth, plunging them into utter darkness, both deeds of no account and deeds which are mighty and worthy of commemoration."

— Anna Comnena

Kalbid Emirate

998-1019 - Rule of Jafar al-Kalbi. Construction of Favara palace in Palermo is attributed to this Emir.

1000 - Norse civilization in northwestern France (Normandy) assimilates with local culture. Approximate period of Norse landings at L'Anse aux Meadows in Newfoundland. *Groenlendinga Saga* (the Greenlanders' Saga) and *Eiriks Saga* (Erik's Story) mention such sea travels.

1016 - Norman knights first participate in battles in Italy. First Turkish raids in Armenia.

1019-1037 - Rule of Ahmed al-Akhal in Sicily.

1037-1040 - Rule by Abdallah Abu Hafs, usurper.

1038-1042 - Byzantine forces of George Maniakes briefly occupy parts of eastern Sicily; army includes Greeks, Normans, Lombards and Norse Varangian Guard under Harald Hardrada.

1040 - Hasan as-Samsam begins his rule; deposed in 1044.

1044 - Island divided into four qadits. Rivalry among emirs worsens.

1053 - Following death of Hasan as-Samsam and extinction of Kalbid dynasty, three important emirs divide control of Sicily: Ibn al Hawas at Kasr' Janni (Enna), Ibn at Timnah at Syracuse and Catania, Abdullah ibn Hawqal at Trapani and Mazara.

1054 - Great Schism between eastern and western Christianity. Sicilian Christians initially remain "eastern" (Orthodox).

1056 - Arab poet ibn Hamdis born; leaves Sicily in 1078.

Norman Period

1060 - Unsuccessful Norman attack in coastal northeastern Sicily.

1061 - Battle of Messina. City and parts of Nebrodian and Peloritan region occupied; permanent Norman presence.

1066 - Battle of Hastings leads to complete Norman conquest of Saxon England. Battle of Messina forms partial pattern of this invasion of an island from a continent; some Norman knights fight at both battles.

1071 - Byzantines lose Battle of Manzikert to Seljuk Turks. Normans attack Palermo; Norman invaders are led by Robert de Hauteville, Arab defenders by Ayub ibn Temim.

1072 - Battle of Palermo ends in early January with Norman occupation under Roger and Robert de Hauteville. Greek Orthodox Bishop Nicodemus removed from authority over Christian community.

1081 - Suppression of revolt led by renegade "emir" Bernavert (Bin al Wardi) at Catania; another of his revolts is suppressed at Syracuse in 1085.

1083 - Roger I appoints Latin (rather than Orthodox) Bishop of Palermo and Gallican Rite is introduced in new churches.

1084 - Bruno founds Carthusian Order in Germany.

1087 - Ibn Hammud, Emir of Kasr' Janni (Enna), last major Arab stronghold, surrenders to Normans in 1087; Noto falls in 1091. Dozens of fortified Arab-founded (or repopulated) towns dot the island: Calascibetta, Caltanissetta, Caltagirone, Mussomeli, Marsala (Mars' Allah), Misilmeri, Cammarata, others.

1095 - Roger II, future King of Sicily, is born.

1096 - First Crusade begins; some Norman knights participate under Bohemond de Hauteville (later Prince of Antioch), brother of Roger I.

1097 - Odo of Bayeux, Earl of Kent, younger brother of William the Conqueror, King of England, dies in Palermo *en* *route* to the Crusade while visiting Roger I.

1098 - Roger I, as Great Count of Sicily, becomes Papal Apostolic Legate, with rights to approve island's Catholic bishops.

1099 - Crusaders conquer Jerusalem.

1101 - Roger I dies, succeeded by Simon, his eldest living, legitimate son, who is still a minor. Roger's consort, Adelaide del Vasto of Savona, is regent.

1105 - Roger II succeeds his elder brother Simon (1093-1105) as ruler of Sicily under Adelaide's regency.

1112 - Roger is knighted (this ceremony marks his age of majority and sovereign authority following "regency" under his mother).

1119 - Knights Templar founded in Palestine. Preceptories in Sicily confiscated by Frederick II following Sixth Crusade. (Order suppressed definitively by Papacy in 1312.)

1123 - First Lateran Council forbids Roman Catholic clerics wives or concubines; until now Catholic priests were permitted to marry before ordination.

1130 - Roger crowned first King of Sicily (known henceforth as "Roger II").

1139 - Second Lateran Council makes celibacy mandatory for Roman Catholic priests, reiterating a canon established in 1123 but not widely enforced.

1140 - Assizes of Ariano, important legal code asserting royal authority, traditionally dated to this year.

1143 - Martorana church (Palermo) built in Norman-Arab style for Greek Orthodox community by George of Antioch. In this year Nilos Doxopatrios authors theological treatise.

1146 - Legal principles expressed in Assizes of Ariano are in force by this time.

1147 - Second Crusade begins but participation by Sicilian knights is very limited.

1154 - *Book of Roger* completed by court geographer Abdullah al Idrisi. Roger dies and reign of King William I "the Bad" begins.

1155 - Frederick Barbarossa crowned Holy Roman Emperor.

1158 - Qaid al Brun (Thomas Brown), treasurer at William's court, returns to England to reform exchequer of Henry II, thus influencing European accounting principles. He uses Hindu-Arabic numerals, later popularized in Christian Europe by Leonardo Fibonacci of Pisa (briefly a guest of young Frederick II in Sicily) in 1202.

1161 - Matthew Bonellus of Caccamo leads revolt of Norman barons. He is killed in the same year.

1166 - Reign of young King William II "the Good" begins under his mother's regency. Queen Margaret gives hospitality to exiled kin of Thomas Becket. Gradual latinization of Sicilian language continues; Latin (Roman Catholic) influence predominates among Christians.

1169 - Major earthquake in Catania and southeast.

1170 - Benjamin of Tudela visits Sicily. Peter Waldo establishes evangelical Waldensian church, precursor of Reform (Protestant) movement.

1171 - Saladin defeats Fatimids in Middle East.

1174 - Work begins on Monreale Abbey in Arab village of Bal'at overlooking Palermo. Style is Norman-Arab on Romanesque plan with Byzantine mosaic icons, including earliest holy image of Thomas Becket (canonized in 1173).

1177 - William II marries Joan, daughter of Henry II of England (sister of Richard Lionheart).

1184 - Bin Jubayr visits Sicily and records his impressions.

1187 - Saladin captures Jerusalem.

1189 - Death of William II. Succeeded by Tancred Hauteville.

1190 - Richard Lionheart, brother of Queen Joan of Sicily, occupies Messina with Philip II of France for several months *en route* to Third Crusade.

1193 - Death of Saladin.

Swabian Period

1194 - Death of Tancred. Holy Roman Emperor Henry VI von Hohenstaufen arrives and rules by right of his wife, Constance Hauteville. Teutonic Knights accompany him, establishing Saint Mary of the Germans (Messina) and obtaining Cistercian properties (the Magione in Palermo).

1198 - Frederick II, son of Henry, is king until 1250, weds Constance of Aragon. Swabian German influences in Sicily. Islam and Greek Orthodoxy permitted but practiced by ever-diminishing minorities. Emergent Sicilian language is Italic with Arabic and Greek influences.

1204 - Latins ("Franks") sack Constantinople during Fourth Crusade, establish "Latin Empire."

1206 - Mongols unite under Genghis Khan (Temujin), who conquers large parts of Eurasia.

1210 - Francis of Assisi meets Pope Innocent III; founds Order of Friars Minor (Franciscans). Albigensian Crusades begin. Birth of John of Procida.

1212 - Frederick II reaches age of majority.

1215 - *Magna Carta* in England. Dominic of Osma (of Caleruega, Spain) founds Order of Preachers (Dominicans or "Blackfriars"), confirmed by Papacy in 1216. By 1500 this is the leading monastic and teaching order in Sicily, supportive of the Inquisition.

1217 - Cleric and scientist Michael Scot (born 1175) translates *On the Sphere* by the Arab astronomer Al-Bitruji (or Alpetragius, who died circa 1204). Fifth Crusade begins.

1220 - Frederick issues Assizes of Capua.

1223 - Following execution of Arab rebel leader Morabit (in 1222), thousands of Muslims from Iato area, who had revolted with their leader Ibn Abbad (or Benaveth), are deported to Lucera in Apulia. Many Muslims have already converted to Catholicism. Jews from occupied Jerba (in Tunisia) invited to Sicily. Expulsions continue until circa 1246.

1224 - University of Naples founded by Frederick II.

1226 - Frederick II summons Imperial Diet of Cremona.

1229 - Frederick II, accompanied by Saracen guards and Sicilian and German knights, goes on Sixth Crusade as King of Jerusalem. Signs peace with Muslims without war.

1230 - Upon his return from Jerusalem Frederick suppresses Templar preceptories in Sicily.

1231 - Constitutions of Melfi become legal code for Kingdom of Sicily under Frederick II.

1233 - Cathars of France persecuted as heretics by first Inquisition.

1240 - Ciullo of Alcamo composes poetry in Sicilian language. First of a series of major revolts by Sicilian Arabs, including some Christian converts, but Frederick retains trusted Saracen guards and court officers.

1241 - Mongol-Tatar army of Batu Khan arrives in central Europe after having sacked Kiev. Leads to foundation of "Golden Horde."

1244 - Fall of Jerusalem to Muslim forces.

1248 - Crusade to Egypt by Louis IX of France.

1250 - Death of Frederick II.

1254 - Death of Conrad IV Hohenstaufen.

1258 - Baghdad falls to Mongols.

Angevin Period

1261 - Byzantine Empire restored when Constantinople falls to Greek control.

1266 - Charles of Anjou (brother of Louis IX of France) becomes king of Naples and Sicily following defeat of Manfred Hohenstaufen, natural son of Frederick II, at Battle of Benevento.

1268 - Young Conradin, a (legitimate) grandson of Frederick II and last Swabian claimant, is executed in 1268 following defeat at Battle of Tagliacozzo. Hohenstaufen Imperial line now extinct. Angevin period begins. It is thought that by now all of Sicily's remaining Muslims have converted to Catholicism. The multicultural golden age is ending.

1270 - Following Eighth (or "Tunisian") Crusade, funeral of Louis IX of France at Monreale, where his heart is preserved; canonized in 1297.

1271 - Charles of Anjou captures part of Albania.

1273 - Rudolf of Hapsburg becomes king in Germany; his dynasty will succeed Hohenstaufens as Holy Roman Emperors.

1281 - Angevin forces defeated by Byzantine troops in Albania and Greece.

Aragonese Period

1282 - Vespers revolt (in March) expels Angevin French and makes Peter III of Aragon King of Sicily. Neapolitan invasion of Constantinople (to restore "Latin Empire") is aborted as military resources must be diverted to Sicily. Death of Michael VIII of Constantinople (in December).

1285 - Deaths of Charles I of Anjou and Peter III of Aragon, succeeded by their sons.

1290 - Approximate date of the writing of the autograph of *Lu Rebellamentu.*

1298 - Death of John of Procida.

1300 - Definitive destruction of Lucera by Charles II.

1302 - Peace of Caltabellotta treaty signed between Aragonese and Angevins. By now, Sicily is essentially monocultural, endogamous and mostly Roman Catholic. Over the next few generations general literacy diminishes.

PERSONAGES

Accardo Latino. A native of Lombardy in northern Italy, he was a knight, and sometime ambassador, in the service of Emperor Michael VIII.

Alaimo of Lentini. A prominent baron, regarded as a competent leader, holder of lands around Lentini in southeastern Sicily. In 1283 he was made the High Justiciar of the Kingdom of Sicily.

Alfonso X "the Wise" of Castile. The *King of Spain* mentioned in the text ruled until 1284. Through his mother, Elizabeth (Beatrice) of Swabia, he was a second cousin, one generation removed, to Constance Hohenstaufen (see below), both being descended from Frederick I "Barbarossa." On that basis, Alfonso was briefly considered a potential claimant to the Sicilian throne.

Baldwin II. Baldwin of Courtenay, the last Latin Emperor of Constantinople, died in exile in Naples in 1273, having been deposed by Emperor Michael's Byzantine Greek supporters. His claim was taken up by his son, Philip I (see below).

Hugh of Brienne. Descended from the same family as John of Brienne, King of Jerusalem, whose daughter (Isabella) wed Frederick II, Hugh took service under King Charles, who restored to him his family's ancestral county of Lecce in Apulia. In 1284 he was taken prisoner with Charles II by Roger of Lauria.

Captain of Palermo. This unnamed knight present in Palermo in March 1282 was responsible for civilian matters, such as police duties and maintaining public order. It appears from the text that he was not French.

Charles of Anjou. King of Sicily from 1266, Charles, known to posterity as "Charles I of Naples," was the erudite younger brother of Louis IX of France.

Charles II of Anjou. Prince Charles "the Lame" of Salerno was the son and heir of Charles I. He was crowned after his father's death, as King Charles II.

Constance Hohenstaufen. Daughter of King Manfred of Sicily, himself a son of Frederick II, Constance was the key to the claim of her consort, Peter III of Aragon, to rule Sicily in her name. She lived until 1302.

Frederick II. Holy Roman Emperor, King of the Germans, King of Sicily, King of Jerusalem. Reigning until death in 1250, Frederick Hohenstaufen was one of the most remarkable monarchs of the thirteenth century, so noted for his intellect that after his death he was nicknamed *stupor mundi,* "wonder of the world."

Cardinal Gerard Bianchi. A native of Parma, Gerard was bishop of Sabina, an important episcopal see near Rome. As a career diplomat, in 1278 he negotiated a treaty between the kings of France and Castile.

Isabella of Aragon, Queen of France. This sister of King Peter III was married to Philip III of France (making the two monarchs brothers-in-law) until her death in 1271. This occurred when she fell from a horse while fording a stream near Cosenza, in Calabria, *en route* to France from Africa and Sicily following the Tunisian Crusade, which saw the death of Louis IX and the succession of Philip III.

Cardinal James Savelli. Born into an aristocratic family, this Papal confidant succeeded Pope Martin IV as Honorius IV in 1285, continuing his predecessor's pro-Angevin policy. He died in 1287.

John Boccamazza (sometimes **Boccamiti**). Archbishop of Monreale from 1282 to 1285, he was related to James Savelli (see above) and, like him, sympathetic to the Angevins. According to the *Rebellion,* his message was the first to reach King Charles explaining that King Peter had arrived in Palermo.

John of Dammartin. Mentioned in Chapter 51, John de Trie was a prominent French count, holder of lands in Picardy, in the service of the Angevins.

John of Procida. The protagonist of the *Rebellion* is described at length in a section of the Introduction. A brilliant physician, he served as chancellor to Frederick II and enjoyed a distinguished diplomatic career under the Aragonese.

Louis IX of France. Canonized in 1297, the ever-crusading Louis of France reigned from 1226 until his death during the Tunisian Crusade in 1270. Preserved in an urn at Monreale

Abbey, his heart is the chief bodily relic of him that survives (except for a finger his corpse at Saint-Denis was removed by revolutionaries in 1793).

Manfred Hohenstaufen. Son of Frederick II, Manfred ruled the *Regnum* for several years until 1266, when he was killed at the Battle of Benevento.

Margaret of Burgundy. The queen consort of Sicily in 1282 was the second wife of Charles I, who she married in 1268. Margaret was a daughter of Odo, Count of Nevers, and Maud of Dampierre. Following Charles' death in 1285, she retired to Tonnerre, where she died in 1308.

Henry of Mari. This Genoan admiral of King Charles is referred to by the narrator as *Alaymu Alkirinu di Mari.* Born around 1250, Henry (Arrigo) of Mari was descended from a prominent family of the Genoan patriciate.

Pope Martin III. This was actually **Martin IV**, born Simon de Brion in Touraine, France. He was an unabashed supporter of his countryman, King Charles, and some historians view him as little more than the monarch's puppet. Indeed, it was most likely through Charles' machinations that de Brion was elected Pope. Succeeding Nicholas III, Martin was Pope from February 1281 until his death in March 1285.

Michael VIII Palaeologue. Ruler of the Eastern Roman "Byzantine" Empire, which he restored following decades of control by Western (Latin) rulers, Michael sought to retain a theologically Orthodox identity in the face of the efforts of the Papacy and King Charles to dislodge him. His autobiography alludes to his funding of the rebellion of 1282.

Guy of Montfort. Born in 1244, he was the son of Simon, sixth Earl of Leicester, and Eleanor of England. He began his military career in England and eventually found his way to Italy, where he became King Charles' vicar-general in Tuscany. Following the Battle of Tagliacozzo he was awarded the county of Nola near Naples.

Muhammad al Mustansir ibn Yahya. This sultan of the Hafsid dynasty ruled northern Africa (Ifriqiya) until his death in 1277. After 1266, he gave refuge to exiled Hohenstaufen sympathizers, and following the Tunisian Crusade of 1270 he paid tribute to Charles. His death provoked a period of unrest that was exploited by the Aragonese. The loss of Sicily entailed the decline in Angevin influence in this part of Africa.

Pope Nicholas III. Born John Gaetan Orsini, Nicholas succeeded John XXI in 1277. His pontificate lasted until his death in 1280. A consummate politician, he became Inquisitor in 1262.

Palmeri Abbati. Viewed by historians as a pragmatist, "Palmer" Abbati (or Abate) was one of the wealthiest barons in Sicily.

Peter, Count of Alençon. Mentioned in Chapter 51, Peter, born in 1251, was the son of Louis IX of France by Margaret of Provence and accompanied his father on the ill-fated Tunisian Crusade in 1270. He subsequently served in the forces of his uncle (Charles) in Italy but died in 1284.

Peter II of Aragon. Grandfather of Peter III, he was killed by French forces at the Battle of Muret in 1213, a defeat which facilitated the eventual annexation of the Occitan regions to the Kingdom of France.

Peter III of Aragon. Married to the daughter and heiress of King Manfred, Peter III ruled Aragon from Barcelona (of which he was Count) from 1276 until his death in 1285. He also ruled Valencia and Sicily while controlling a coastal region of northern Africa.

Peter Santafede. Archbishop of Palermo during the Vespers uprising, he was not present when King Peter arrived.

Philip I. As the son and heir of Baldwin II, Philip of Courtenay was the pretender to the throne of the "Latin" Empire of Constantinople that Charles of Anjou wished to restore. He wed Beatrice, a daughter of Charles of Anjou. Philip died in 1283.

Philip III of France. Succeeding his father, Louis IX, as King of France, Philip was the nephew of Charles and much influenced by him.

Richard of Lauria. Nobleman who held the fiefs of Lauria and Scalea in Calabria, Grand Justiciar of Manfred Hohenstaufen. Richard's wife was the nurse of Constance Hohenstaufen (who married Peter III of Aragon). Richard was killed at the Battle of Benevento in 1266. His son, Roger, became an admiral in Aragonese service.

Robert II, Count of Artois. Mentioned in Chapter 51, Robert was a nephew of Louis IX and served as viceroy at Naples following the death of Charles I until Charles II (who was then still imprisoned) was released by the Aragonese.

Roger of Lauria. Son of Richard of Lauria, Roger was born in Lauria or Scalea around 1245 during the reign of Frederick II. He became one of the greatest naval tacticians of his era.

Roger went to the Aragonese court following his father's death and the fall of the Hohenstaufens in Italy, and eventually became a fleet admiral.

Walter of Caltagirone. One of the more outspoken barons, holder of a large manor around the town of Caltagirone in southeastern Sicily.

King William II of Sicily. Mentioned in Chapter 55, this was the penultimate Norman king of the House of Hauteville, ruling from 1166 to 1189. He was known for wielding power ably while treating his subjects fairly. A reflection of the esteem in which he was held is that Dante placed him in Paradise, while Boccaccio, in his *Decameron,* refers to "the days when good King William ruled Sicily."

GENEALOGICAL TABLES

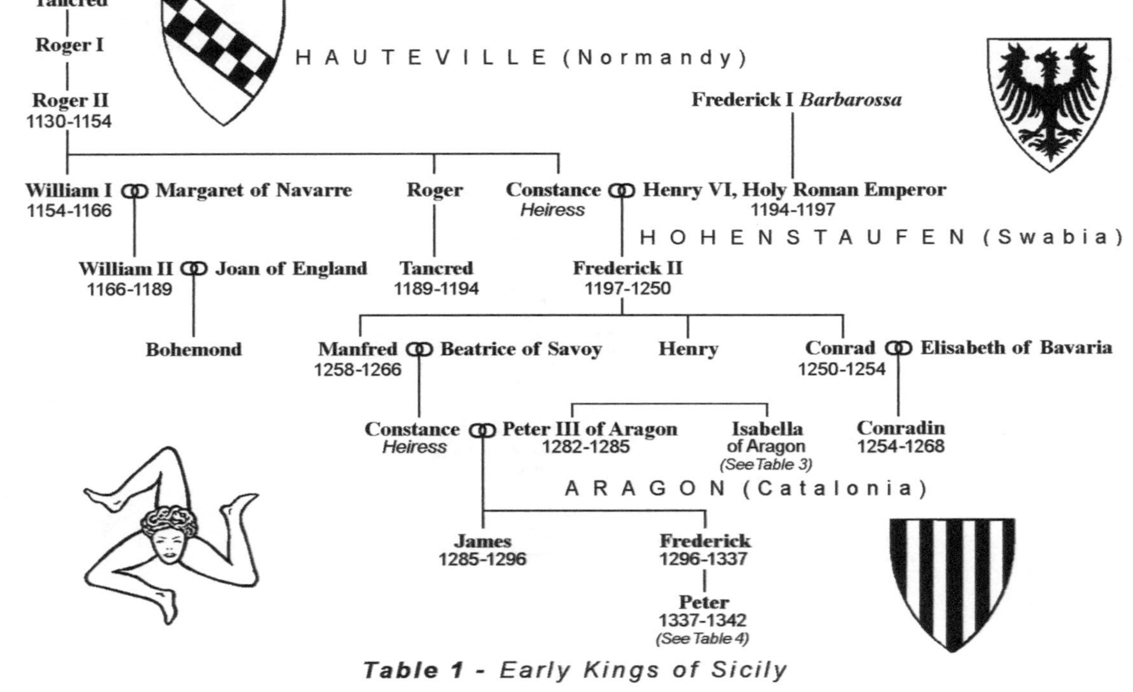

Table 1 - Early Kings of Sicily

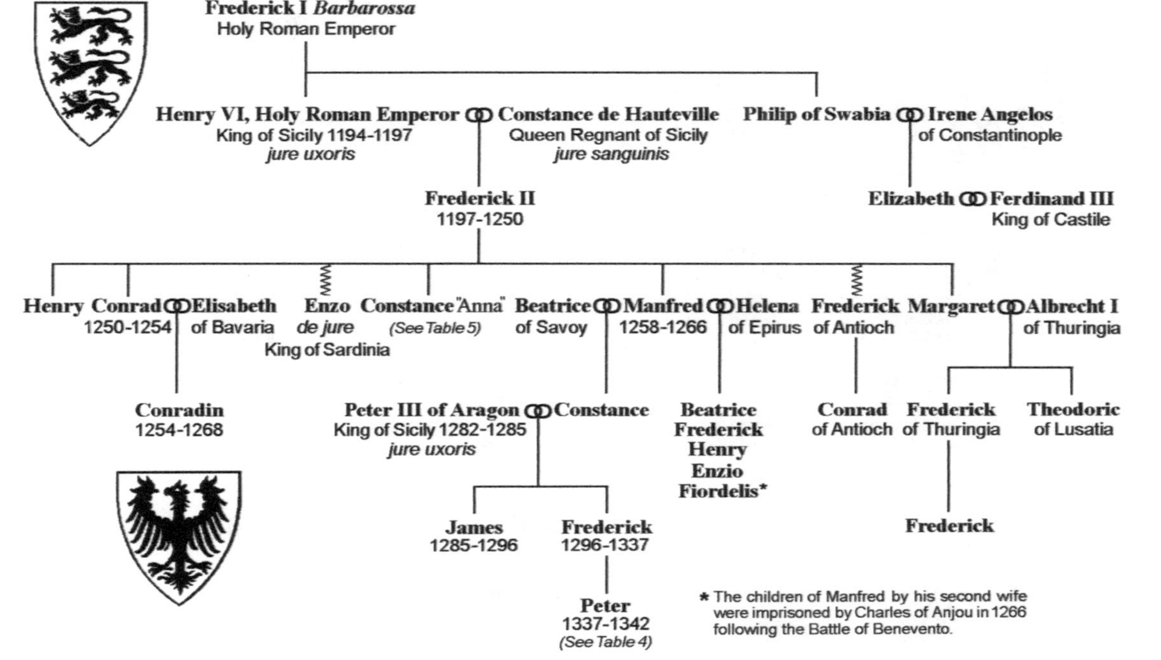

Table 2 - Hohenstaufen Heirs: Claims to the Sicilian Throne through Frederick II

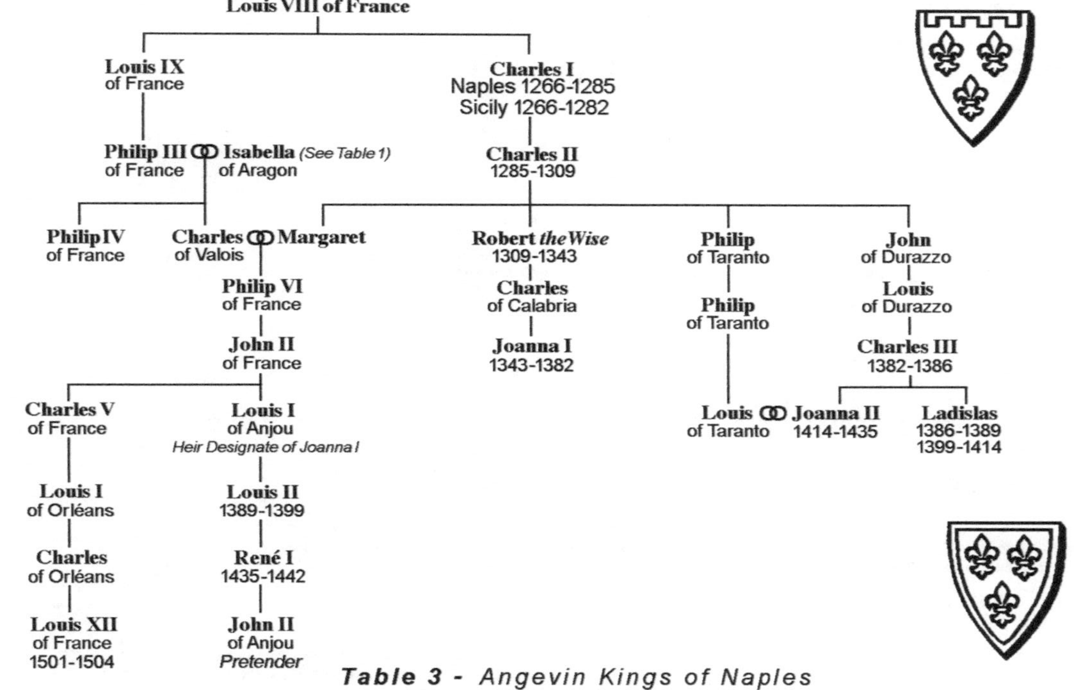

Table 3 - Angevin Kings of Naples

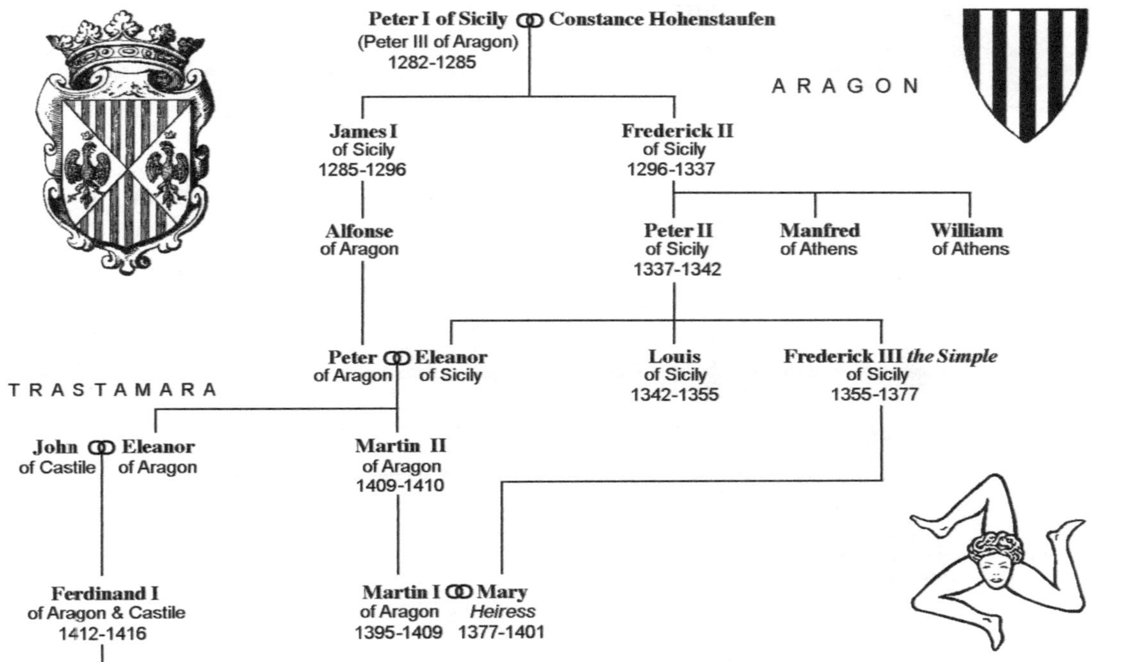

Table 4 - *Legacy of the Vespers: Aragonese Kings of Sicily*

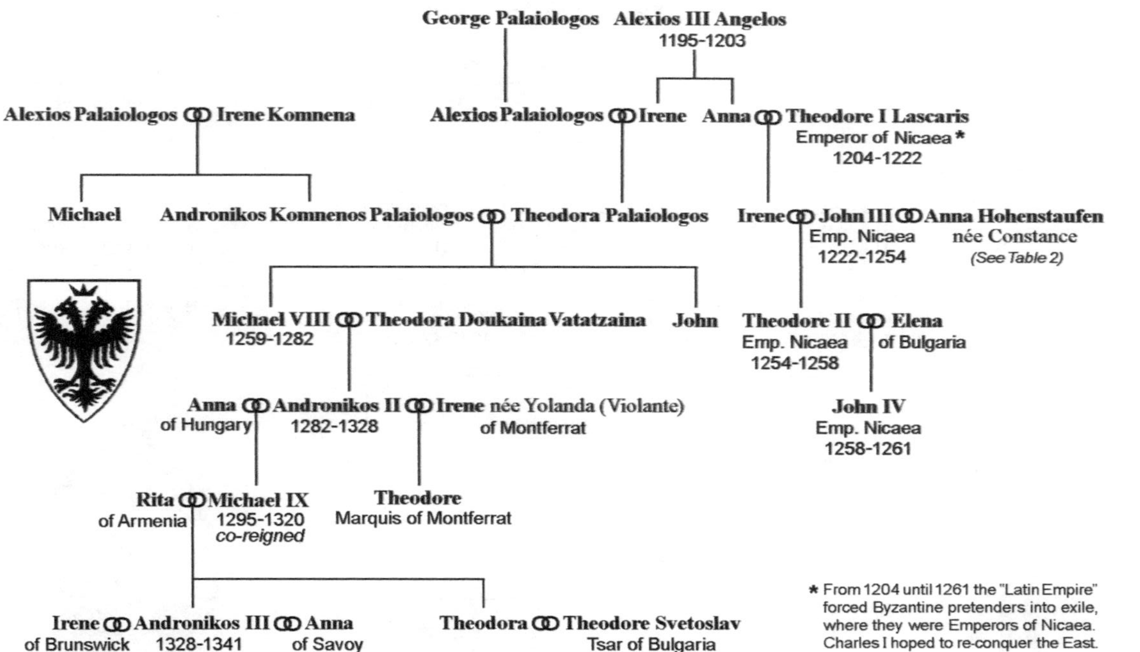

Table 5 - Byzantine (Eastern Roman) Dynasties in the 13th Century

LU REBELLAMENTU DI SICHILIA

Quistu esti lu Rebellamentu di Sichilia lu quali hordinau e ffici fari Misser Iohanni di Prochita contra Re Carlu.

1

A li milli dui chentu sictanta novi annj di la Incarnationj di nostru Signurj Ihu Xpu, lu Re Carlu havia prisa una grandi guerra cum lu Imperaduri Plagalogu di Rumania. Et per quilla guerra lu dictu Re Carlu fichi fari multi navj grossi et galei, per passari in Costantinopuli cum tuctu lu so ifforzu, et supra zò avia invitata multa bona agenti di Francza et di Provenza et Italia, kj li fachissiru conpagna a quillu passaiu per putiri vinciri lu Plagalogu et tuctu lu sò inperiu di Rumania.

Et standu Misser Iohannj di Prochita in Sichilia, si pinsau in chi modu putissi sturbari l'andata la qual facta havia Re Carlu contra lu Plagalogu, et comu putissi fari distrudiri, et muriri lu Re Carlu, et ribellari Sichilia, et auchidiri tucta sua genti. Dundi si pensau di andari in Rumania a lu Plagalogu per audari cum ipsu, azzò kj li intencioni di lu Re Carlu vinissiru mancu.

Et incuntinenti Misser Iohannj si partiu, et andau in Costantinopoli a lu Inperaduri Plagalogu. Quandu Misser Iohannj fu iuntu a Costantinopuli, illu mandau per dui cavaleri di lu Regnu, li quali si eranu rebelli di Re Carlu, et eranu in curti di lu Imperadurj di Costantinopuli, et secretamenti li parlau, et cuntauli comu illu era vinutu in Costantinopuli, "inperò chi eu su cachatu di mia terra et di Sichilia, et vayu per cachandu mia vintura. Undi eu vi pregu caramenti, chi vi placza di putirimi acconzari cum lu Imperaduri, et ki eu fussi di sua famigla, et preguvj, mictitimi multu innanti, et dichiti comu eu su dassai et grandi, et comu eu su homu multu necessariu a ssì et comu per meu saviu consiglu sì putria beni viviri et essiri ayutatu a li soi bisogni."

Et li cavaleri audendu quisti palori foru multi allegri et dissiru chi vulinteri farrianu la sua imbaxata. Dundi si mossiru li cavaleri et andaru a la Plagalogu et dissiru,

"Signuri nui vi portamu boni nuvelli, chi di lu Regnu di Sichilia, unu di li migluri di fisica chi sia a lu mundu, lu quali è vinutu per stari cum vui in vostra curti, et cuntasi chi illu esti cussi saviu homu, chi vui indi avirissivu unu bonu consigleri, lu quali sì esti scachatu di sua terra, et sapi meglu li facti di lu Re Carlu, et di lu sou putiri. Et ancora di li soi barunj."

2

Quandu lu Imperaduri intisi quista inbaxata, issu fu multu allegru. Incontinenti cumandau chi lu minassiru dananti di ipsu, chi lu Imperaduri lu vulia vidiri. Allura andaru li cavaleri, et minaru Misser Iohannj dananti lu Imperaduri, et quandu Misser Iohannj li fu davanti, li fichi quilla reverencia chi si convuinia fari ad omni imperaduri, et lu Imperaduri lu richippi graciusamenti, et fichilu so mastru consigleri generali. Et cussi stecti Misser Iohannj tri misi in la curti, et richipia multi grandi honuri da li Grechi et Latinj.

3

Standu Misser Iohannj in quistu sou essiri, si dissi unu iornu a lu Plagalogu,

"Signuri, per Deu vi pregu hordinati unu secretu locu di putiri parlari secretamenti, azò ki lu nostru parlamentu non si poza sapiri per altrui."

Et lu Imperaduri dissi, "Chi vui mi vuliti parlari cussì secretu?"

Et illu rispusi, "Per lu più grandi bisognu ki vui haviti in quistu mundu."

Et incontinenti andaru supra alta turri di lu palazu, undi stavanu tucti li secretanczi di lu Inperaduri.

4

Intandu dissi lu Imperaduri,

"Misser Iohannj, vi dichu, et sachati chi nui simu in secretu locu."

Misser Iohannj dissi, "Qualunca persuna si sia chi a vuy aya per saviu et prudu homu, chi eu vi tegnu et ayu per lu plui vili et folli et cussi comu una bestia, chi non si movi, si non esti punta di lu punturu. Et quistu vi dicu imperò ki illu avi circa tri misi, chi eu sugnu statu a la tua curti, et ayu audutu parlari di tou periculusu statu, zò è di la morti la quali ti veni adossu. Or non penczi tu folli, et mactu, di prindiri riparu, et difencza contra lu impericulu chi lu Re Carlu veni per livariti la coruna, et per auchidiri a ti et ac tuctu lu tou lignaiu, et veni cum ipsu quillu chi di raxuni sì esti sua conquesta et sua coruna, zò esti lu Imperaduri Balduynu, et veniti adossu cum tucti li cristiani cruchiati et cum chentu galei armati et cum vinti navj grossi, et dechi milia cavaleri beni adubati, et cum quaranta conti, tucti cum li loru conpagni per conquistari tou riamj."

5

Lu Imperaduri audendu quisti paroli, li quali Misser Iohannj li havia dictu, accuminzau fortimenti a plangiri, et dissi:

"O Misser Iohannj, chi voliti ki eu faza, chi eu stayu et vivu sì comu homu disperatu, chi eu sì mi su volutu acconzari cum lu Re Carlu per multi volti, et jammai non hayu potutu trovari per nixunu modu di accordarimi cum ipsu? Chi eu sì mi su misu in putiri di Sancta Ecclesia di Ruma et di li cardinali, et in manu di lu Re di Franza et di lu Re di Ingliterra et di lu Re di Spagna et di lu Re di Aragona? Dundi chascunu mi rispundi di lictri a lloru mandati? Et dichini chi jasquidunu timi di muriri, non tantu di parlari, considerandu sua grandi pussancza la quali lu Re Carlu havia. Dundi non hayu cunsiglu et non hayu riparu di homu. Hayu spirancza chi Deu m'ayutirà, poi chi di li cristiani non trovu ayutu non consiglu."

6

Et Misser Iohannj li rispusi et dissi,

"Or cuj ti livassi di supra tuctu quistu fururi et quista morti et affannu, miritirissilu tu di alcuna cosa?"

Et lu Imperaduri rispusi, "Eu lu miritiria di tuctu quillu chi eu fari putissi. Ma cui fora tantu arditu chi, per sua bona et plachivili voluntati, chi di mi havissi merzì et prindissi guerra per mi contra la potencia di lu Re Carlu di Franza?"

7

Et Misser Iohannj dissi,

"Eu sirrò quillu, si tu lu vurrai, chi mictirò a distrucioni lu Re Carlu, mictendu lu tou ayutu cum lu meu consiglu. Eu dirrò chi bisognu ti farrà, et di farj. Et imperò ti plaza di ascutarmi a mi et alcuni autri soi ribelli, chi ben divingirimu nostra injuria, et vui haviriti la vostra intencioni, et lu vostru inimicu non vi porrà nochiri non sucta mectiri, si a Deu plachirà."

8

Intandu dissi lu Imperaduri,

"In chi modu vui putiti fari quistu factu?"

Et Misser Iohannj dissi, "Eu non vi lu dirria jammai, excectu chi vui non mi promictiti chentu milia unczi, dundi eu ti farrò viniri unu chi prindirà la terra di Sichilia a lu Re Carlu et darrali tanta briga chi jammai non sapirà di ki lu modu porrà spichicari di ipsu."

Di chi lu Imperaduri audendu quisti palori fu multu allegru et dissi, "Misser Iohannj, prinditi tuctu lu meu trisoru et fandi quillu chi vi plachi et fa chi sia lu plui tostu chi si pocza fari."

9

Et Misser Iohannj rispusi dichendu,

"Signuri Imperaturi, ora mi jurati cridenza et sigillatimi la lictra di quillu lu quali mi haviti promisu, et eu mi partirò in quistu modu et chirkirò di mectiri a ffini quillu ki eu vi aju inpromisu lu plui prestu chi si potirà fari."

10

Intandu lu Imperaduri fichi sacramentu a Misser Iohannj et partiri di intru di quilla cammara, di chi Misser Iohanni dissi a lu Imperaduri,

"Signuri, eu mi voglu partiri di vui in quistu modu, chi vui mi faczati donari bandu et appellarimi per tradituri dananti tucta agenti et specialimenti dari davanti li mei amichi latini, et eu dirraiu comu eu vi aiu offisu, et para chi eu fuya per quista accaxuni, et quista via et modu voglu tiniri azò ki altra genti non pensanu lu nostru secretu."

Intandu si partiu l'unu di l'autru cum grandissima alligriza et confortu.

11

In quistu annu videmmi si partiu Misser Iohanni di Prochita di Costantinopuli, et andau in Sichilia, vistutu a modu di frati minuri. Et parlau cum Misser Palmeri Abati et cum Misser Alaymu di Lintini, et autri baruni di Sichilia, dichendu a quisti nobili homini,

"O miseri, vinduti comu cani mali disavinturati et mali tractati, haviti li vostri coragi impetrati? Or non vi muviriti jammai, ma sempri serriti servi putendu essiri signurj, divinjandu li iniurij, et li virgogni vostri?"

Et in quistu tucti insembli incominzaru a plangiri dichendu,

"Misser Iohannj, comu putimu nui fari altru, ki nui semu suctamisi assì altu signurj potenti chi mai fussi a lu mundu, dundi a nuj pari ki per nixuna causa potissimu xiri di servituti."

Et Misser Iohannj li rispusi,

"Eu vi poczu liberari axivilmenti, puru chi vui voglati tiniri cridencza quillu ki è ordinatu per li vostri amichi."

Et quilli signurj supradicti rispusiru,

"Nuj simu apparichati di sequiriti fina a la mortj."

12

Dundi Misser Iohannj dissi,

"A vui si convinirà di ribillari tucta la terra di Sichilia a quillu tempu lu quali esti ordinatu per lu signurj di lu quali vui tucti serriti allegri di la sua signuria."

Et intandu dissi Misser Galteri di Calatagirunj,

"Comu poti cusì esseri zò ki vuj dichiti? Non pensati chi nui avimu per signuri lu plui potenti signuri di lu mundu chi ogi sia in li cristiani? Si ki lu vostru parlarj et consiglu mj pari vanu."

13

Quandu Misser Iohanni intisi lu parlari di quilli nobili homini, et ipsu rispusi, et sì dissi,

"Crediti vui chi eu mi fussi misu a ffari una grandi imprisa si eu non havissi im prima pinczatu quillu chi si convinia di fari et comu divissi andari lu factu? Dundi vui non haviti a ffari altru si non di tiniri cridenza, ki a mminu di unu annu vidiriti fari per opera li nostri facti."

Incontinenti li baruni foru accurdati et iuraru cridenza a lu dictu di Misser Iohannj et fichiru li licteri chasquidunu cum loro sigilli, li quali licteri dichianu in quistu modu:

14

A lu magnificu et egregiu et potenti signurj Re di Aragona, et Conti di Barsilona, cum tuctu vostru putiri et signuria, di ki nuj ni arricumandamu tucti a la gracia vostra.

Imprimu lu conti di Lintini, zò esti Misser Alaymu, et Misser Palmeri Abbati, et Misser Galterj di Calathagirunj, et tucti li altri barunj di la ysula di Sichilia, sì vi salutanu cum omnj reverencia. Havendu sempri mercì di li nostri persunj, sì comu hominj vinduti et subjugati comu bestij, ricomandamunj a la vostra Signuria et a la signura vostra muglerj, la quali è la nostra Donna a ccui nuj divimu purtari liancza, mandamuvj prigandu chi vui ni digiatj liberari e trayri et livari di li manu di nostri et di li vostri nimichi, sì comu liberau Moises lu populu di li mani di Faraguni, actali chi nuj poczamu tiniri li vostri figloli per signurj et divinjari di li perfidi lupi malvasi devoraturj, di zò chi omni jornu vi scrivirimu, et quandu non potissimu per nostri lictrj scriviri, criditi a Misser Iohanni lu quali esti nostru secretu.

15

Et quandu sigillati happiru li licterj, sì li pregau Misser Iohannj chi quisti gintilominj tinissiru cridenza di zò kj ipsu avia ordinatu di fari. Et Misser Iohannj mustrau a li dictj nobili li licterj li quali lu Plagalogu avia factu, et comu li havia promisu multa munita et comu lu Imperaturj Plagalogu avia iuratu cum lu dictu Misser Iohannj cridenza et conpagnia in quista tali fachenda. Et cussì si partiu Misser Iohannj cum li licteri et cum fidi di Misser Palmerj et di Misser Alaimu et di Misser Galterj.

16

In quillu tempu signuriava et sidia in la Sancta Sedia di Ruma Papa Nicola terzu di casa di Ursini di Ruma, chi avanti havia nomu Misser Iohannj Gaytanu cardinali. Et standu lu dictu papa in un castellu chi avia nomu Surianu, sì vinni a lu Papa Misser Iohanni di Prochita et dissi,

"Sanctu Patri, eu vurria parlari cum vui in unu locu secretu."

Et lu Papa rispusi, "volinteri" inperò kj lu Papa lu canuxia, et richippilu graciusamentj.

17

Intandu dissi Misser Iohannj,

"O Sanctu Patri, tu lu quali tuctu lu mundu mantenj et divi regiri in pachi, rincrixati di quilli miseri scachati di lu Regnu di Sichilia et di Pugla, chi non trovanu cui li regiri non cuj ritiniri, chi illi su peyu chi sunu librusi. Plazati di rimictirili in casa loru, li quali sunu boni cristianj, cussì comu li altri di lu mundu!"

18

Et lu Papa rispusi,

"Comu purria andari contra di lu Re Carlu nostru figlu, lu quali mantenj lu factu et lu honurj di la Ecclesia di Ruma?"

Et Misser Iohannj dissi,

"Eu sachu ki la Re Carlu non obedixi li vostri comandamenti in nixunu casu."

Et lu Papa dissi,

"In quali casu non mi à volutu obediri?"

Et Misser Iohanni dissi,

"Quandu vui vulistivu apparintari cum ipsu et donavivuchi una fimmina di vostru lignaju, et ipsu non volsi, avanti vi disdignau et straczau li vostri lictri. Ben vi divirissivu ricurdari."

Di chi lu Papa si'ndi maraviglau multu, quandu audiu diri a Misser Iohanni quisti cosi. Et Misser Iohanni dissi,

"Comu vi'ndi maraviglati? Quistu esti in palisi per tucta Sichilia et lu Regnu, chi non voli obediri li vostri comandamenti nè voli fari parintatu cum vostru lignaju, et disdignauvj."

19

Intandu lu Papa fu multu iratu, et dissi a Misser Iohannj,

"Beni esti la veritati zò kj vui dichiti, dundi volinteri indi lu farria pentiri."

Intandu dissi Misser Iohanni,

"Illu non è nixunu homu a lu mundu chi lu pocza fari cussì comu vui."

Et lu Papa dissi,

"Comu lu pozu eu fari?"

Et Misser Iohannj rispusi,

"Si vuj mj vuliti dari palora, eu li farrò livari Sichilia, et lu Regnu."

Et lu Papa rispusi,

"Comu dichitj, chi illi sunnu di la Ecclesia?"

Et Misser Iohanni dissi,

"Eu lu farrò fari a ssignuri, kj voli essiri fidili di la Ecclesia; lu quali vi rindirà beni lu vostru inchensu, et esti signuri chi vulinteri farrà parintatu cum vuj et cum lu vostru lignaju, et rimictirà a tucti nui in nostru locu."

Et lu Papa dissi,

"Cuj sarrà quillu signuri chi zò putissi fari oy fussi contra di lu Re Carlu, et kj pensassi tali ardirj oy chi potissi abastari a tali inprisa?"

Et Misser Iohanni dissi,

"Si vuj mi lu vulissivu tiniri in cridenza supra la vostra anima, eu vi dirraju et mustriraju comu quistu poti tuctu essiri."

Et lu Papa dissi,

"Supra la fidi mia, eu ti promectu di tenirilu chilatu."

20

Et Misser Iohannj dissi,

"Sanctu Patri, illu serrà lu Re di Aragona, et quista cosa farrà cum la forza di lu Plagalogu, si vui lu vuliti consentirj, et cum la forza di li sichilianj, li quali su jurati insembla di fari quista cosa, et eu indi su procuratorj di zò."

21

Et intandu dissi lu Papa,

"Sia factu zò chi plachi a vuj senza nostri lictrj."

Et Misser Iohanni rispusi,

"Quistu non potì essiri, ma vuj mi darriti vostri lictri, ki eu la purtirò cum li altri li quali eu aju, a tali chi eu sia crictu."

22

Et lu Papa dissi,

"Eu vi li farro fari, poi chi vui li voliti," et fichiru li lictri. Et si li fichi sigillari non di bulla di plumbu papali, comu si costuma, ma foru sigillati di lu sigillu propriu di lu Papa secretu. Et incontinenti si partiu Misser Iohanni di lu Papa in grandi pachi et concordia. Et lu tinurj di li lictri dichianu in quistu modu:

23

A lu xpranissimu figlu nostru Petru Re di Aragona Papa Nicola terzu la nostra benedicioni ti mandamu.

Cum socia cosa chi li nostri figloli fidili di Sichilia, signuriati non rixuti boni per lu Re Carlu, sì vi pregamu et comandamu chi vuj digiati andarj a ssiguriari per nuj la ysula di Sichilia e li sichiliani, iudicanduvj tucti lu Regnu di piglarj et mantiniri per nuj, si comu figlu conquestaturi di la Sancta Matrj Ecclesia Rumana. Et di zò chi indi voglati cridiri Misser Iohannj di Prochita nostru secretu tuctu quillu lu quali vi dirrà a bucca, tinendu chilatu lu factu, chi jammai non si'ndi sacha nenti. Et però vi plaza prindiri quista inprisa, et di non timirj di nixuna cosa ki contra a ti volissi offendirj.

24

Or si partiu Misser Iohanni cum quistu processu sigillatu di lu Papa, et sì si partiu per andari in Cathalogna.

Et quandu yunsi andau davanti lu Re di Aragona, et lu Re li fichi assai honurj et richippilu allegramenti. Dundi Misser Iohannj adimurau certu tempu cum lu Re, ma non comu homu canuxutu. Et quandu appi statu un certu tempu cum ipsu et lu Re lu minau cum ipsu in Mayorca, et Misser Iohanni dissi a lu Re,

"Eu vurria parlari cum vui in chilatu locu di mei grandi cridenzi, li quali non si conveninu di sapiri si non Deu et nui duj."

Et lu Re li dissi,

"Dichiti sicuramenti tuctu quillu chi vi plachi, chi eu lu tirrò ben chilatu."

Et Misser Iohannj dissi,

"Non sapiriti di mi nixuna cosa, exceptu chi vuj non mj tiniti cridenza cum fidi e vostru sacramentu."

Et lu Re li jurau di tiniri cridenza et secretu. Intandu dissi Misser Iohannj,

"Re Petru, or sachati chi, per aventura quista cosa si sapissi di zò kj eu vi dirrò oy per dictu oy factu, vui et lu vostru lignaju indi sarria distructu, tantu eu aju factu et misu quistu factu innanti."

Intandu lu Re appi grandi pagura et dissi,

"Kj è zò, Misser Iohannj, chi vuj mi dichiti?"

Et Misser Iohannj rispusi,

"Eu aju misu lu factu tantu a conplimentu chi, si vui mi tirriti cridenza et fidi, eu vi pozu fari signurj plui grandi."

Intandu dissi lu Re,

"Eu ti lu promectu tinirj fidi et cridenza, si a Deu plachirà."

25

Et Misser Iohannj dissi,

"Vurrissivu vuj divinjari di li offisi li quali vi su stati facti per lu tempu passatu? Chi aviti richiputu plui virgogni chi signuri kj sia in cristianj? Chi jà comu vui sapiti kj lu Re Manfré lassau lu Regnu di Sichilia, a ssua figla, la quali è vostra mugleri, et vui comu debili et cutardu jamaj non vulistivu viniri ad recuperari la vostra raxunj. Ancora vi diviria ricordari di vostru avu, kj villanamenti lu auchisiru li franchiski a Morellu in Tulusa. Ora vi'ndi potiti vinjari et satisfari tuctu lu tou dammaju si vui vuliti essiri prudu et arditu."

26

Intandu rispusi lu Re,

"Comu pò essiri quista cosa kj tu vui chi eu facza? Sì tu

paczu oy exutu di ti? Non sai ki casa di Francza signuriya tuctu lu mundu et specialimenti lu Re Carlu? Comu putira xiri ki un signurj di sì pichulu putiri comu su eu putissi contrastari cum ipsu? Ma si tu mi mustri alcunu modu chi eu lu pocza fari, lu farrò volinterj."

Et Misser Iohannj dissi,

"Si eu vi darrò la terra tucta guadagnata senza colpu di spata, non la prindiriti? Et ancora vi darrò chentu milia unzi di oru per fornirj omnj spisa et la terra."

27

Et lu Re Petru di Aragona rispusi,

"Comu farrissivu vui quista cosa, chi eu non lu poczu cridiri et ceptu kj tu non mi mustrassi altra cridenza?"

Incontinenti Misser Iohann ixiu li lictrj di lu Papa et ancora li lictrj di lu Plagalogu et quilli dili barunj di Sichilia, et misili in manu di lu Re, et lu Re li guardau effundi multu allegru et dissi a mMisser Iohannj,

"Ben siti bonu amicu ki tanta cosa ay chircata per honuri to et per aviri to intendimentu. Et eu mi proffiru di la parti di Deu, poi ki lu Sanctu Papa voli, et ancora mj rendu ben sicuru di issu, chi zò ki illu mj promecti poti ben fari, et per nixuna accaxuni soi promisi non virranu minu. Et promectu, eu Petru Re di Aragona, et iuruvi fidi et cridenza, ma sempri vi arricordu, fa tu chi quista fachenda vegna facta, et eu farrò zò ki a cti plachi et prindirò lu factu e la briga supra di mj."

28

Et Misser Iohannj dissi,

"Ora apparicha chilatamenti di 'zà ala mia tornata, et eu andirò a lu Papa et a lu Plagalogu et a li sichilianj, et tornandu eu sì ti portirò multa monita per forniri tuctu to factu, et mustriroctj tucti quilli secreti kj zò sapinu comu vuj aviti richiputa quista imprisa. Et per nixuna accaxunj non lu manifestati ad altruj, ne per morti ne per vita, chi troppu serria grandi periculu."

29

Parlati kj foru di tucti cosi comu ia aviti intisu intru Misser Iohannj et lu Re dj Aragona, Misser Iohannj si partiu cum lu Re da Catalogna per andari in Mayorca insembli. Or prisu l'unu conviatu di l'altru et dissi lu modu chi avissi a tiniri di quistu factu 'per fina a la mia tornata,' imperò kj ipsu havia ad ordinari cum lu Plagalogu et cum li sichilianj et cum lu Sanctu Patri Papa Nicola terzu. Et cussì si partiu l'unu da l'altru et andausindj per mari et lu Re di Aragona rumasi in Barsilona.

Dundi Misser Iohannj si'ndi vinni per fina a pPisa per marj et cavalcau chilatamentj fina a Vitelbu et illocu trovau lu Sanctu Papa. Et quandu lu Papa lu vidj, sì li fichi grandi honuri et fu multu allegru et dissi,

"O Misser Iohannj comu haviti factu cum Re di Aragona di tucti quisti cosi?"

Et Misser Iohanni rispusi, "Sanctu Patri, eu aju factu tuctu vostru intendimentu complitamentj, avi richiputa lu Re di Aragona la signuria per lu vostru comandamentu et multu si recomanda a la vostra sancta benedicioni et mandavi quisti lictrj chi lu factu sia ben chilatu, actalkì aja bonu fini et ki lu factu ni vegna a puntu a vostru intendimentu."

Et lu Papa adimandau a Misser Iohannj, "Chi vi pari di lu Re di Aragona?"

Et Misser Iohanni rispusi, "Fachiti chi illu esti lu plui saviu homu di lu mundu et lu plui prudu cavaleri kj ogi sia in xanitati."

Et lu Papa dissi, "Ben mj plachi dj cutali homu, inperò kj a nnuj fachia bisognu in quistu factu, ancora bisugnava a li sichilianj, inperò vactindi in Sichilia et dilli di mia parti et di lu Plagalogu chi si spachanu di ixiri di lu manu di lu Re Carlu et di la sua signuria, cum la mia palora eu li ayutirò chilatamenti, et dichitili chi tostu avirannu bon signuri, si a Deu plachirà."

30

Allura si partiu Misser Misser Iohannj di lu Papa et andau a Cornitu, et illocu trovau unu lignu di pisanj, e muntau di supra quistu lignu, et vinnisindj in Trapanj et fu cum Palmeri Abbati et mandau per tucti li autri barunj di Sichilia.

Dundi illi vinniru tucti in Trapani di kj Misser Iohannj li cuntau comu lu Papa avia concessu e datu la signuria di Sichilia a lu Re Petru di Aragona et comu lu dictu re Petru la avia richiputa vulinteri et allegramenti e comu avia iuratu la morti di lor inimichi, undi vi manda a diri,

"Tiniti chilatu lu factu per fina a la mia tornata, ki cum quilli ordinj ordinatamenti kj eu aju a ffari kj eu voglu andari per fina a lu Plagalogu, per cuntari tuctu lu factu comu è stactu, et per portarj la monita per lu incomenzari di la guerra, et farrimu l'armata grandi e grossa, e ffarrimu tuctu beni, si a Deu plachirà. Preguvi per honuri di Deu, chi vuj tiniti chilatu, chi vinutu esti lu tempu chi vuj ixiriti di servituti et di li vostri inimichi et divingirimu beni tucti nostri virgogni e displachirj."

Et poi prisi conviatu di Misser Palmerj Abbati, et per mari muntau di Trapanj cum una galia di vinicianj et misirulu in terra in Rumania ad unu locu lu quali avia nomu Nigruponti, et poi si'ndj andau in Costantinopuli vistutu ad modu di frati minurj per andarj chilatamentj, actali, chi ipsu non fussi canuxutu.

31

E quandu illu fu chicatu in Costantnopuli, fu davanti lu Inperaturi Plagalogu, et illocu secretu dissi,

"Signuri or ti allegra, chi lu tou intendimentu ti esti vinutu factu cum la veritati, comu lu Papa avi conchidutu la morti e la distrucionj di lu Re Carlu, cum lu tou ayutu et cum quillu di li sichilianj, e di li nostri amichi, di kj ni esti datu per signuri et capitanu di lu Re Petru di Aragona, lu quali esti capu di la guerra et havi iuratu conpagnia cum ticu ad vita et a morti, et avirai per amichi li toi amichi et tucti li toj nimichi avirai per inimichi. Et però vidi si ti veni factu quillu lu quali eu ti promisi. E cum li lictri di li barunj di Sichilia et di lu Papa. Vidi zò kj nuj avimu ordinatu, kj in lu tenpu di li milli et duj chentu octanta duj annj Sichilia serrà ribellata a Re Carlu et serranu morti tucti li soi franchischi, et prindirimu a lloru tucti loru galei et lignj et omnj altri navili et tuctu altru fornimentu li quali divinu vinirj supra di ti, tucta lu so intendimentu serrà perdutu, imperò kj lu Re Carlu avirà a ffari tantu di quilla parti di 'llà chi non purrà izà."

32

Quandu lu Plagalogu vidi tucti li lictrj bulati, dissi,

"Eu sugnu per diri, e ffari tuctu quillu kj ti plachi, chi tu ay factu cosa chi homu di lu mundu non lu haviria potutu fari, et pari ki Deu ti aya datu tou vulirj et conplimentu."

Et Misser Iohannj dissi,

"Or datimj trenta milia unzi di oru, per fari apparichari armata et suldari cavaleri, di ki eu vi pregu chi vui mi donati unu vostru secretu et veru vostru amicu, lu quali vegna cum nuj in Cathalogna per assignari quista munita."

Allura lu Plagalogu rispusi,

"Eu vurria fari parintatu cum ipsu, di darj mia figlola ad unu sou figlu, actali kj inchi fussi plui fidi e pluj fermiza a lu nostru factu."

33

Et isser Iohannj dissi,

"A mmj ben mj parj chi quista cosa si facza, chi lu Re di

Aragona lu farrà volinteri. Dundi eu vi pregu, chi tostu sia factu quillu ki eu adimandu, imperò chi in quisti parti eu non poczu troppu starj. Ancora vorria ad homu kj a nuj canuxissi."

Et lu Imperaduri incontinenti fichi pisari l'oru e mmisili supra di una galia cum Misser Iohannj insembli, la quali galia era di ginuisi, a lu qualj portaru in Barsilona insembli cum unu cavalerj di lu Imperaduri chi era missaiu secretu, chi per nomu si chamava Misser Accardu Latinu, chi era natu di lu planu di Lumbardia, lu quali era prudu e ssaviu et valenti cavalerj.

34

Et vinendu per mari Misser Iohannj per andari in Sichilia si ascuntraru in una navj di pisani et illi adimandaru di novellj di Italia et quilli di la navj arrispusiru kj Papa Nicola era mortu, et "altri novelli non avimu."

Misser Iohannj dissi, "Andati cum Deu," et finsisi di non dunari cura a cutali novelli, actalkj Misser Accardu non si 'ndi adonassi. Ma ipsu in sì midesmj prisi confortu et andau in Sichilia et arrivau in Trapanj, et parlau cum Misser Palmerj Abati et a li altri barunj di Sichilia kj divissiru andari in lysula di Malta a pparlamentu.

E quandu foru tucti assinblati tucti insembla, illi fichiru gran festa e grandi honuri a lu imbaxaturj di lu Imperaturi Plagalogu, lu quali havia nomu Misser Accardu. Et Misser Iohanni di Prochita dissi comu lu Imperaturi di Costantinopuli avia iuratu ferma conpagna cum lu Re di Aragona "et cum vui signuri e barunj di Sichilia," et dissi comu illu havia portata multa monita per incomenzari lu factu.

Poi si livau Misser Alaimu di Lintinj, e dissi,

"Misser Iohannj, multu reingraciamu lu signori Inperaturi Plagalogu di tanta fatiga kj iorni e nocti haviti patuta per trayirinj et livarinj di servitutu di li nostri nimichi, ma sachati kj novellamenti si'nchi esti ascontrata una traversa la quali esti multu ria a lu nostru factu, si comu esti la morti di lu Sanctu Patri Papa Nicola, lu qualj era capu di tuctu quistu factu, kj per so culurj tuctu si potia fari. Undi, poi chi ipsu è mortu non mi plachi chi quistu factu vaya chuj indavanti, et quillu kj indi esti factu si tegna ben chilatu, chi non pari kj Deu vogla chi si facza, per tali signu chi ni esti mostratu, di lu Papa lu quali è statu mortu. Et però mi pari chi si tucti nui stamu a lu vidiri cui sirrà factu Papa, si per avventura illu fussi amicu di lu signuri lu quali esti nostru amicu, et tandu vidirimu si sì sarrà di fari. E quistu mi pari kj sia lu migluri consiglu."

Et a quistu diri si accordaru tucti li barunj di Sichilia e quasi kj foru rumasi di lu factu e discorati, et cussì eranu dubitusi e spagnati di la morti di lu Papa.

35

Et quandu Misser Iohannj audiu quistu parlamentu, fu multu curruchatu in lu visu e dissi,

"Signurj mei, multu mj maraviglu di quistu chi vui dichiti. Et illu esti veru, chi lu Papa esti mortu, et imperò era cosa la sua morti, kj sia contraria a lu nostru factu. Et imperò non si divi lassari quista cussì facta inprisa cussì grandi per quista raxuni: chi si lu Papa chi si farrà, sirrà nostru amicu, accominzamu questioni, chi la Ecclesia di Ruma perduna tucti li peccaturj, et si non cuj veni factu quistu chi nuj cridimu, la terra a lu mal dispectu di lu Papa e di la Ecclesia di Ruma la terrimu per forza, imperò kj majur forza fu quilla di lu Inperaturj Fidericu chi quilla di lu Re Carlu et sì vinissivu fina kj vui vulistivu essiri liali e boni. Undi vi dicu e pregu chi siati liali a lu signurj a ccuj vuj aviti datu fidi et ki vaya innanti lu factu valentimenti."

Sì kj lu diri di Misser Iohannj cum soi veri raxunj et chascunu curaju fu aplacatu. Et cussì fu furnitu chi tucti dissiru chi si divissi mandari per lu Re di Aragona in sua curti per sapiri la sua voluntati. Et Misser Iohannj dissi,

"Eu voglu andari eu, et Misser Accardu, lu imbaxaturi di lu Plagalogu, volia vidiri darj la monita, la quali da lu Inperaduri havia avuta per forniri li soldati et l'armata e mectirj a ffinj lu factu."

36

Or si partiu Misser Iohannj et Misser Accardu, et foru chicati in Barsilona vistuti a mmodu di frati minurj, et andaru davanti lu Re di Aragona. Et quandu lu Re li vidi, fu multu allegru et prisi a Misser Iohannj per la manu et minaulu in cammara, et fichi cum ipsu grandi lamentu di la morti di lu Papa et dissi,

"Ben ni esti fallutu lu nostru pinsamentu, poi ki esti mortu lu nostru capu, zò esti lu Papa, non è di diri nè di andari pluj innanti quistu factu."

37

Et Misser Iohanni rispusi,

"Non dichiti nenti in quista cosa, chi nuj avimu spiranza di aviri cussì bonu Papa chi serrà nostru amicu. Et inperò non timiti. Anantj ajati plui studiu in quista cosa chi iammay, a tali chi nuj ni pozamu arricordari di li nostri amichi di Sichilia, chi di la morti di lu Papa non dubitamu nenti, per tali modu esti lu loru vidiri. Et sachati chi quistu meu compagnu sì esti un cavalerj chi lu Signuri Plagalogu lu manda, et havi nomu Misser Accardu Latinu, saviu homu. Preguvj, fazatilj grandi honuri et audiritilu quillu chi vorrà diri. Et sachati kj nuj avimu portatu trenta milia unzi dj oru, actalkj vuj apparichati l'armata."

38

Et quandu lu Re appi audutu quisti palori, sì fu tuctu incorajatu e dissi, "Eu viyu chi a Deu plachi chi quista cosa sia, or sì zò kj tu voi."

Et Misser Iohannj dissi, "Signurj, quistu cavaleri chi esti cum micu sì esti cavalerj di lu Inperadurj di Costantinopuli et esti so inbaxaturj."

Allura ixiu di la cammara et Misser Accardu lu salutau da parti di lu Inperaturi dichendu chi, "lu Imperadurj avia grandi vogla di vidirilu, et di fari parintatu cum vuj et cum vostru lignaju."

Et poi li prisintau la munita. Et comu l'unu si recomandava all'autru. Et standu tuctj tri insembli supra tuctu lu factu parlaru, et in kj fini di divissi mectirj, et zò fu a lu tempu di li milli e dui chentu octanta duj annj.

Di kj vinnj unu missaiu di curti di Ruma et dissi chi era factu ellivatu papa unu cardinali lu quali avia nomu Misser Simunj Cursu di Franza, et poi sì li fu postu nomu Papa Martinu terczu. Et quandu auderu zò, dissiru,

"Multu chi esti di diri e di penzari imperò chi esli factu papa franchiscu, però kj esti amicu di lu Re Carlu, et porriani dari grandi sconzu a quistu nostru factu."

39

Allura dissi lu Re di Aragona a mMisser Iohannj, "Per Deu, pinzamu zò kj si divj penzari supra stu factu."

Et mMisser Iohannj dissi, "Lu migluri amicu chi lu Re Carlu avissi in curti sì è quistu Papa, ma pertantu fazamu nostru apparichamentu et vidirimu quillu chi serrà di fari, pinzirimu zò chi bisugnirà di fari supra quistu factu, inperò non lassamu di non intendiri di aviri adiminticati nostri facti."

Et stantu insembli intisiru supra lu accomenzamentu di l'armata.

Sì kj vinnj lu misi di aprili, di kj yunzi unu inbaxaturi di lu Re di Franza, e ffu davanti lu Re dj Aragona, e dissi,

"Lu Re di Franza vi manda multi saluti per lu bonu amurj

kj ipsu vi porta, di kj mj à mandatu a vuj cum socia cosa chi ipsu avi intisu chi vuj fachiti grandi armata et grandi naviliu per andari supra sarachini. Però ipsu si po fari in avirj et in persuna et a ctucti plachiri, et pregavj kj per lu so amuri vui li dichiti e ssignificati, per vostri lictrj et per vostru missaiu, lu vostru passaiu in quali parti sirrà et in quali secta di sarachinj. Si vj bisogna munita, chi forsi in quistu essiri non di siti cussì beni adaxatu, chi ki lu fazati a ssapiri, chi ipsu vindi inpruntirà allegramenti quantu vindi bisugnirà."

40

Et lu Re di Aragona rispusi,

"Eu rendu multi gracij a lu vostru signurj Re dj Franza di tanta proferta, la quali per sua bontatj mj avi facta a li mei bisogni, chi a mmj non bisogna a pparlari per lictrj a ssì, chiià sa kj ipsu fu meu cugnatu, si kj parlandu a vuj bastirià si comu esso cavalerj, lu quali si fidirà benj a li vostri palori, li quali eu vi dirrò a bucca. Or dichiti a lu Re di Franza di mia parti, kj vera cosa esti chi eu fazu armata furnita supra sarachinj, ma eu non dirria a nnixuna persuna la accaxunj in quali parti, ma eu criyu chi di prestu lu sapirà et tuctu lu mundu di quista cosa parlirà."

41

Cum quista preposta si partiu lu imbaxaturi et tornau alu Re di Franzca. Et illu videndu et parlandu cum lu missaiu so et avuta la risposta, di ki lu Re di Francza incontinenti mandau in Parisi, undi era sou trisoru, et fussiru portati quaranta milia libri di turnisi di sua parti a lu Re di Aragona, et cussì fu factu. Et incontinenti fichi unu imbaxaturj a lu Re Carlu, mandandulj dichendu li novelli, li quali ipsu avia havutu da lu Re di Aragona, et comu dissi chi ipsu va supra sarachini cum grandi isforzu, non voli dirj in quali parti va, "et inperzò vi mandu pregandu chi vui ajati cura et guardia di vostra terra, zò esti di vostru Regnu, et kj vi'ndi consiglassivu cum lu Sanctu Papa."

42

Lu imbaxaturj si mossi per andarj in Pugla, et quandu fu a Viterbu sì trovau lu Re Carlu et lu Papa insembli, et cuntauli tucta la inbaxata, la quali li avia conmissu sou signurj Re di Franza.

Et quandu lu Re Carlu audiu quisti palori, si'ndi andau a lu Papa e dissi,

"Patri Sanctu, unu imbaxaturi mi esti vinutu di lu Re di Franza, lu quali cunta novelli comu lu Re di Aragona fa grandi armata di marj e non voli diri undi voli andari. Illu esti un gran follunj, inperzò vi pregu chi vuj li mandatj a diri in quali parti ipsu intendi di andari, e kj si illu va supra sarachinj promictitili di darili grandi ayutu, et si illu va supra cristiani sì li mandati comandamentu, sucta la pena di la terra chi tenj di vuj, chi no vaja supra lj fidili di la Ecclesia di Ruma per donari nixunu dampnu."

43

Quandu lu Papa audiu quisti palorj, li quali lu Re Carlu avia dictu, dissi,

"Figlolu nostru, factu sia quillu chi vuj volitj." Et mantinenti mandau per Frati Jacupu di lu ordini si Sanctu Dominicu, et dissi,

"Va a lu Re di Aragona di nostra parti, et dichitili comu a nnuj esti vinutu et datu ad intendiri, chi 'vui fachiti grandi armata per marj per andarj supra sarachinj,' et si zò esti viru, vaya cum la parti di Deu, chi Deu li lassa ben fari e dugnali gracia di ogni honurj et victoria. Et dichi li chi, si li bisogna ayutu, chi volinterj chi lu darrimu. E pregatilu da parti nostra, chi vi dica undi va, oy in terra di Egiptu oy in Barbaria oy puru in Granata, kj in omnj modu nuj li vulimu puru sapiri, inperò kj la sua andata tocca troppu a la Ecclesia di Ruma in sou honuri, non pò ixiri senza lu nostru cumandamentu. Ancora li comandati, supra pena di la terra kj teni di nuj, kj non vaya supra nullu fidili cristianu per fari guerra. Et dichitilj chi ni renda certa e vera risposta."

44

Lu dictu Frati Jacupu di lu ordini di Sanctu Dominicu prisi unu sou conpagnu et andau a lu Re di Aragona et dissili la sua inbaxata comu lu Papa li avia commandatu.

Et lu Re di Aragona chamau Misser Iohannj di Prochita e dissi, "Auditj zò ki lu Papa mj manda a dirj."

Incontinenti fichiru consiglu infra illi duj et in quillu videsmj locu e iorno fichi la risposta a lu dictu Frati Jacupu:

"Or dichiti a lu signurj Sanctu Papa chi nuj lu reingraciamu cussì comu a nostru patri dj tanta bona pruferta quantu ipsu ni avi factu a quista nostra inprisa e di tantu amuri quantu chi mustra. Et dichitili kj quandu ni fussi bisognu lu sou ayutu, nuj lu riquidirimu et ricurririmu a ssì comu a nostru patri. Et dichitilj chi, di lu factu di sapiri dundi nuj andamu, chi ipsu non lu pò sapiri per nixunu modu, chi si una di li nostri manu lu dichissi allura nuj ni li farriamu taglari, et inperzò si'nchi perdunj in quista volta, kj altru non po essiri. Ma si a Deu plachi eu andirò in parti chi lu Sanctu Patri et soi frati cardinali havirannu a gracia et alligriza, perzò li plaza chi prega a Deu per nuj a lu nostru intendimentu."

45

Quandu Frati Jacupu appi richiputa la risposta di lu Re di Aragona, si partiu e chicau a Munti Flascunj, et illocu trovau lu signuri Sanctu Papa et lu Re Carlu, et quandu lu Papa lu audiu si maraviglau multu.

Allura dissi lu Re Carlu, "Sanctu Patri, ben vi dissi viru eu chi Re di Aragona è gran fulluni. Auditj bella risposta chi à facta! Ma faza cum Deu zò ki li plachi, chi si illu va supra sarachini vuj diviti esseri allegru et tucta la curti di Ruma."

Supra zò non fu plui parlatu, anti dissi lu Papa, "Ajati cura e custodia di la vostra terra, chi eu aju audutu diri ki lu Re di Aragona è unu di quilli signuri chi sia in quistu mundu di la mayuri inprisa kj nixunu altru."

Et lu Re Carlu rispusi, "Sanctu Patri, nuj starrimu a lu vidiri zò ki ipsu farrà."

46

In quillu tempu si partiu Misser Iohanni di Prochita et Misser Accardu di lu Re di Aragona et dissi,

"Eu voglu andari in Sichilia per ordinari chi in quist'annu si rebella Sichilia contra di lu Re Carlu."

Et lu Re di Aragona li donau comandamentu dichendu chi secretamenti fachissiru lu factu, azò ki lu loru intendimentu vegna factu.

Et Misser Iohanni si partiu lu misi di ginnaru et iunsiru in Trapani et mandaru per Misser Palmeri Abbati e per Misser Alaymu di Lintini e per Misser Galteri di Calatagirunj et per li altri baruni di Sichilia chi venissiru a lu parlamentu. Dundi tucti foru venuti, et cussì Misser Iohannj si livau e dissi,

"Belli signuri, sachati chi lu Re di Aragona à facta la pluj bella armata di marj chi sia per lu mundu e di multa bona agenti et assai, di kj indi esti factu almiragla lu pluj francu e valirusu homu kj in mari putissi stari, lu quali si chama Misser Rujeri di Lauria, di Calabria, lu quali è sempri statu in Aragona cum lu Re di Aragona, et esti lu pluj grandi guirreri et homu saputu in quisti facti chi nixunu homu di lu mundu, et quillu kj di li franchiski esti grandi nimicu, imperò ki li auchisiru a sso patri. Et inperò pinzati in qualuncata modu vuj pozati livari la terra a lu Re Carlu ma non si pò farj mai meglu di ora chi lu Re Carlu esti in curtj di lu Papa et lu princhipi so figlu esti in Provenza. Ma ananti chi sachanu quisti cosi sì passirà multu tempu et potiriti meglu fornirj li terri vostri per tucta Sichilia."

Et a zò si accordaru tucti, e prisiru hordini di livari a rrimurj la terra e di lu putiri di lu Re Carlu.

47

Eccu kj fu vinutu lu misi di apprili (sic) l'annu di li milli e dui chentu octanta duj, lu marti dij (sic) di la Pascua di la Resurreccioni.

Eccu kj Misser Palmeri Abbati e mMisser Alaimu di Lintinj et Misser Galteri di Calatagirunj et tucti li altri barunj di Sichilia, tucti accordati ad un volirj pir loru discretu consiglu viniru in Palermu per fari la ribellacionj.

Dundi in quillu iornu predictu si soli farj una gran festa fora di la chitati di Palermu in unu locu lu quali si chama Sanctu Spiritu.

Dundi unu franchiscu sì prisi una fimmina toccandula cum li manu disonestamenti, comu ja eranu usati di farj. Di kj la fimmina gridau, et hominj di Palermu cursiru in quilla fimmina et riprisirusi in briga. Et in quilla briga intisiru quisti barunj predicti et in calzaru la briga contra li franchiskj et livaru a rimuri e fforu a li armi li franchischi cum li palermitani.

Et li homini a rrimuri di petri e di armj gridandu: "Moranu li franchiskj!"

Et intraru intra la chitati cum grandi rimuri et foru per li plazi, et quanti franchiskj trovavanu tucti li auchidianu. Infra quistu rimuri lu capitanu chi era tandu per lu Re Carlu si ascontra cum quista genti e non pocti stari di avanti loru, anti fugiu et misisi in unu steri in lu quali illu stava, et li palermitani andavanu aconpagni per la chitati et quanti francischi trovavanu tuctj li auchidianu.

Di kj poi andaru allu steri di lu capitanu et lu capitanu si rindiu cum in certj pacti, et poi kj fu in putirj loru non li foru actisi anti lu auchisiru et tucta la sua conpagna ancora andaru a li lokj di frati minurj et frati predicaturj et quanti chi'ndi trovaru chi parlassiru la lingua franchisca li auchisiru intra li ecclesij.

Or quandu li baruni di Sichilia appiru vidutu tuctu quistu factu, tucti si'ndi andaru in loru terri et fichiru lu simiglanti per tucta Sichilia salvu Missina, chi ad dimurau un certu tempu. Di ki sì trovaru morti franchiskj in Palermu tri milia.

48

In quillu tempu standu lu Re Carlu in curtj di lu Papa si li vinnj missaiu, lu quali li mandau lu archi episcupu di Murriali, et cuntauli sì comu li sichiliani sì avianu rebellatu tucta la terra di Sichilia, e comu avianu mortu tuctu li soy franchiskj, et non sapia per quali actu sianu morti, nè comu esti andatu quistu factu, "et perzò pinzati supra quista cosa quillu kj vuj aviti a ffari, comu saviu."

49

Quandu lu Re Carlu audiu tali novella, fu multu curruchatu, et incontinenti andau a lu Papa e dissi,

"Patri Sanctu, malj novelli vi ayu portatu di mei facti, chi illu mi esti vinutu unu missaiu di lu archiepiscupu di Murriali, chi mj cuntau sì comu li sichilianj mj sunu rebellati et ànnu morti tucta mia genti, la caxunj perchi è stata eu non so perchi. Et imperò vi pregu chi vi plaza di darimj cunsiglu quillu chi sia migluri, imperò kj lu dannu e lu malj indi aviti vui e la Ecclesia di Ruma."

E lu Papa rispusi,

"Figlu nostru, non timirj chi tuctu lu ayutu e cunsiglu chi vi fa misteri di tucti vi ayutirimu. Vatindj a lu Regnu e ffa tua armata et passa in Sichilia et conquesta la tua terra per pachi e per accordu, si vuj potiti. Et mina cum ti unu nostru legatu cum nostri lictri, et dirrà di nostra parti a li sichilianj, chi la terra nostra chi teninu, chi esti speciali cammara nostra, chi ti la rendanu."

Et cussì si partiu lu Re Carlu di quistu parlamentu cum lu Papa.

50

In quillu videmmj iornu andau lu Re Carlu in consiglu con tucti li cardinali et tucti li soi amichi et clerichi di la curti di Ruma preganduli per Deu chi lu divissiru consiglari di lu sou bisognu, chi li sichilianj li avianu rebellati, et avianu morti tucta la sua gentj. Allura si levau Misser Iacopu Savelli, cardinali, e dissi,

"Signuri Re Carlu, sachati kj tucta curti di Ruma plachi chi vuj siyati ayutatu e consiglatu per kj lu divimu farj per tucti raxunj, chi troppu haviti misu ad honuri la Ecclesia di Ruma et di soy facti. Inperò eu primu voglu chi andati in Sichilia, et minati cum vuj unu ligatu cardinali cum tucti li prochessi chi si pozanu diri et fari, sì kj la terra si recuperi per pachi, si essiri sì pò, et si non, si aquesti per guerra."

Et in quistu modu si accordaru tucti et lu Papa plazi. Et incontinenti comandau a Misser Girardu di Palma, cardinali, chi si acconzassi per andari in Sichilia in serviciu di la Ecclesia et di lu Re Carlu, et illu sì fichi lu comandamentu di lu Papa.

51

Intandu mandau lu Re Carlu multi missagi per multi parti et a lu Re di Franza et a lu princhipi so figlu, significandu a lloru comu li sichiliani eranu rebellati a ssì et avianu morti tucti li soy franchischi, l'accaxunj non si sa, "e preguvj chi supra vuj Re di Franza dijati darj consiglu," et cussì a lu primu chi l'ayutassiru, chi incontinentj vinissiru oy mandassiru per sou amurj. Lu Re di Franza audendu quillj novelli fu multu iratu e ssuspirau e dissi,

"Fratelli mej, gran pagura aju eu chi quista non sia opera di lu Re di Aragona, chi non mj volsi significarj la sua andata, nè in quali parti gissi quandu eu li inprestai quaranta milia librj di tornisi. Troppu mi'ndi pari mali ma zò esti chi illu sia veru, eu non criyu jammai portari coruna si eu non indi lu fazu pentiri si ipsu à factu quistu tradimentu a la casa di Franza!" Et incontinenti dissi a lu principi, "Vatindi in Pugla. Et poi mandau a lu Conti Artisi, quillu di Lanzola et quillu di Martinu, et multi altri barunj et cavalerj, significandu quistu factu, dichendu chi si apparichassiru cum socia cosa kj li vulia mandarj illu ayutu a Re Carlu."

52

Or vinni in quillannu videmmi di millj e duj chentu octanta duj, lu Re Carlu si partiu di Brandizi cum grandi hostj di mari, et per terra vinniru in Calabria a rRigiu cum grandi isforzu di franchischi e provinzanj et lumbardj et tuscanj et di terra di Ruma. Et passau in Missina et misi campu undi Sancta Maria di Rocca Amaduru, et era cum ipsu Misser Girardu di Palma, cardinali elligatu in Sichilia per la Ecclesia.

Quandu li missinisi victiru quista cussì facta armata et essiri invaduti, appiru gran pagura comu homini li quali avianu servutu di richipiri morti, et mandaru a lu Re Carlu et a lu cardinali chi divissiru viniri a richipirj la terra sì comu legitimj signurj, preganduli per misericordia chi avissi di loru.

Et si lu Re Carlu fussi intratu intandu haviria avutu la terra a lu sou comandamentu.

Ma non volsi anti li mandau disfidandu sì comu trayturi di sua coruna, chi non volia promictirj a lloru vita si non morti ad issi et a lloru figlolj, chi di tali offisa la quali avianu facta et pinsata contra la Ecclesia di Ruma et di la casa di Franza, chi mai non aviria misericordia di loru si non morti, chi ben l'avianu servutu et "chi mai non mj tornassivu pluj davanti."

Et cum quista risposta si partiu unu missaiu di Re Carlu et tornau a mMissina et cuntau la risposta di Re Carlu. Et tandu li missinisi appiru grandi pagura di morti, et stectiru quatru iornj in consiglu, oy difendirisi oy rendirisi per mortj.

53

Un iornu vinni quillu conti di Munfortj et cum lu conti di Brinda et cum multj cavalerj et pidunj et andaru inver di una terra chi avia nomu Milazu, et andaru ardendu et guastandu omni cosa. Et quandu quilli di la terra vidiru quista cosa, ixeru fora cridendusi difendiri, et quandu li franchischi li vidiru, sì ficheru adossu et prisirundi et auchisirundi assai missinisi et di quilli di Milazu. Et quandu indi vinnj la novella a mMissina, si tinniru tucti per morti, et mandaru per misser lu ligatu chi divissi vinirj a mMissina per acconzarili cum lu Re Carlu.

Et quistu factu fu di lu misi di jugnectu, chi lu legatu intrau a mMissina, et apprisintau li lictri di lu Papa a lu comunj di Missina et lu processu chi la Ecclesia avia factu contra di loru, si per via di pachi vi donassiru la terra et portassiru li chavj a lu Re Carlu, sì comu e lligitimu signurj, chi li potissi prindirj per via di morti. Et li lictrj dichianu in quistu modu:

54

A li perfidi 'judei' di l'isula di Sichilia, Martinu Papa terzu manda quilli salutj sì comu ecorrumpituri di pachi, di cristianj alchiditurj et isbanditurj di lu sangu di li nostrj fidili.

A vuj comandamu chi, viduti li nostri lictrj, incontinenti, vi dijati rendirj e darj la terra a lu nostru figlolu campiunj, zò esti Carlu Re di Iherusalem et di Sichilia, per l'antiquitati di la Sancta Ecclesia di Ruma. Imperò dijati vuy obedirj a lu dictu Re Carlu, sì comu vostru legitimu signurj, et si zò vuj non obedissivu, annunciamuvj per iscomunicatj et interdicti, e ssupra lu so undi avj raxunj annunciamuvj instracta specialj et temporalj.

55

Quandu li missinisi intisiru quisti lictri e cussì facti comandamentj, sì appiru gran pagura, et sillissiru trenta hominj di lu populu, di li quali divissiru pinzarj lu modu per putirinj accordarj cum lu Re Carlu et cum lu legatu di lu Papa. Et quandu quisti trenta hominj appiru ben pinzatu et consiglatu insemblj, illi sì andaru davanti di lu legatu, et li missinisi sì dissiru, "Nuj simu vinutj a dirivj quillu chi si divi fari."

Et illu dissi, "Dichiti vostru vuliri."

"Nuj volimu quisti pacti di lu Re Carlu: Nuj li darrimu la terra et paghirimu in quillu modu comu pagavamu antiquamenti in lu tempu di lu Re Guillelmu, et non volimu signurj altru si non latinj, zò è officialj nostri, e non franchischi nè provinzani; et volimu chi ni perdugna la offisa chi nuj avimu facta et li nostri figloli a li soi cavalerj et soy genti. Et si quista cosa nj fa, nuj li sarrimu boni e ffidili."

Quandu lu ligatu audiu quistu diri, sì dissi, "Mandamu a lu campu undi esti lu Re Carlu et audirimu lu so vulirj. Si plachirà a Deu, nuj farrimu omni beni."

Et incontinenti lu ligatu chamau un so cambilingu et a lu legatu sì mandau a lu Re Carlu cum tucti quisti pacti scripti, ancora da partj di lu legatu chi li divissi plachirj di partj di Deu chi divissi prindiri quisti pacti et perdonarilj, actali chi Deu perdonassi ad ipsu.

56

Or quandu lu Re Carlu audiu talj adimanda chi li missinisi fachianu, fu multu adyratu e dissi,

"Quilli chi su dignj di morti sì fanu dimandanu pacti! Ipsi non mj liviranu la mia signuria, anti adimandanu la signuria antica di lu Re Guillelmu, kj non avia nenti terra a lu paysi nè nixuna rendita! Dichitili kj eu non indi voglu farj nentj, ma poichi plachi a lu legatu, eu a lloru perdugnu la morti, salvu chi eu voglu chi ipsi stayanu a mmeu putirj e ffari di loru tucta mia voluntati, dimandu a lloru quilla signuria chi a mmj plachirà sì comu liberu signurj, pagandu colti, e dunandu sicundu esti usanza. Si non li plachi a lloru, sì lu faczanu, et si non sia a llor plachirj, si difendanu, chi a lloru fa bisognu."

Intandu lu cambirlingu di lu ligatu chicau a mMissinau cum la risposta la quali vuj aviti audutu. Et quandu li trenta missinisi audendu zò, sì lu cuntaru davanti tuctu lu populu la risposta la quali avia facta lu Re Carlu. Et lu populu rispusi tucti ad una vuchi,

"Ananti volimu manjari l'unu all'autru chi quista cosa sia, chi chasquidunu di loru semprj vurria vindicta. Ananti volimu morirj in nostra terra, ananti chi venirj in perdicioni et in li manu di li nostri nimichi!"

E quistu fu dictu a lu legatu, dundi lu ligatu fu multu iratu e dissi,

"Poy chi vuj non voliti fari quistu acconzu cum lu legatu et cum Re Carlu, eu vi dinunciu per escominicati et interdicti da parti di lu Sanctu Papa e di la Ecclesia di Ruma."

Et senza pluj parlari ixiu di Missina, et anantj chi partissi comandau actucti quilli chi avissiru ordini sacri kj di llà a trj jornj divissiru ixiri di la terra, et ancora riquersi lu comunj di Missina chi di zà a quaranta jornj si divissiru apprisintarj dananti di lu Papa ad audirj la sentencia, sucta pena di la terra kj teninu da ipsu, zò è da la Ecclesia di Ruma.

57

Et quandu lu re vidi lu legatu et sappi la risposta, fichi consiglu cum li soy conti per fari quillu chi avissi a ffari. Et li baruni lu consiglaru chi ipsu divissi stringiri la terra per bactagla, in tali chi la terra s'avissi per forza.

Et lu Re Carlu stecti a quillu consiglu unu jornu et una nocti, e ppoi la matina vinendu mandau per li soi barunj e dissi,

"Signuri, non mj accordu cum vuj di lu qonsiglu lu quali nuj avimu terminatu, inperò kj, si fussi cussì comu lu consiglu, eu guastiria mia terra, non voglu auchidirj li pichulillj, inperchì non ànnu culpa. Anti eu li voglu assijarj sì strictamenti et per necessitati di manjari illi pozanu murirj, et innanti chi ipsi moranu, avirimu la nostra terra et tuctu lu nostru vuliri, et ancora nostrj ingegni et instringimenti per spagnarili et avenirj a nostra intencioni."

Et cussì fu factu.

Un jornu, volendu darj bactagla a la terra, tucti li missinisi cursiru cum loru donnj e ffimminj et ancora li pichulillj, et fichiru unu muru di quilla partj dundi era l'osti, et accuminzarusi a difendiri. Et tandu fichiru un capitanu et rigiturj per quilli. Si difisiru in quistu actu ben duj misi contra Re Carlu.

58

Et in quillu tempu si mossi Re Aragona di Cathalogna e ffichi vuchi dj andarj in Tunisi. Dundi prisi in Barbaria una terra chi si chama Alcoy et dunanduchi una bactagla, e stecti in quillu locu per quindichi jorni, e ffu di augustu. Et Misser Iohannj di Prochita cum li altri inbaxaturj di Sichilia andaru per mari perfina in Cathalogna a lu Re di Aragona, chi in tuctu vinissi a pprindiri la ysula di Sichilia.

Et li inbaxaturj sì foru Misser Iohannj di Prochita et l'altru Misser Guillelmu di Missina, e duj sindaki di l'isula di Sichilia. Et junsiru undi era lu Re di Aragona, et lu re li richippi volinteri et fichili grandi honuri.

Di ki lu Re di Aragona adimandau a mMisser Iohannj, chi lu Re Carlu ja esti a Missina cum grandi hosti et avi multu strictu la terra,

"Consiglatimi chi eu dija fari supra zò?"

Et Misser Iohannj dissi, "Non dubitati nenti ma viniti al-l'isula di Sichilia et mandiriti a diri a lu Re Carlu chi scumbra la terra vostra, inperò kj lu Sanctu Papa Nicola vi l'à conchessu, inperò kj era di vostra mugleri, et intandu audiriti la risposta. Et sachati chi quistu Misser Guillelmu esti imbaxaturi di Missina, imperò audiriti quillu chi ipsu dirrà et ancora quisti altri sindakj di Missina e di Sichilia."

59

Allura si livau lu imbaxaturj di Sichilia e li altri et imsembla dis-siru,

"Signurj re, multu vi disiyanu li nostri fidili di Sichilia, et mandanuvj pregandu chi vuj vegnati per la terra di Sichilia e kj fazati livarj lu campu a lu Re Carlu et lu sou osti, chi altru re-cuperu non aspictamu si non lu vostru, pertantu plazavj di fari quista deliberacionj per lu amuri di Deu. Et si vuj non voliti vinirj a ssuccurrirj et ajutarilj, issi si excusanu si farranu li co-mandamenti di lu Re Carlu e di la Ecclesia di Ruma."

Et quandu fu finutu quistu dictu, tucti li altri sindakj et im-baxaturi dissiru lu simiglanti parlarj a lu Re di Aragona.

60

Et lu Re di Aragona dissi,

"Eu virrò volinteri in l'isula di Sichilia in ayutu di li mej fidili, et inperò andati e dichiti a chasquidunu locu chi la mia vinuta serrà tostu, et stayanu allegramenti, chi tostu serrò illocu a lloru ayutu."

Et cum quista risposta si parteru di lu Re di Aragona.

61

Incontinenti lu Re di Aragona si partiu d'Alcoy et vinnisindi in Sichilia, et incontinenti sì fu davanti di Misser Palmerj Abbati et li altri barunj di Sichilia e ffichiru consiglu di zò kj avianu a ffari, et Misser Iohannj di Prochita si livau e dissi,

"Signurj re, a nnuj nj pari chi vuj de presentj dijati andarj in Palermu. Si pinsirimu quillu chi si divi fari, il locu sapirimu zò kj fa lu Re Carlu, zò kj avirà factu a Missina et a lu paisi. E ssupra zò prindirimu bonu consiglu, si a Deu plachirà."

E cussì fu factu.

62

In lu annu di li milli e dui chentu octanta dui annj di lu aventu di Xristu, in lu misi di agustu, cavalcau lu Re di Aragona di Trapani in Palermu.

Et li palermitanj fichiru grandi sollempnitati di la sua vinuta, sì comu hominj li quali aspictavanu liberacionj di morti. Di kj lu ascuntraru ben sej migla, cum grandi gazara: donnj e dunzelli, hominj e ffimmini, conti e baruni.

L'archiepiscupu di Murriali non sì vosi trovarj a darilj coruna, chi in Palermu avia statu mortu lu loru archiepiscupu, sì kj quillu di Murriali fugiu et andausindi a lu Papa, et cussì non fu incoronatu si non chamatu di lu populu.

Di kj un jorno vinniru tucti li barunj di Sichilia ad ipsu in Palermu, e ffichiru gran consiglu cum ipsu.

63

Livausi Misser Palmerj Abbati, e dissi,

"Signuri re laudatu sia Deu, chi ben esti vinutu e ffactu nostru intendimentu per vostra bontati e quilla di Misser Iohannj di Prochita. Inperò vi plaza di quista cosa aja bon mezu e bonu finj, sì comu à avutu bonu incomenzamentu. Ma ben vurria kj vuj fussivu vinutu cum pluj genti, chi si lu Re Carlu dixindi per tucta la ysola di Sichilia, lu quali avi ben quindichi milia hominj a ccavallu, sì kj nui avirimu troppu a ffarj a ccumbactirj cum ipsu. Et inperò mj pari kj penzamu di avirj pluj agentj di quali parti avirj si'ndj putissi, inperò eu cryu kj Missina sia perduta, tantu era ristricta et in succaru di vidanda."

64

Quandu lu Re di Aragona audiu quisti palori, sì appi grandi dubitanza, audendu chi lu Re Carlu avia tantu putirj. Et incontinenti mandau currerj per l'isula di Sichilia, chi si Re Carlu vinissi inver Palermu.

Et in quilla nocti vinni unu notaru inbaxaturi di parti di lu comunj di Missina, e quillu missaiu dissi a lu Re di Aragona comu in Missina non avia vidanda exceptu per octu iorni et non per chuj e kj "vuj nj dijati dari ayutu e ssiccursu di gentj e di victuagli, chi per nixunu modu nuj non putimu pluj resistiri dananti di lu Re Carlu, sì kj nuj nj rindirimu ad ipsu, kj nuj non putimu altru farj."

65

Et quandu lu Re di Aragona audiu quistu parlamentu, fichi chamari tucti li barunj di Sichilia e cuntau a lloru tuctu lu factu. Allura si livau Misser Galteri di Calatagiruni e dissi,

"A mmi pari chi vuj, signuri re, cavalcati per fina a mMilazu, lu quali esti appresu Missina, perzò chi a mmi pari chi, sì tostu kj lu Re Carlu lu sintirà, sì si livirà di l'osti et dananti la terra, chi si Missina sì perdi, nuj avirimu factu mali di nostra inprisa."

Et poy si livau Misser Iohannj di Prochita et dissi,

"A mmj pari chi zò si faza in quistu modu, chi lu Re Carlu non esti homu chi si spagni e fuya. Ma fazamu cussì. Mandamu una lictra a lu Re Carlu di parti di lu Re di Aragona e dirrimu sì comu

Papa Nicola sì dedi la terra a lu Re di Aragona et inperò illu la dija lassari. Et si per avintura illu non voli lassari non partirisi, difinditila comu cosa vostra. E quandu kj zò non voli, mandati chi lu vostru miragla cum vostri galei fina a mMissina et comandatili chi, tucti lu naviliu chi porti victuagla a lu Re Carlu et a lu sou hosti, chi illu li prinda. Di kj conveni chi lu Re Carlu pera et Missina serrà assicursa et indi ajati vindicta di sì e ssua genti chi fussi iammai facta di nixunu signurj chi jammai a lu mundu. Et si di llocu illu si leva, putirà andari, e starrimu a lu vidiri si andirà in alcuna parti di l'isula oy ipsu si 'ndi andirà a lu Regnu oy in Calabria."

66

Et quandu lu Re e li barunj auderu quistu, sì si accordaru. E di prisenti sì mandaru duj cavaleri cathalani a lu campu di lu Re Carlu cum lictri, e l'unu si chamava Misser Guillelmu et l'altru Misser Almingu, et li lictrj dichianu in quistu modu:

67

Petru di Aragona, di Sichilia Re, a vuj Carlu di Iherusalem e di Provenza conti.

Significamuvj lu nostru avinimentu di l'isula di Sichilia, sì comu nostru riamj judicatu per l'autoritati et voluntati di la Sancta Ecclesia di Ruma et di lu sanctu apostolicu Papa Nicola terzu. Et imperò vi comandamu a vuj, chi viduta la nostra lictra, livarivj di l'isula di Sichilia cum tucta vostra genti. Sachati chi, si zò vuj non fachiti, li nostri cavaleri fidili vidiriti prisentj in vostru dampnu e di vostra genti.

68

Et quandu lu Re Carlu appi viduta quista lictra, sì fichi cunsiglu cum li soy baruni. Et multu si maraviglavanu li barunj, chi audendu dirj a lu Re Carlu tantu ultraju quantu li lictri continianu inver di sì et di soy cavaleri.

Allura si livau lu conti Guidu di Munforti e dissi chi multu li paria cosa strania chi un signuri di sì pocu potencia avissi ardiri di livari la terra ad unu di li miglurj e di li mayuri signurj di lu mundu.

Intandu lu Re Carlu dissi chi chasquidunu dichissi lu sou vulirj.

E ppoi si livau lu conti di Brinda e dissi chi a ssì paria chi arrispundissi a lu Re di Aragona per lictri, dichenduli kj li avj factu grandi fauzia et tradimentu, e zò non divia fari, chi lu Re Carlu non li avia factu ultraju, e comu quilli terri lu Re di Aragona non avia di la Ecclesia di Ruma non per Papa, anti l'avia falsamenti comu e traydituri.

"Inperò li mandati comandandu chi illu si parta di prisenti di vostra terra, chi di quillu chi à factu vui indi lu farritj pentiri, sì comu e traditurj, chi maj non si trovau nixunu signuri chi andassi l'unu contra di l'altru sencza accaxunj, e quistu, sì comu trayditurj misi vuchi e dichia chi vulia andari supra li sarachini, et ora esti vinutu supra cristiani e contra la Ecclesia di Ruma 'et di mi, di ki eu vi mandu per voluntati di li baruni li quali si accordanu ad un diri.'"

Dundi lu Re Carlu fichi fari una lictra a li imbaxaturj di lu Re di Aragona, e quistu esti lu tinurj di la lictra:

69

Carlu per la gracia di Deu Re di Iherusalem et di Sichilia et Conti di Provenza et Princhipi di Capua fina a Pedi Munti e fFulcalorio, a cti Petru di Aragona Re et Conti di Barsilona.

Maraviglandunj in tuctu comu tu fusti usanti di intrari intru la ysula di Sichilia, iudicata nostra per la vitilitati di la Ecclesia di Ruma, et per zò ti comandamu per l'autoritati di nostru cumandamentu chi incontinenti, viduti nostri lictri, tu digi partirj di lu riamj di Sichilia sì comu malvasu traditurj. Et di prisentj vidiritj lu meu avinimentu et di li nostri cavaleri, li quali disiyanu trovarisi cum la tua genti.

70

Et li missagi si parteru per lu comandamentu di lu Re Carlu et iunsiru in Palermu et andaru davanti lu Re di Aragona et aprisintarichi la lictra. Et lecta e viduta la lictra lu Re di Aragona appi consiglu cum li soi barunj. Dundi si livau Misser Iohannj di Prochita e dissi,

"Per Deu, ordinati tostu et mandati la miragla vostra per mari a mMissina, et comandatili chi prinda tucti li navili di lu Re Carlu, dapoi chi vuj l'aviti disfidatu, ordinatj et pinzati omnj so dampnu. Et inperzò vi dicu chi illu vi virrà factu, et lu Re Carlu sirrà prixunj, et farritilu periri e ssiccari di famj, di kj li convinirà chi sia mortu."

Et incontinentj mandaru per la miragla, lu quali era Misser Rujeri di Lauria. Et cumandau lu Re di Aragona a mMisser Rujeri chi incontinenti fachissi acconzarj l'armata et andassi a mMissina, et prindissi et ardissi tucti li navili di Re Carlu.

Et intandu era vinutu unu spiunj di Misser Alaymu Alkirinu di Mari di Genua lu quali era miragla di Re Carlu, et incontinenti si partiu di Palermu et vinnj all'osti et dissi a lu sou ammiragla tucta la vinuta di l'armata di Misser Rugeri di Lauria.

Di kj Misser Alkirinu di Amari si'ndi andau a lu Re Carlu, e dissi,

"Signuri, spachativi di passarj in Calabria cum socia cosa chi una spiya è vinuta di Palermu, et cuntamj comu lu miragla di lu Re di Aragona veni a mMissina cum tucta sua armata et voli prindirj tucti li nostri navilj. Et sachati kj eu non aju galej, anti avimu ligni disarmati, di kj illu nj prindirà senza nixunu consiglu, sì ni perdirimu e ssenza bactagla, et rumaniriti di quista parti senza vidanda e convirravi di morirj di fami, e quistu serrà di 'zà a tri jorni. Et inperò pinsati di passari di quilla parti per quista raxuni, et lu vernu nj venj adossu, et vuj non aviti bonu portu chi vuj e li navilj pozati stari. Et si per aventura quistu no vi plachi, li ligna rumpiranu, undi vi penzati di passari in terra ferma, sì kj zò kj vi bisogna vi vegna di terra di li nostri cuntratj."

71

Et allura lu Re Carlu fu multu corruchatu e ffici consiglu cum li soy barunj et cuntau zò kj Misser Alkirinu di Amarj li avia dictu. Li baruni, audendu quisti palori, appiru grandi doluri et dissiru a lu Re Carlu,

"Multu nj dolimu, imperò kj non vulistivu chi prindissimu Missina non per pachi nen per guerra. Ora non la porrissivu per nixunu modu avirj, di kj simu multi dolurusi et non potimu fari. Et però passamu in terra ferma et serrà quillu chi a Deu plachirà."

Et cussì fu ordinatu per tucti li barunj.

72

Quandu lu Re Carlu audiu quisti palorj, fu ismarritu, zò esti ixutu di sì, et suspirandu dissi infra sì midesmj, dichendu,

"Eu su mortu, poi chi tanti disaventuri mj su vinuti, chi eu aju perdutu mia terra, et àmmila prisa homu a ccuj jammaj eu non displachivj. Multu mj doli kj eu non vosj prindirj Missina, ma poi kj cussì va lu factu, passamu in Calabria, et cui mj avirà culpatu a quistu tradimentu, oy cuj chi fu a darinchi ayutu, cumveni chi sia mortu."

E cussì finiu sou parlarj. Et quistu fu lu misi di sictembru, chi si livau l'osti davanti Missina et andau in Calabria.

73

Lu primu jornu passau la rigina, e lu secundu jornu passau lu Re Carlu con multa genti, et lassau duj capitani cum duj milia cavaleri e dissi,

"Stati chilatamenti, et quandu quilli di Missina ixiranu fora per prindiri la roba, sì intririti in fra loru, et firendu intrati in Missina. Si vi venj factu, eu turnirò a vui."

E cussì fu ordinatu. E quilli di Missina sappiru quisti palorj per loru spiya et incontinenti fichiru comandamentu chi nixunu nixissi di la terra, e cussì fu factu. E quandu li franchiskj vidiru chi quilli di Missina non nixianu fora, incontinenti conzaru loru naviliu et passaru in Calabria e dissiru a lu Re Carlu,

"Signurj, lu nostru pinsamentu nj esti vinutu mancu, kj quilli di Missina non nixeru jammai fora di la terra."

74

Altura lu Re Carlu fu pluj adiratu, intandu dissi,

"Nuj starrimu a lu vidirj zò kj serrà di loru et ancora di lu Re di Aragona e di sua genti."

L'altru iornu di appressu junsi la miragla Misser Rugerj di Lauria per comandamentu di lu Re di Aragona et intrau in bucca di faru di Missina, fachendu gran gazara cum dechi galej, et firiu intru lu naviliu di lu Re Carlu, e prisi et abruscau navj e galej, e fforu prisi chincu galej di lu comunj di Pisa, e fforu minatj in Missina, cridendu putirj prindirj lu Re Carlu in mari.

E lu Re Carlu, sapendu quistu factu, appi tali doluri chi vorria essiri statu mortu. Et tandu lu Re Carlu era a rRiju di Calabria, et dedi conviatu a tucta maynera di genti li qualj eranu strayneri e ssuldati, excectu quilli kj teniano terra ad sì, e quistu fu di lu misi di octobru.

75

In quistu misi di octubru vinnj lu Re di Aragona in Missina cum Misser Iohannj di Prochita, e fforu ascuntrati di li missinisi cum grandi festa e gran gazara, di kj si ascuntraru una grandi via cavaleri et donnj e donzellj e tucta altra bona agenti di lu paysi, fachendu gran sollempnitati cussì comu si divj farj ad omnj principi et regij et a lloru signurj.

E quistu esti lu finj.

76

La raxunj perchì Misser Iohannj di Prochita si misi ac tractarj et ordinarj quista rebellionj contra di lu Re Carlu, sì fu chi unu grandi barunj di lu Re Carlu fichi forza ad una figla di Misser Iohannj et illu si'ndi lamintau a lu Re Carlu, di kj lu Re Carlu di quista falla non indi appi plena justicia comu a mMisser Iohannj si convinia.

Et Misser Iohannj si propossi in corj comu potissi distrudirj lu Re Carlu et vinjarisi di la injuria la quali avia richiputa, di kj l'ordinau quistu tractatu comu tucti avitj intisu.

77

Et imperò tucti quilli signurj chi teninu regni, chitati, terrj e castelli, et omnj altrj officij, prindanu quistu exemplu di non vulirj usarj virgogna nè injuria ad soy vassallj nè serviturj, nen consentirj a lloru nixunu ultraju ma farj plena iusticia.

GLOSSARY OF MIDDLE SICILIAN

Most of these words occur in the original text of the *Rebellion,* some differing in diction or usage from their modern counterparts in common use in recent centuries. Whilst those most obviously similar to Italian, such as *castellu* for *castello* (castle) and *pagari* for *pagare* (to pay), have not been included, the reader should resist the temptation to presume that every word is identical in meaning to its modern cognate. Here the intent is merely to provide the reader with a general idea of the nuances of Middle Sicilian and the meanings of certain terms in the specific context of the *Rebellion,* where some of these words were written for the first time in history. It should be borne in mind that even within the chronicle the precise meanings of some words vary according to context.

a - to.
abastari - to suffice.
abruscari - to burn.
accanzari - to purchase, buy.
accaxuni - cause, reason.
acconzari, accunzari - to give consent.
accordari - to agree.
actali - to that end.
actu - act or method.
aczò chi - to that end, also *azò ki.*
ad - to.
adimanda - request.
adimandari - to ask or request.
adirare - to become angry.
adossu - in front of.
adubati - armed.
agenti - See *genti.*
agustu - August.
aia - See *aviri, haviri.*
alcunu - some.
allegru - happy, cheerful.
alligriza - happiness.
allura - then. See also *intandu.*

almiragla - admiral. Also *amiragla.*
altru - other, another.
altrui - another person.
amiragla - admiral.
ananti - rather than.
ananti chi - before.
ancora - still, already.
andari - to go.
andata - military expedition.
anti - instead, rather; compare Italian *anzi.*
aplacari, placare - to please.
apparichari - to prepare.
appellari - to declare.
apprili - April.
ardiri - to have courage.
arditu - brave.
armata - army or armada.
armata di mari - armada, fleet.
arricomandari - to recommend.
arricordari - to remember.
arrispundiri - to respond.
ascontrari - to meet.
ascutari - to listen to.
assai - much, great.
assignari - to consign.
assijari - to besiege.
assinblati - assembled.
auchidiri - to kill.
audiri - to hear, to listen to.
augustu- See *agustu.*
autru - See *altru.*
ava - grandmother.
aviri, haviri - to have.
avu - grandfather.
axivilmenti - easily.
ayutu, ajutu - help, aid.
azò ki - See *aczò chi.*
bactagla - battle.
baruni - baron, barons, baronage.
bastari - to suffice.
bella, bellu - beautiful.
benedicione - blessing.
bestia - animal; stupid.
bisognari - to be needed.
bisognu - need, necessity.
bulla - Papal bull (document).
cachari - to chase from.
cammara - room, possession.
campiuni - defender.
canuxiri - to know (be acquainted with).
capu - leader, guide.
casa - house, dynasty.
caxuni - See *accaxuni.*
cerveru - deerhound.
chamari - to call, to acclaim.
chascuno - somebody, everybody.
chasquidunu - every, everybody.
chavi - key (also figurative).
chelatu - See *chilatu.*
chentu - a hundred.
chi, ki, kj - what, that.

chicari - to arrive.
chilatu, chilatamenti - hidden, secretly.
chincu - five.
chitati - city.
chui, plui - more.
comandamentu - an order, command.
comu - like, as.
conti - count (nobleman); also *cunti*.
conzari - to prepare.
coruna - crown.
cridenza - belief, trust, credential.
cu, cum - with.
cuntari - recount, tell.
cunti - count (nobleman); also *conti*.
cuntrati - villages, lands.
curaiu - heart, courage.
curti - court.
cussi, cussì - so, therefore.
dampnu, dapnu - damage, harm.
dananti, di avanti - before (in front of).
dari - to give.
davanti - See dananti.
debili - weak.
dechi - ten.
dedi. See *dari*.
di - of.
dictu - said (stated), a discourse.
diri - to say.
disaventura - misfortune, failure.
discordari - to forget.
disiyari - to desire.
divinjari - to seek redress.
diviri - duty.
doliri - to displease.
donna - lady.
donzella - damsel, maiden.
dubitanza - fear, doubt.
dubitari - to fear, to distrust.
dugnali, dunari - to give.
dui, duj - two.
dundi - where.
dunzella - See *donzella*.
e - See *et*.
è - See *essiri*.
ecclesia - church.
eo - See *eu*.
essiri - to be.
et - and.
eu - I (pronoun); also *eo*.
exceptu - safe, except.
excominicatu - excommunicated.
exutu - exited. See ixiri.
fachenda - matter, problem, task.
factu, fattu - fact, event, undertaking.
falla - offense, failure.
famigla - family, dynasty.

fari - to do, to make.
faru - coastal beacon tower.
fauzia - deception.
ffari - variant of *fari.*
fidi - faith, loyalty, fealty.
fidili - faithful (religiously), followers.
figlola - daughter.
figlolu - son (usually literal)
figlu - son (spiritual).
filluni - fool.
fimmina - woman.
fingiri, finsiri - to lie or feign.
firiri - to attack.
fisica - medicine.
folluni - felon, disloyal person.
fora - outside, beyond.
forniri - to supply, to effect.
franchiscu, franchisku - French.
frati - friar.
fuya - to flee, flight.
galia - galley.
gazara - discord, loud noise, confusion.
genti - people, nation, followers; also *agenti.*
ginnaru - January.
gintilomini - noblemen.
ginuisi - Genoans.
guastari - destroy, devastate.
guirreri - warlike, aggressive.
haviri - See *aviri.*
homu - man.
honuri - honors.
hosti - See *osti.*
ià, jà - already.
iammai, jammai - now, at any moment.
illa - she, her.
illi - they, them.
illocu - (over) there.
illu - See *ipsu.*
imbaxata - See *inbaxata.*
imbaxaturi - ambassador.
imperaduri - emperor.
imperaturi - See *imperaduri.*
imperò - accordingly, consequently.
imperò ki - as, because.
imprima - before.
imprimu - foremost, above all.
in - in, within.
inbaxata - embassy, diplomatic mission.
inbaxaturj - See *imbaxaturi.*
incalzari - intensify.
incontinenti - immediately.
incoraiari - to encourage.
incoronari - to crown.
indi - neither.
infra - during.
inperiu - empire.
inperò - See *imperò.*
inprisa, imprisa - enterprise, undertaking.
insembli - together, assembled.
intandu - then, meanwhile.

intencioni - objective.
intru - inside, within.
inuria, injuria - offense.
inver - toward.
iornu, jornu - day.
ipsu, issu - he, him. Also *illu.*
isforzu - military force.
ismaritu - annoyed, disturbed.
issu - See *ipsu.*
isula - See *ysula.*
ixiri - to exit, to leave.
izà - here.
ki, kj - See *chi.*
kistu - See *quistu.*
la, lu - it (definite article).
latini - Latins (contextual).
legatu - legate.
legiri - to read.
liancza - loyalty.
librusu - leper.
lictra - letter.
ligatu - representative, legate.
lignu - cargo ship.
lloru - variant of *loru.*
locu - place, locality.
loru - they.
lu - see *la, lu.*
lumbardi - Lombards.
lupi - wolves (also figurative).
mancu - less.
mastru - master craftsman.
matra, matri - mother(s).
mayuri - major, greater.
mectiri - to place, to complete.
meglu - better, best.
mercì - mercy, pity.
mi - me (pronoun).
mia, meu - mine, belonging to me.
migla - thousand.
milia, mille - thousand(s).
miseri - miserable.
misi - month.
missaiu - messenger.
misser - lord.
Missina - Messina.
missinisi - Messinians.
modu - way, manner.
monita - money.
moranu - See *moriri.*
moriri - to kill. Also *muriri.*
mugleri - wife.
mundu - world.
muriri - to die, to kill.
muru - wall.
navi - cargo ship.
naviliu - fleet.
ne, nen - neither, nor.
nenti - nothing.
nixiri - See *ixiri.*
nixunu - nobody.
no - no, none.
nocti - night.
nomu - name.
non - not, none, neither.
nostru - ours.
notaru - notary.
novella, novelle - news.

novellamenti - recently.
nui, nnui - we, us.
nullu - nobody; see also *nixunu.*
octanta - eighty.
octubru - October.
ogi - today.
ogni - See *omni.*
omni, onni - every, everybody.
or - or, now.
oru - gold.
osterio - See *steri.*
osti - army, encampment.
oy - either, or.
pachi - peace.
pacti - conditions (pacts), agreements.
paczu - irregular, crazy.
pagura - fear.
palazu - palace.
Palermu - Palermo.
palora - word.
parlamentu - meeting, discussion.
paroli - words; plural of *palora.*
Pascua - Easter.
passaiu - military expedition.
paysi - town, city.
pera - see *periri.*
perdiri - to lose, be defeated.
perdugnu - pardon, forgiveness.
periri - to perish, die.
però - See *imperò.*
persuna - person.
peyo - worse.
pichulilli - young children.
piduni - footmen.
pinsamentu - plan.
placare - See *aplacare.*
plachiri - consent, agree, approve, like.
plui - See *chui.*
plumbu - lead (metal).
poi, poy - then, later.
portu - port, harbor.
potencia - power.
poy - See *poi.*
Prochita - Procida.
proferta, pruferta - offering.
proffiriri - to offer.
prudu - wise.
puru - also; more profoundly.
pussancza - See *potencia.*
putiri - power, authority.
quali - which, what.
quandu - when.
quandu ki - in the event that.
quantu - how much.
quillu - that one.
quistu - this one.
raxuni - reason, purpose.
rebellamentu - rebellion.
recomandari - See *arricomandari.*
recuperu - help, protection.
regii - royal, of the king.
regiri - govern or reign.

regnu - kingdom.
rendita - financial payment ordered by a court.
riami - realm, kingdom.
ribellacionj - See *rebellamentu.*
rigina - queen.
rigituri - governor.
rimuri - noise or confusion.
riparu - safety, retreat.
ritiniri - to accommodate.
riyuti - See *regiri.*
rumanu - Roman.
sacru - sacred, holy.
saldare - to pay.
salvu - except for.
salvu ki - but.
sanctu - holy.
sangu - blood.
sapiri - to know.
saputu - expert.
saviu - wise.
scachari - to expel. See also *cachari.*
secretanczi - secrets, secret things.
secretu - secret; person privy to a secret; secretary.
secta - nation; a people.
sedia - see (as the Holy See).
sentencia - verdict, sentence.
sequiri - to follow.
servi - serfs.
serviciu - service.
si - if.
Sichilia - Sicily.
sichiliani - Sicilians.
sictembru - September.
sicundu - according to.
sigillari - to seal (a document).
sigillu - seal.
significari - to declare, explain, inform.
signu - sign, indication.
signuri - lord, lords.
signuria - lordship, dominion.
silligiri - to choose, to decide.
sindaku - delegate, representative.
sintiri - hear, learn of.
so, sou, soy - his, hers, its.
soldati - soldiers; mercenaries.
spagnari - to frighten.
spata - sword.
spichicari - to free oneself from.
spisa - expenses.
spiuni - See *spiya.*
spiya - spy.
stari - to be present, to stay.
steri - fortified tower or keep. See also *osti.*
straczari - to rip or tear.
stu - See *quistu.*
studiu - task.
sturbari - to impede.
sua - See *sou.*
succaru - scarcity.
suldari - to recruit mercenaries.

suldati - See *soldati.*
supra - above.
suzu - above.
tandu - then, at that moment. See also *intandu.*
tantu - much, as much.
tarì - a gold coin.
tempu, tenpu - time, times, era.
terra - land, country, territory.
ti - you (pronoun).
tiniri - to hold, to keep, to retain.
tinuri - tenor, tone.
to, toi, tou, tua - yours.
tornata - return (noun).
tostu - soon, now, immediately.
trayri - to free, liberate.
trayturi - traitor.
tri - three.
trisoru - treasury, funds.
tucti - everybody.
tuctu - all.
turnisi - silver coins, also *tornisi.*
turri - towers.
ultraiu, ultraju - outrage, offense.
undi - where, there. See also *dundi.*
unu - one
unzi - gold coins.
usatu - ordinary.
valenti - valiant.
veniari - to seek revenge.
vernu - winter.
veru - true, factual.
vidanda - victuals.
videmmi - the same, similar.
vili - vile; peasant.
villanamente - cruelly.
vinchiri - to win.
vindicta - revenge, vendetta.
viniciani - Venetians.
vinti - twenty.
viru - variant of *veru.*
vitilitati - authority.
vogla - a wish or desire.
vostru - your, yours (plural).
vuchi - voice
vui - you (plural); also *vuy.*
vuliri - to want.
vuy - See *vui.*
xiri - See *ixiri.*
xp - Christ.
ysola - See *ysula.*
ysula, isula - island.
Zisa - palace in Palermo.
zò - this (or that) which.

APPENDIX 1

The Contrasto

Composed before 1240, the *Contrasto,* or *Dialogue,* of Ciullo of Alcamo is for its length considered by many to be the quintessential poem of the Sicilian School, although more work of Giacomo of Lentini survives. Little is known of the author, sometimes *Cielo,* except that he served at the Hohenstaufen court and presumably had some association with the town of Alcamo; we know not whether he was born in Sicily.

The *Contrasto* is regarded as a milestone in the development of an Italian language. Its oldest manuscript source is Codex Vaticanus 3793 (later 4817), a copy written in Florentine script toward the end of the thirteenth century, of which a successive copy exists as number 4823.

Readers will note the obvious variations in spelling and orthography from the Middle Sicilian text of the *Rebellion* composed some fifty years later. The lost autograph of the *Contrasto* was almost certainly less "italianized" than the texts of the surviving manuscripts, just as the *Spinelli Codex* is more "Sicilian" than later copies of *Lu Rebellamentu.*

This text combines the eloquent translation by Lorna Lancaster de'Lucchi (the first fourteen stanzas) published in 1922 and the more classical translation of Dante Gabriel Rossetti (the last eighteen stanzas) effected in 1861. Great as they are, neither renders more than perhaps half the poem's original Sicilian very closely, and both were edited for clarity. Indeed, certain stanzas bear little more than a passing similarity to the Middle Sicilian. While these translations in the public domain might be considered the standards for this material, they are no substitute for Ciullo's own words.

Knight:
Rosa fresca aulentissima, chi apparj inver la state,
le donne ti disirano, pulzelle et maritate,
Trajimi de 'ste focora, si de'ste a boluntate,
per te non aviu abbento notte e dia,
penzando pur di vuy, madonna mia.

Most fragrant rose, born on a summer's day,
Thou dost both damsels and dames with envy sway,
Out of this raging flame, rescue me, I pray.
From thoughts of thee my lady, I never cease,
Day and night am I bereft of mortal peace.

Damsel:
Si di meve trabagliti, follia lo ti fa fare:
lu mari potj arromperj avanti a semenare,
l'abere de 'sto seculo tutto quanto assembrare.
Avereme no' poteri a 'sto monnu,
avanti li cavelli m'aritonno.

If I be thy desire, foolish indeed art thou,
Easier it were by far to strip of bark and bough,
All forests of the world, and sow the seas and plough,
Than to subdue my heart, for ere 'twas done
I would have shorn my hair off like a nun.

Knight:
Si li cavelli attònniti, avanti fossi morto,

ca eu sì mi pèrdera lu sullazzo e diporto.
Quanno ci passo e veioti, rosa fresca dell'orto,
bono conforto donimi tutt'ore,
poniamo chi s'aiunga nostro amore.

Before thy hair be shorn in death let me bow low,
For solace and delight forthwith from me would go.
Flower of the garden close, whenever I see thee blow
Your beauty takes my hours away.
If only your passion could I sway!

Damsel:

Chi nostro amori aiungasj?! No'boglio maltalenti!
Si ci ti trova patremo co' l'altri miei parenti,
guardanò t'aricolgono questi forti currenti.
Como ti seppi bona la venuta,
consiglio chi ti guardi la partuta.

It cannot be, though I change my mind one day.
If father, kith and kin should chance hereby to stray,
Thy body in the swift stream would be whirled away.
Therefore I counsel you straightly to flee
By the good road that brought thee unto me!

Knight:

Si toy parenti trovammi, chi mi pozzono farri?
Una difensa mettoci di dumilia gostari,
non mi toccara patreto per quanto ave a Bari.
Viva l'imperaduri 'n grazi'a Deu!
Intendi, bella, chi ti dico eu?

If thou called upon father, cousins and nieces,
For my life they'd win two thousand golden pieces.
For all his riches in Bari your father'd find only caprices.
Long live the Emperor, unto God be praise!
Dost ponder well, enchantress, what thy lover says?

Damsel:

Tu mi no' lasci vivere né sera né mattino!
Donna mi so' di perperi, d'àuro massamotino,
si tant'avé donassemi quant'ave Saladino,
et per aiunta quanto lu Soldanu,
toccaremi no' poteri a lu manu.

Then neither morn nor eve thou willest I should rest,
I too have golden coins piled high in a great chest.
Could'st thou give me for dower the richest and the best,
Twice over Saladin's vast hoard of gold,
I vow today this hand thou should'st not hold!

Knight:

Multi sono le fimmini c'hanno dura la testa,
et l'omo, co' parabole, l'adimina et ammonesta,
tanto intorno percazzala, fin chi l'ave in podesta.
Femmina d'omo non si po' tenere,
guàrdati, bella, pur di ripentere.

I've known full many a maid and obstinate no doubt,
But man by flattery may wheedle her about.
He presseth her so close her strength must needs give out.
My lady, bear in mind against a future day,
Man is the stronger and will have his way!

Damsel:

Ch'eu mi repentéssendi? Avanti fossi accesa,
ca nulla bona femmina per mi fosse ripresa.
Aersera passastici, correnno a la discesa,
acquistiti riposo, canzoneri!
Le to' paraole no' me piaczo gueri.

Art fain that I relent? Nay, better 'twere to die
Or ever a modest maid be scorned by such as I!
Last evening hitherwards I saw thy footsteps fly,

This is my answer, flatterer, know withal
Such words from thee belike me not at all!

Knight:

Quanti sono le schiantora chi m'hai mise a lu cori!
E solo purpenzànnonde, la dia quanno vo fori!
Fimmina de 'sto secolo tanto no'amai ancori,
quant'amo teve, rosa invidiata,
bene creo chi mi fosti distinata.

Alas, how many bonds hast cast about my heart!
I weep remembering thee in loneliness apart!
No lady in my life was cherished as thou art,
Was half as well beloved, oh rose divine,
And I believe one day thou wilt be mine.

Damsel:

Si distinata fosseti, cadèra de l'altezze,
ché male messe forano in teve mie bellezze,
Si tutto addivenissemi, tagliàrami le trezze!
Eu consori m'arenno a una magione,
avanti chi m'attoccano persune.

If it so came to pass, downfallen were my pride,
That to enhance thy fame my beauty should abide!
Indeed I'd shave my head before this could betide,
And to the shelter of a convent flee,
From thy unwelcome wooing to be free.

Knight:

Si tu consore arenneti, donna col viso cleri,
a lu mosteru venoci et arennomi confreri,
per tanta prova vencierti, faràllo volonteri!
Con te co'stao la sera et lu mattino,
besogna chi ti tenga al meo dimino.

If thou to be a nun, proud maid, didst flee away,

Thy convent I would find, and where I was I'd stay,
To win so fair a maiden gladly would I pay.
I'd be there at the dawn and twilight hour,
Until at last I had thee in my power.

Damsel:
Oy me tapina misera, com'ào reo distinato!
Gesù Cristo l'altissimo, de 'ntutto se' airato?
Concepistimi a 'mbàttere in omo blestiemato?
Cerca la terra, ch'este granne assai,
chiù bella donna di me troverai.
Alas, most hapless maid, destined to suffer wrong!
Dear Jesus Christ, to Whom my hopes belong,
Silence this man, I pray, he doth blaspheme too long!
Let him go seeking through the world so wide,
He'll find a lovelier lady for his bride.

Knight:
Cercat'aio Calabria, Toscana et Lumbardia,
Pugla, Costantinopoli, Genoa, Pisa, Soria,
Lamagna et Babilonia, tucta Barbaria.
Donna non ci trovai tanto cortese:
per donna sovrana di mi te prese.
Calabria, Lombardy and Tuscany all through,
Constantinople, Rome, Pisa and Genoa too.
Babylon, Barbary, I've searched and searched anew,
But found no woman lovely as thou art,
Dearest and sovereign lady of my heart.

Damsel:
Poy tanto trabagliastiti, faccioti meo prigheri,
chi tu vai et domannimi a mia mare et a mon peri.
Si dare mi ti degnano, menami a lu mosteri
et sposami davanti da la iente:

eu poi farò le to' comannamente!

Since thou dost love me so I need no more repine,
Go ask me, love, of both mother and father mine;
If they thereto agree lay thou my hand in thine,
Then in the abbey take me soon to wife,
And I will do thy bidding all my life!

Knight:

Di ciò chi dici, vitama, neiente non ti bale,
ca de le to' parabole fatto n'ao ponti e scale,
penne penzasti mettere, sonti cadute l'ale.
Eu dato t'aio la bolta sottana,
dunque, si poy, manteniti villana.

These thy conditions, my lady, are altogether nought,
For still I'll make a net wherein thou shalt be caught.
If thou put on wings to fly, of wax they shall be wrought,
They'll let thee fall to earth, not rise with thee,
So, if thou canst, then keep thyself from me.

Damsel:

En paura no' mettimi di nullo manganiello!
Eu staomine 'n 'sta groria de 'sto forte castiello,
prezzo le to' parabole meno de 'no zitiello.
Si tu no' levi e vàitine di quace,
si tu ci fosse morto ben mi chiace.

Thou dost not frighten me with nets and suchlike gear,
I am safe pent within the walls of this strong castle here.
A boy before he is a man could give me as much fear.
If suddenly thou get not hence again,
It is my prayer thou mayst be found and slain.

Knight:

Dunque vorresti, vitama, ca per te fosse 'strutto!
Si morto essere debboci od intagliato tutto,

di quaci no' mi mossera, si non ayo lu frutto
lo quale staci ne lo to' jardino
disìrolo la sera et lu mattinu.
Wouldst thou in very truth that I were slain, and for thy sake?
Then let them hew me to such mince as a man's limbs may make!
But meanwhile I shall not stir hence til of that fruit I take
Which thou hast in thoust garden, ripe enough
All day and night I thirst to think therought

Damsel:
Quello frutto non àvvero conti né cavaleri,
molto lo disirarono conti et iustizieri,
avere no' nde pottero, gìronde molto fieri.
Intendi bene chi bole dicére
me n'este di mill'unzi lo to' abere.
None have partaken of that fruit, not counts nor cavaliers,
Though many have so desired it, barons and great seigneurs.
They've all went hence in wrath because they could not make it theirs.
Then how canst thou think to succeed alone
Who hast not a thousand ounces of thine own?

Knight:
Molti so' li garofani, ma non chi salma nd'hai
bella, no' dispregiaremi s'avanti no'massai.
Si vento è 'n proda, et girasi, agiunge da li prai,
arimembrare t'ao 'ste parole,
ca de 'st'ira, animella, assai mi dole.
How many carnations I have sent unto thy house, sweet soul
At least till I am put to proof this scorn of thine control.
For if the wind, so fair for thee, turn ever and wax foul.
Be sure that thou shalt say when all is done,
Now is my heart heavy for him that's gone.

Damsel:

Macara, si dolesseti, chi cadesse angosciato
la iente ci corressoro da traverso e da lato,
tutt'a meve dicessoro 'accorri 'sto malnato!
Non mi degnara porgere la mano,
per quant'ave lu Papa et lu Soldano.

If by my grief thou couldst be grieved, God send me a grief soon!
I tell thee that though all my friends prayed me as for a boon,
Saying, 'Even for the love of us, love thou this worthless loon,'
Thou shouldst not have the thing that thou dost hope.
No, verily, not for the realm o' the Pope.

Knight:

Deu lo volesse, vitama, ca fossi morto in casa
l'arma n'andèra cònsola ca di notte fantasa,
la iente ti chiamarano 'oi periura, malvasa
c'ha' morto l'omo in càsata traìta,
sanz'ogni colpo levimi la vita!

Now could I wish that I were dead here in thy house,
My soul would get its vengeance then the thing would rouse.
They'd point at she who breaks her vows
And in her own chamber stabs her love.
It is curtly done, with a knife strike from above.

Damsel:

Si tu no' levi e vàitine co' la maladizione,
li frati miei ti trovano dentro chissa magione,
bell'omi so s'eu soffero, perdici le persone,
ca meve se' venuto a sormonare.
Parente oy amico non t'ave a itare.

If now thou do not hasten hence, my curse companioning,
That my stout friends will find thee here is a most certain thing.
After the which, my gallant sir, thy points of reasoning

May chance, I think, to stand thee in small stead.
Thou hast no friend, sweet friend, to bring thee aid.

Knight:

A meve non aì tano amichi né parenti
stranio mi sono, carama, enfra 'sta bona ienti.
Ora fa 'n'anno, vitama, ch'entrata mi se'n menti,
dicènnoti: 'Vististi lu'ntaiuto?'
Bella, da quello jorno so' feruto.
Thou sayest truly, saying that I have not any friend.
A landless stranger, lady mine, none but his sword defend.
One year ago, mine love began. And now, is this the end?
Oh! the rich dress thou worest on that day.
Since when thou art walking at my side alway?

Damsel:

A tanto 'namorastiti, Iuda, hàilo traìto,
como si fosse porpora, iscarlatto o sciamito!
S'a le Vangelie iurimi chi mi sia marito,
avereme no' poteri a 'sto monno,
avanti in mari ièttomi a perfonno.
So't was my dress enamoured thee! What marvel I did wear
A cloth of samite silver-flowered, and gems within my hair.
But one more word, if on Christ's Book to wed me thou didst swear,
There's nothing now could win me to be thine,
I had rather make my bed in the sea-brine.

Knight:

Si ne lu mari ièttiti, donna cortesi et fina,
deretro mi ti misera per tucta la marina.
Da poi ca annegàsseti, trobàrati a la rina
solo per questa cosa adimpretare,
con teco m'ayo a junjiri et peccare.
And if thou make thy bed therein, most courteous lady and bland,

I'll follow all among the waves paddling with foot and hand.
Then, when the sea hath done with thee I'll seek thee on the sand.
For I will not be conquered in this strife,
I'll wait, but win; or losing, lose my life.

Damsel:
Segnomi in Patri et 'n Filio ed in santo Matteo,
si ca non se' tu retico, figlio de lu giudeo,
e cotale parabole n'odio redire anch'eu!
Mortasi la fimmina, a lo 'ntutto
perdeci lu saboru et lu desduttu.
For Father, Son, and Holy Ghost, three times I cross myself.
Thou art no godless heretic, nor Jew, whose God's his pelf
Even as I know it then, meseems, thou needs must know thyself
That woman, when the breath in her doth cease,
Loseth all savor and all loveliness.

Knight:
Bene lo faccio, carama; altro no' pozzo fare,
si quisso non accomplimi, lassone lo cantare.
Fallo, mia donna, plàzati, chi bene lo poi fare.
Ancora tu no' m'ami, molto t'amo,
sì m'hai preso come lu pesci a l'amo.
Oh it must be said, no craft could then avail,
So that if thou be thus resolved, I know my suit must fail.
Then have some pity, of thy grace: Thou mayst very well.
For though thou love not me, my love is such
That 'tis enough for both, nay overmuch.

Damsel:
Sazzo chi m'ami; amoti di core paladino,
lèvati susu e vattene, tornaci a lu mattino.
Si ciò chi dico facimi, di bon cor t'amo e fino.
Quisso eu ti 'mprometto sanza faglia,

te' la mia fede, chi m'hai in toa baglia.
Is it even so? Learn then that I do love thee from my heart.
Tomorrow, early in the day, come here, but now depart.
By thine obedience in this thing I shall know what thou art.
And if thy love be real or nothing worth,
Do but go now, and I am thine henceforth.

Knight:
Per zò chi dici, carama, neiente non mi movo.
Innanti prenni e scannami, to 'sto cortello novo,
'sto fatto fare potesi innanti scalfi 'n'ovo.
Accompli mio talento, amica bella,
ché l'arma co' lu cori mi si 'nfella.
Nay, for such promise, my own life, I will not stir a foot.
I've said, if thou wouldst tear away my love even from its root,
I have a dagger at my side which thou mayst take to do't,
But as for going hence, it will not be.
Please hate me not: My heart is burning me!

Damsel:
Ben sazzo: l'arma doleti, cumo mo ch'ave arsura.
'Sto fatto no' potèrasi per null'altra misura,
si non hai le Vangelie, chi mo ti dico: 'Jura!'
Avereme no' poi 'n toa podesta.
Innanti prenni et tagliami la testa.
Think'st thou I know not that thy heart is burning thee to death?
Of all that thou or I can say, but one word succoreth.
Till thou upon the Holy Book give me thy bounden faith,
God is my witness that I will not yield.
For with thy sword't were better to be killed.

Knight:
Le Vangelie, carama? Ch'eu le porto 'n sino,
a lu mostero presile, non c'era lu patrino.

Sovra 'sto libro juroti: mai non ti vegno mino.
Accompli mio talento in caritate,
ché l'arma me ne sta 'n suttilitate.
Then on Christ's Book, borne with me still to read
from and to pray,
That I stole fairest, in a church, the priest being gone away,
I swear that my whole self shall be thine always from this day.
And now at once give joy for all my grief,
Lest my soul fly, that's thinner than a leaf.

Damsel:
Meu sire, poy jurastimi, eu tucta quanta incenno.
Sono a la toa presenzia, da voy non mi difenno.
S'eu minespreso àioti, merzè, a voy m'arenno.
A lo letto ne gimo, a la bon'ora,
chi chissà cosa n'è data in ventur.
Now that this oath is sworn, sweet lord, there is
no need to speak.
My heart, that was so strong before, now feels
itself grow weak.
If any of my words were harsh, thy pardon I do seek.
Now, I will give thee entry presently.
Be it best so, since so it was meant to be.

APPENDIX 2

Concordance

The *Rebellion,* though told from what is essentially the Ghibelline and Aragonese perspective, is remarkably accurate in its details regarding geography, major events, personages, royal kinship, political relationships and military alliances, facts unequivocally corroborated by contemporary sources. These established facts far outnumber the few original (unconfirmed) details.

The chief Aragonese source is the *corpus* of decrees and correspondence issued by King Peter in Sicily, Calabria and Aragon in 1282 and 1283. The original manuscripts are kept at the Archivo de la Corona de Aragón in Barcelona. This registry was published as *De Rebus Regni Siciliae* in 1882, with a useful appendix added ten years later and several subsequent supplements published before 1900.

The contents are varied, with some items having a wider importance than others. Many relate to feudal rents collected to raise funds for the war, and the supply of arms and victuals. A rather large number deal with the appointment of judges (justiciars) around Sicily to replace the Angevins who had been expelled or killed, and with specific legal cases. Some concern the treatment of castles and other property confiscated from the Angevins. Malta and Gozo are mentioned. Some charters refer to Angevins still present in remote localities when King Peter arrived in Sicily.

The betrothal between children of Peter of Aragon and Michael of Constantinople is the subject of a letter of 20 September 1282 sent to Michael with Hugh of Romanino as Peter's delegate.

On 12 December 1282, King Peter gave royal assent to the betrothal of a feudal heiress, Stolfa de Sacco, to a certain George, of Caltagirone, who was landless. Under the Constitutions of Melfi of 1231, women could inherit feudal property. This decree indicates that certain legal principles established by Frederick II were to be respected. Brief commentary on the legal rights of women guaranteed by the Constitutions of Melfi is presented, from the Italian (and male) point of view, in Mazzarese Fardella, Enrico, "La Condizione Giuridica della Donna nel Liber Augustalis" in *Archivio Storico Siciliano,* Series 4, Volume 21-22 (Palermo 1997), pages 31-44.

Several letters written during the same month of 1282 outline the conditions for the duel or joust proposed between Peter and Charles in France, which never took place.

A charter of 14 January 1283 makes reference to the Angevin attack on Milazzo.

Decrees issued at Messina on 26 January 1283 summon knights from around Sicily, with their names listed. Orders were also given to muster archers and foot soldiers. We see Peter raising a Sicilian army to complement the forces he brought from Spain. A number of knights and nobles are mentioned in addition to those summoned in early 1283.

Of particular significance is the decree of 4 May 1283 appointing John of Procida as the chancellor of the realm, effectively its viceroy. A letter to John sent from Logroño (see the map of regions and languages in northeastern Spain) on 29 July of the same year details numerous undertakings in Sicily; here the king is ruling Sicily from afar. John's younger brother, Andrew, is mentioned in several decrees.

A decree of 22 October 1283 appoints Alaimo of Lentini as the High Justiciar of the Kingdom of Sicily. A charter issued a month later addresses the circumstances of a riot that occurred in Palermo between Pisans and Genoans.

Although they do not constitute anything like a legal code, these decrees, considered *in toto,* set the stage for the rule of Sicily by Spanish dynasties over the next few decades, if not the next four centuries.

Complementary to this record is the *Codice Diplomatico del Regno di Carlo I e Carlo II d'Angio 1265-1309*, compiled by Giuseppe del Giudice in 1863. This is a compendium of most of the more significant decrees and correspondence of Charles I and his son. See also *Codice Diplomatico dei Re Aragonesi di Sicilia 1282-1355,* compiled by Giuseppe La Mantia and published in 1917, which contains, for example, the last will and testament of King Peter.

Various records similar to these have been published over the years, for example *Documenti Relativi all'Epoca del Vespro* (Palermo 1983), extracted from the Domenico Schiavo manuscripts.

The chronicle of Saba of Malaspina, *Rerum Sicularum Historia,* was consulted for comparative and supplementary information; this was completed in 1285. Salimbene's chronicle considers this period but is less detailed than Malaspina's where the Vespers are concerned.

De Vita sua Opusculum, the memoir of Michael VIII of Constantinople, was first published in Saint Petersburg in 1885. Michael alludes to his support of the Aragonese conquest of Sicily.

Some 380 registers containing most of the extant manuscripts from the Angevin Chancery (1265-1435) retained by the Archive of State of Naples, and kept outside the city at San Paolo Bel Sito during the Second World War, were burned by German troops in September 1943 in reprisal for Italy changing allegiance in that month. Fortunately, some of these documents had already been transcribed and published over the last few centuries, and a few, like the invaluable *Catalogus Baronum* (later translated by the erudite Evelyn Jamison and published in 1972), had been photographed.

There are, of course, other records. Though an exhaustive examination of its content lies beyond the scope of this work, a slightly later source of information on some of the participants in the War of the Vespers is a feudal roll, the *Descriptio Feudorum sub Rege Friderico,* completed around 1335 (see Appendix 3). Published by Bartolomeo Muscia in 1692, it contains entries which are traditionally (and misleadingly) dated collectively to 1296. It is likely that many of these feudatories were the heirs (perhaps sons or grandsons) of Aragonese, Catalans or Sicilians to whom King Peter ceded estates confiscated from Angevins in 1282. This roll was republished in 1925 in an appendix to Volume 3 of *La Storia dei Feudi* by Francesco San Martino de Spucches.

Hugh Falcandus is mentioned in the text by way of a loose analogy to "Athanasius of Iaci." While an examination of the *Liber de Regno Siciliae* lies beyond the scope of this book, it should be mentioned that there is no clear academic consensus on its authorship.

Among the various medieval manuscripts consulted were those of the *Tabulario della Commenda della Magione* (in Palermo).

Clearly, a number of barons and enfeoffed knights *floruit* 1282 lived into the next century; David Abrazalem, who was quite possibly Jewish, is mentioned in both the registry of royal decrees and the roll of 1335 as holder of the fief of Scanzafridi. (For more about Jewish ennoblements in the Kingdom of Sicily, see the author's "Jewish Nobles in Late Medieval Sicily" in *Sicilian Genealogy and Heraldry,* pages 275-278.)

The author is inclined to concur with Steven Runciman that

the *Rebellion* most likely recounts, at least in part, some of the movements of one of the sons of John of Procida rather than the protagonist himself. However, Sir Steven errs in stating that John was granted Procida by Frederick II; in fact, the island was a possession of John's ancestors at least since 1194, the feudal right to it being, at best, *confirmed* by Frederick to John *ad personam* as its rightful heir. Confusion may result because (by most accounts) John, his father and grandfather all bore the same Christian name, the John of Vespers fame being referred to by some Italian historians as *Giovanni III*.

The Introduction mentions that John of Procida served at three courts. These were those of Frederick II, Manfred and Peter III. There is no evidence that he spent any time at the court of Michael of Constantinople.

APPENDIX 3

Vespers Armory

"The age of chivalry is gone. That of sophisters, economists and calculators has succeeded, and the glory of Europe is extinguished forever." The words of Edmund Burke ring true.

A few years ago, a Chiaramonte sword from the fourteenth century was unearthed in the crypt of a church not far from the family's imposing castle outside Mussomeli. The weapon is no mere artefact. To the medieval nobility, swords symbolized something akin to the sacred status accorded crowns by royalty, and by 1250 knightly (feudal) investiture, like coronation, was a religious rite held in a church or chapel. Coats of arms, like swords, represented the knightly class.

Armorial insignia (heraldry) came into use in Europe during the middle of the twelfth century, though the art was not much known in Sicily before 1200. (Hence the Norman shields of the Monreale knight figures shown on the cover of this book are devoid of heraldic embellishments.) At first, these designs on shields and surcoats distinguished friend from foe in battles and tournaments. By 1282, armorial bearings were commonplace in coinage and seals, and coats of arms were hereditary, the right to a certain design, or *blazon,* being passed from father to son. Early plate armor was supplanting chain mail, and the shields used in combat and tournaments were smaller than the long escutcheons of the Norman era. In Sicily, this is seen in the depictions of shields painted on the wooden ceiling of the hall of barons in Palermo's Palazzo Steri, rendered during the fourteenth century.

Coats of arms were incorporeal property, rather like (in our times) a copyright, patent or genome. Most seals impressed into wax were heraldic, and usurping a nobleman's coat of arms was a criminal form of impersonation similar to what we now call "identity theft."

In theory, no two armigers in the same kingdom could use the same blazon, and even brothers might "difference" their coats of arms by altering the designs slightly, usually by changing the tinctures (colors) or minor details. One branch of the La Rocca family displayed a cross *or* (gold) while another displayed a cross *argent* (silver). The two unrelated Mendola families bore slightly different coats of arms; one displayed a comet while the other displayed stars.

No formal system of differencing for "cadency" (sibling birth order) was ever introduced in Sicily along the lines of that used in England, and in Italy coats of arms might be said to be more familial than personal.

Do we know the heraldic blazons of the knights and barons present in Sicily in 1282?

Although the following list does not indicate every known feudatory holding a manor or barony in Sicily in that year, it gives those few families of that era whose coats of arms were recorded for posterity and survived into later times. The scope of this concise compilation is chiefly genealogical; there is little doubt that most enfeoffed knights living in the Kingdom of Sicily in 1282 were armigerous, but precious few records of their heraldic blazons are known to us, perhaps because many of the families themselves were extinct within a few generations of the Vespers.

That is to say, our focus is a *visual* one. We know very little of the physical appearance of the knights and barons who fought in the War of the Vespers, but if we could visit the year 1282 we would see shields and surcoats emblazoned with these designs.

Some of these families flourished in Sicily under the Normans and Swabians, whereas others arrived with King Peter in 1282 or settled on our island very soon afterward.

To arrive at this (incomplete) list, meticulous research was effected to determine which coats of arms recorded by Mugnos, Galluppi, Mango di Casalgerardo, Palizzolo Gravina and other modern heraldists were most likely known and borne before 1300, or at least attributed to families holding feudal tenure before that time as indicated in the *Descriptio Feudorum sub Rege Friderico* (1296-1335), published as the *Roll of Muscia,* and in compendia of royal decrees and charters, such as those in *De Rebus Regni Siciliae* (Barcelona) and the *Tabulario della Commenda della Magione* (Palermo). Also consulted were specialized works like *Lo Steri di Palermo e le sue Pitture* (2003) by Ettore Gabrici and Ezio Levi, and *Il Soffitto della Sala Magna allo Steri di Palermo* (1975, 2002) by Ferdinando Bologna.

Published collectively here in English for the first time, blazons of the following familial coats of arms were translated by the author from Italian or (in a few instances) from Norman French or Latin.

Between the use of toponyms and patronyms, we encounter during this period the earliest use of hereditary surnames among the Sicilian aristocracy.

Here in Sicily, being a "Vespers descendant" used to confer a social cachet comparable to that of aristocratic English families boasting patrilineal descent from the Normans who arrived at Hastings in 1066, often engendering the same degree of wishful thinking.

Many families ennobled in the Kingdom of Sicily centuries long after the Vespers lay claim to prior antiquity as armigers, but very few can prove it through an ancestor's presence confirmed by medieval records. Indeed, the greater part of the extant Sicilian nobility descends from progenitors ennobled after 1500, typically through the purchase of feudal property — a practice that survived in law until 1812. In 1882, the parade in Palermo of nobles "whose ancestors fought in the Vespers" was based on the most tenuous historiography, whilst nowadays many "aristocratic" Italian lineages submitted as "proof of nobility" to the Sovereign Military Order of Malta and like institutions consist of less fact than fiction. (This observation is based on personal experience; in the past the author was sometimes consulted by the late Prince Cyril Toumanoff, the order's High Historical Consultant, to investigate and review Italian pedigrees of dubious accuracy.)

Not for nothing did an aristocrat in an Oscar Wilde play advise an ambitious young man to study the *Peerage,* with its flattering family histories, because the hefty volume was, after all "the best thing in fiction the English have ever done."

Most heraldic blazons of extant families ennobled in the Kingdom of Sicily before 1860 will be found in *Nobiliario di Sicilia,* compiled by Antonino Mango di Casalgerardo and published in two volumes in 1912. (Extensive research in archival records would be the only way to find a blazon overlooked by Mango.) Further information on Sicilian coats of arms and titles of nobility will be found in the author's book *Sicilian Genealogy and Heraldry.* For information on the use of blazonry (in English) the reader is referred to *Boutell's Heraldry* by Charles Boutell and John Brooke-Little, and *A Complete Guide to Heraldry* by Arthur Fox-Davies.

Many of the following families are long extinct in the direct, legitimate male line, *videlicet* Abbatellis, Chiaramonte, Sclafani, Ventimiglia and numerous others.

Abbati (Abate) - per fess vert and argent.

Abbatellis (Abbatello) - or a griffon rampant sable.
Abbracciabene (Abrazabeni or Abrazalem) - or a lion rampant gules clutching a column in pale argent.
Abela (Abello) - azure a chevron or in chief 3 mullets or.
Accardo - or 3 mounts gules in chief a mullet of 6 points gules.
Afflitto - gules a palm tree or between 2 peacocks proper.
Agon - or 3 mounts vert in chief a mullet of 6 points gules.
Agosto (de Agosta) - azure between a chevron argent 3 mullets of 6 points argent.
Alagona - or 6 roundels sable.
Alaimo - per fess azure and argent in chief an eagle displayed or.
Alberti - azure in saltire a chain or.
Alemagna (Alamanno) - argent a leopard rampant gules.
Aloisio - or 4 pallets gules a lion rampant argent.
Altavilla - azure a cypress argent in sinister a greyhound rampant of the second.
Amari - argent a mermaid affronte proper in base a bar gemel undy azure.
Amato - azure 6 mullets of 6 points or.
Amico - or a bend azure in sinister chief a sparrowhawk close sable.
Amore - or an arrow argent in bend through a heart gules.
Andrea - azure a bend or in sinister chief a sparrow close argent.
Ansalone (Ansalono) - azure 6 bendlets or.
Anselmo - or a castle of 3 towers vert.
Antiochia - argent an eagle displayed sable.
Aragona - or 4 pallets gules.
Arezzo - per fess or and azure 4 hedgehogs counterchanged.
Armenia (Armonia) - or 2 bears combattant gules.
Auria. See Doria.
Bancherio - or a bend gules.
Barrese (sometimes Bavario) - Vairy gules and argent over all 3 pallets or.

Branciforte - azure a lion rampant crowned or bearing a pennant gules charged with 3 fleurs de lis or, in dexter 2 lion's paws crossed in saltire or.
de Cabrera - or a goat salient sable within a border checky or and sable.
Calafato - azure a griffon rampant argent a fess or over all.
Caltagirone - vert a tower or.
Cappello - per fess argent and sable an antique cap counterchanged.
Cardona - gules 3 cardoons vert flowered or.
de Caro - or 4 pallets gules a palm tree proper over all.
Cassaro (Alcassar) - argent 2 bendlets gules a pale gules over all.
Castellar - gules a castle argent, over all a bend azure charged with 4 bezants.
Castello - azure a castle argent in chief a fleur de lis or.
Cavalcante - azure semy of crosslets potent gules.
Cavarretta (Gavarretta) - or 3 dragons volant gules.
Cesareo - azure 2 bends or.
Chiaramonte - gules 3 mounts argent.
Cirino - or on a fess azure 5 lozenges of the first.
Doria (de Auria) - per fess or and argent an eagle displayed gules.
Emanuele. See Manuele.
Espatafora. See Spatafora.
Especiale (Speciale) - vert on a bend or a lion's paw gules in sinister chief a mullet of 6 points or.
Falcone - per fess azure and gules a falcon volant proper.
Federico - bendy or and azure.
de Ferro - gules a fess or.
Filesio - paly or and azure a chief gules, over all a bend gules.
Filingeri (Filangerio) - argent a cross azure.
Gargano (Gargono) - azure a bend or.
Grimaldi - lozengy argent and gules.

Grua - per pale embattled or and gules over all a crane in its vigilance proper.
Guccia - azure goutty d'eau.
Homodeo. See Omodei.
Incisa - azure 4 pallets or a bend argent over all.
Inveges - gules 4 bars or.
La Grua. See Grua.
Lancea (Lanza) - sable a lion rampant crowned or.
Landolina - party per pale, in dexter per bend sinister argent and sable, in sinister per bend sable and argent, on a chief sable 3 fleurs de lis argent.
Leone - or a lion rampant sable.
Leontino (Lentini) - gules 5 fusils in bend or.
Lucchisio (Lucchese) - gules 3 bezants.
Luna - per fess argent and checky sable and argent, in chief a crescent inverted checky argent and sable.
Maletta - barry or and sable.
Maniscalco (Mariscalco) - azure 3 mullets of 6 points argent in base 2 bars undy argent.
Manuele (Emanuele) - argent a lion rampant gules.
Martini (de Martinis) - gules 3 antique crowns or.
Mazzarino - argent a fasces proper on a fess azure over all 3 mullets of 6 points or.
Mendola (Mendula) - azure an almond tree fructed proper.
de Michele - barry or and azure, 21 bezants counterchanged.
de Modica (Moac) - azure a mullet of six points or.
Moleti (Muletta) - or on a mount vert a lion rampant proper holding a mullet argent.
Moncada - gules 8 bezants.
Monforte - gules a lion rampant or holding an inescutcheon azure ermined argent.
Montalto - paly gules and argent.
Montaperto - azure between 4 bendlets sinister argent 9 roses argent.

Monteliano (Murtillano?) - or in base 5 mountains gules.

Naselli (Nasello) - azure a fess or in base 3 bezants in chief a demi-lion rampant issuant or.

Nassari (Nasaro) - argent in pale a serpent undy azure crowned or.

Omodei (Homodeo) - per pale argent and gules a lion rampant counterchanged.

Orioles (Oriolis) - gules a lion passant or atop a mount of 3 summits or.

Pace (Pactis?) - argent a lion rampant gules.

Palici (Palizzi) - azure 3 pallets argent.

Pancaldo - per fess gules and azure, 3 bezants between a chevron or.

Pepoli - checky argent and sable.

Peralta - per fess azure and argent.

Perollo - azure a tower or.

Perrotta (Perrocta) - azure a fess or in chief a lion rampant bearing a cross or.

Podio (Poggio) - azure in base 3 mounts or in chief a fleur de lis or between 2 mullets of the same.

Pollicino - per fess argent and gules in chief 3 pullets close gules in base a chestnut branch or.

Prefolio - checky or and gules.

de Procida - bendy or and azure a chief or.

Queralt (Queralto) - checky argent and gules on a chief or a lion passant sable.

Raneri - or a lion sable with a head azure.

Reina - gules an arm proper issuant from sinister holding a crowned sceptre or.

Riccio (Rizzo) - argent a hedgehog passant sable.

la Rocca - argent upon a mount of 3 summits a cross gules.

Rosso (Rossi) - gules a bend or.

Ruffo - per fess indented argent and sable in chief 3 escallops gules.

Sacco - gules a lion or.
Sanfilippo - azure a lion rampant or over all a bend gules.
Santapace (Santapau) - or 2 bars gules.
Santo Stefano - azure upon a tower or a soldier sounding a horn proper.
Sclafani - per pale sable and argent 2 cranes close respectant counterchanged.
Spatafora - gules an armored arm issuant from sinister bearing a sword argent.
Speciale. See Especiale.
Spina (de Spinis) - or 3 bars dancetty azure, on a bend argent 3 roses gules.
Squillace (Schillaci) - azure in base an eel naiant argent in chief a mullet of 6 points or.
Tagliavia - azure a palm tree vert fructed or.
Taranto - azure a crescent or.
Tomasi (Tommaso?) - azure on a mount of 3 summits vert a leopard rampant or.
Tornabene - or a lion rampant azure in chief a crosslet saltirewise of the same.
Valguarnera - argent two bars gules.
Ventimiglia - gules a chief or.

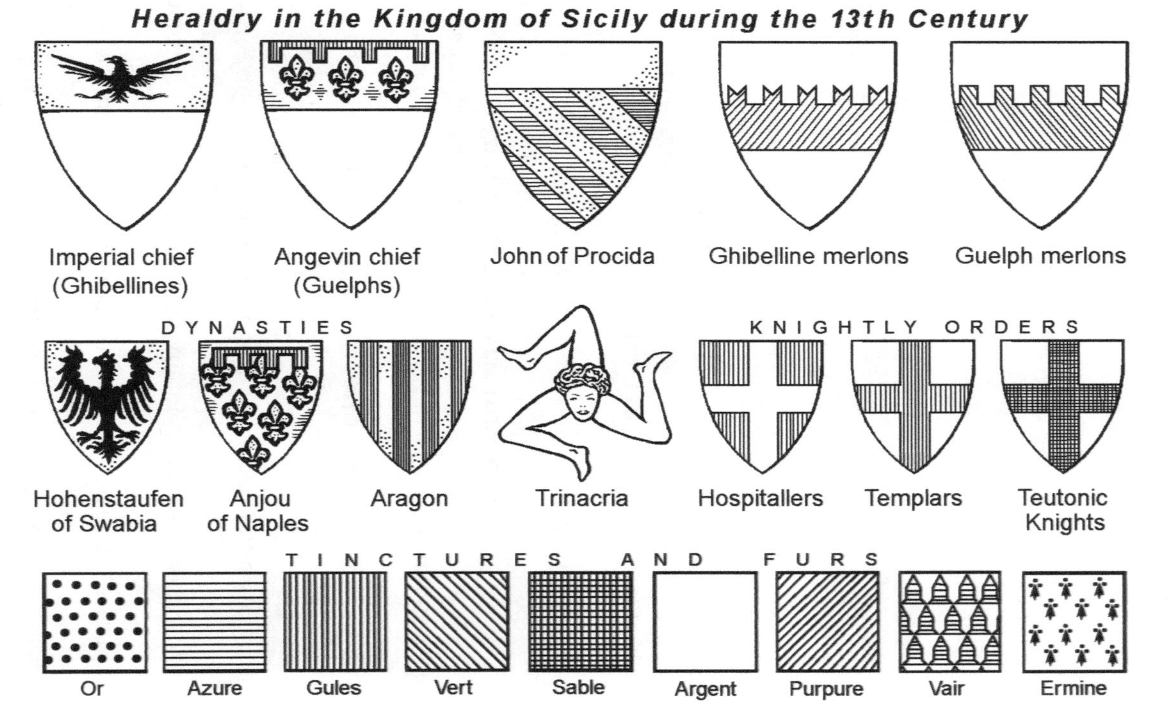
Heraldry in the Kingdom of Sicily during the 13th Century
Imperial chief (Ghibellines)
Angevin chief (Guelphs)
John of Procida
Ghibelline merlons
Guelph merlons
DYNASTIES
KNIGHTLY ORDERS
Hohenstaufen of Swabia
Anjou of Naples
Aragon
Trinacria
Hospitallers
Templars
Teutonic Knights
TINCTURES AND FURS
Or
Azure
Gules
Vert
Sable
Argent
Purpure
Vair
Ermine

Some Early Sicilian Coats of Arms

Coat of arms above the portal of Palazzo Abbatellis, a Catalan Gothic residence erected in 1490

APPENDIX 4

People and Places

How were the Sicilians defined as a people in 1282?

By 1282, as we have seen, there was a vernacular Sicilian language and it was possible to identify "native" Sicilians as distinguished from the Angevin French, at least linguistically. During the next century, the chief distinction and conflict among the nobility was between these Sicilians (or "Latins") and the "Catalans" (families that arrived with the Aragonese dynasty of King Peter).

Cultural assimilation and familial amalgamation (through intermarriage) are facts of life. In 1282, it was possible to speak of a specific Sicilian identity, and a generally endogamous population. Most Sicilians were Roman Catholic, with a dwindling number of Greek Orthodox, while the Jews comprised less than a tenth of the general population. The Arabs had converted to Catholicism or had been expelled (to communities like Lucera in Apulia) by Frederick II; it is fair to say that there were no "native" Sicilian Muslims in Sicily by 1300, although there were many Sicilian Christians descended from them.

We now look to the genetic record to complement what we know from contemporary documentation. In Sicily, the genetic record closely confirms the historical record.

Each of us has millions of ancestors, but it is possible, in a very approximative way, to identify historical "ethnic" ancestry along a few lines through the use of phylogeography based on genetic (DNA) haplotyping. As regards Sicily's population, this is described in Appendix 4 of the author's book *The Kingdom of Sicily 1130-1860* (New York 2015). Analysis must take into account variables resulting from such phenomena as "genetic drift" over time and the isolation of sub-clades.

As Sicily's genetic diversity reflects its historical ethnic diversity, there exists no single "Sicilian haplotype" or haplogroup, no "Sicilian DNA" *per se.* By percentage of the population, Sicily's Y (patrilineal) haplogroups are today approximately: J (35), R (25), I (15), K (10), H (10), Others (5).

Before the arrival of the Normans, entire localities were founded or repopulated by Arabs, who were then Muslim, particularly those places whose names begin with the Arabic *Kal, Kalta* or *Kasr,* or *Regal* or *Rahal,* and *Gibel,* among others, and of course Sicilian is full of words derived from Arabic. A good reference is *Sichillia* (2004), a three-volume work by Antonino Di Gregorio.

The Normans who arrived in 1061 identified the populations of certain communities, such as Troina, based principally on language, namely as "Greeks" and "Arabs."

Although certain historians, such as David Abulafia in his biography of Frederick II, refer to the various expulsions between 1222 and 1246, there were most likely fewer than forty thousand Muslims in Sicily (mostly in the west) who were transferred to towns such as Lucera. Precise numbers do not exist, and there were isolated revolts by some of Sicily's "former" Muslims for decades after 1222. Generic references to "Arabs" during the Hohenstaufen reign are imprecise because, in fact, the vast majority of Sicily's Muslims had already converted before 1222. There is no evidence of Arabic-speaking populations in Sicily in 1282. Alexander Metcalfe's *Muslims and Christians in Norman Sicily: Arabic Speakers and the End of Islam* (2011) is an insightful study into a specific period. By the same author is the more general work *The Muslims of Medieval Italy* (2009), which covers the status of the Muslims until 1300. See also *Muslims in Medieval Italy: The Colony at Lucera* (2003) by Julie Anne Taylor.

Unfortunately, in trusting certain studies conducted here in Italy, some superb historians have been fed inaccurate information. Fortunately, the inaccuracies usually concern rather insignificant details of little import to our general view of Sicilian history.

For example, archeological excavations indicate that the monastery of Saint John of the Hermits may stand on the site of a mosque (as some historians report), but based on the same research it is highly likely that, like Palermo's cathedral, this was the site of an earlier church before the arrival of the Arabs. Numerous are the Sicilian ritual and fortified sites that were occupied for many centuries before the Middle Ages, hence the cathedral of Syracuse is built on a Greek temple while Palermo's Norman Palace stands on a Punic citadel (in both cases the ancient structures are clearly visible).

Two sites studied since 1990 relate specifically to the Jews. The mikveh excavated in Syracuse, with its stout Romanesque arches, dates from the Byzantine era and has come to be regarded as the oldest surviving Jewish ritual bath in Europe. However, according to five experts from Israel who came to examine it, the crudely-carved mikveh in Palermo (under what is now the Jesuit cloister behind Palazzo Marchese) may well be several centuries older.

A good general work on the Sicilian Jews is *Between Scylla and Charybdis: The Jews in Sicily* (2011) by Shlomo Simonsohn, the leading expert on the subject. See also David Abulafia's "Economic Activity of the Sicilian Jews around 1300" presented at the *Italia Judaica* conference held in Palermo in 1992, and Scandaliato and Gerardi's "Gli Ebrei in Sicilia nel Medioevo: Cultura e Lingua," in *Archivio Storico Siciliano,* Series 4, Volume 21-22 (Palermo 1997), pages 114-133.

John of Procida was one of the most famous physicians of his time. For the state of medicine during this period, see "Medicine in Southern Italy, Twelfth-Fourteenth Centuries: Six Texts," translated by Monica Green, in *Medieval Italy: Texts in Translation* (2009), pages 311-327.

No fewer than three different locations are indicated in various sources as the site of the beginning of the insurrection in Palermo that sparked the War of the Vespers. They are the Holy Spirit church, the cathedral of Monreale, and the square near Saint Ann's convent where it is believed that John of Saint Rémy, the High Justiciar for Val di Mazara, resided (although some sources imply that he lived at the Norman Palace).

All of the names mentioned in this book's Prologue were drawn from contemporary sources; none are hypothetical. As most were extracted directly from Latin manuscripts or transcriptions, some surnames may differ slightly from their Italian or English translations by other authors.

The modern translations of medieval surnames recorded in Latin are rarely precise. For example, the surname of John of Walehorn, sometimes Walkorn, a German preceptor of the Teutonic Order in Sicily during the reign of King Manfred, is variously reported by Italians as *Guallechorn* and *Vualehorn,* among other interpretations. (See the charter reproduced in this volume.) In Latin the name of Palmeri Abbate is given in the royal charters of King Peter as *Palmerius Abbas.*

All of the edifices mentioned in the Prologue were standing in 1282. Prosopography was applied to specific details. In the Magione complex, the visitor may view a pillar taken from a nearby mosque, and similar exemplars (bearing Koranic inscriptions) are preserved in the Palazzo Abbatellis museum, the Steri Palace and the portico of Palermo Cathedral. The *cerveru,* or Norman deerhound, is known from heraldic sources and a few manuscripts; related to the Scottish deerhound, it is depicted in this volume in the line drawings adapted from

Frederick's treatise on falconry.

The knightly orders, including the Teutonic Knights, are described in Desmond Seward's *Monks of War: The Military Religious Orders* (the revised edition of 2000 is recommended). See also Lynn Townsend White's *Latin Monasticism in Norman Sicily* (1938), pages 234-240. A fine history of the Magione is *La Magione di Palermo negli Otto Secoli della Sua Storia* (1975) by Rocco Russo.

The precise role of the Teutonic Knights in the revolts of 1282 is not known, but the author supports the very credible thesis that they destroyed the tomb of King Tancred in the Magione in 1194 or shortly thereafter, almost certainly on the orders of King Henry or his consort, Constance of Hauteville. The Magione was severely damaged during the Allied carpet bombings of 1943, and subsequent restorations revealed no trace of a corpse that could be identified as Tancred.

Despite occasional claims to the contrary, the precise location of Mategriffon Castle in Messina is unknown. Whatever may have remained of it by the twentieth century was probably destroyed by the earthquake of 1908. In the same city, Saint Mary of the Germans, built for the Teutonic Knights, is the nearest thing in Sicily to a purely Gothic church; it has been partially restored.

For the heraldic blazons of Guelph and Ghibelline armigers known during the Vespers period in Florence, Milan, Venice and elsewhere in Italy, the best general compendium is Giovanni Battista Crollalanza's three-volume *Dizionario Storico-Blasonico* (1886). By the same author is the *Annuario della Nobiltà Italiana,* first published in 1878 and still issued every four or five years in its distinctive red cover.

Caveat lector. Pseudohistory is not unknown in Italy.

In stark contrast to the charters, letters, chronicles and feudal rolls mentioned in Concordance (Appendix 2), some "secondary" narratives, such as *I Raguagli Historici del Vespro Siciliano*

(1645) by Filadelfo Mugnos, present certain details unsupported by the extant historical record. These should be read critically.

From time to time, fabulists emerge in public life (or on the internet) as the *soi-disant* "pretenders" to the headship of one or another historical Sicilian dynasty. Sicily's principal medieval dynasties (namely Hauteville, Hohenstaufen, Aragon, Trastámara) are long-extinct in their legitimate male lines, as are the imperial Byzantine dynasties. In the same bailiwick are the ever more numerous individuals who claim titles of nobility lacking any genealogical foundation. Legally, this is unimportant because Italian nobiliary titles have not been recognized by the Italian government since 1948, nor by the Vatican since 1984.

For commentary on distorted historiography, see Professor Denis Mack Smith's insightful "Documentary Falsification and Italian Biography," in *History and Biography: Essays in Honour of Derek Beales* (Cambridge 1996), page 181, and the introduction of his *Italy and Its Monarchy* (1989); also *The Pursuit of Italy: A History of a Land, Its Regions, and Their Peoples* (2011) by David Gilmour. A candid essay is Gianni Oliva's *L'Alibi della Resistenza* (2003). See also "Italy's Bloody Secret" by Rory Carroll in *The Guardian,* London, 25 June 2001.

Mention was made of lingering censorship as a vestigial effect of zealous nationalism (and Fascism). In 1981, for example, Italy banned the theatrical release of *The Lion of the Desert,* a motion picture (starring Anthony Quinn, Oliver Reed, Rod Steiger, Irene Papas, John Gielgud) depicting civilian massacres in Italian-occupied Libya. The censorship, which forbade licensing for commercial screenings, finally ended when the film was broadcast on Italian satellite television on 11 June 2009. For a contemporary review see "Lion of the Desert: Bedouin vs Mussolini" by Vincent Canby in *The New York Times,* 17 April 1981.

As regards Italian universities, see "Higher Education in Italy: A Case for Change" in *The Economist,* 15 November 2008, page 32.

NOTES

1. See Jensen, Frede, *The Poetry of the Sicilian School* (1986). Jensen's book is the lengthiest compilation of these poems in English translation.

2. Issued in installments ("books") beginning in 1558, Fazello's tome was published in its final form in 1560. Fazello wrote from a Palermitan point of view; Francesco Maurolico's *Sicanicarum Rerum Compendium* advocated for Messina as the focus of Sicilian history. The rivalry was more geographical than political, but it was rooted in history.

3. For sober observations about Amari's political motives, see Salvatore Tramontana's *Gli Anni del Vespro: L'immaginario, la cronaca, la storia* (1989), pages 102-106, 112-114, 116. In English, insightful commentary is provided by Steven Runciman in *The Sicilian Vespers* (1958), pages xi, 288-289; and by Karla Mallette in *The Kingdom of Sicily 1100-1250: A Literary History* (2005), pages 36-42. This is not the place to present an analysis of the effects of the Italian unification movement. Suggested histories are Denis Mack Smith's *Italy and Its Monarchy* (1989) and his paper "Documentary Falsification and Italian Biography" in *History and Biography: Essays in Honour of Derek Beales* (Cambridge 1996), as well as *The Fall of the House of Savoy* (1972) by Robert Katz, *The Pursuit of Italy: A History of a Land, Its Regions, and Their Peoples* (2011) by David Gilmour, *The Risorgimento Revisited: Nationalism and Culture in Nineteenth-Century Italy* (2012) edited by Silvana Patriarca and Lucy Riall, and *The Kingdom of Sicily 1130-1860* (2015) by Louis Mendola.

4. We find John of Procida in the Kingdom of Sicily witnessing one of Manfred's charters dated 18 July 1262, a document (reproduced in this volume) conserved in the *Tabulario della Commenda della Magione.* The signatures of the monarch and

chancellor do not appear on the only surviving copy (catalogued as manuscript TM 95 in the Palermo Archive of State), made on 22 August at the request of the Preceptor (Commander) of the Teutonic Order, John of Walkorn. Specifically, the decree orders the justiciar Pandolf of Petruro to exempt the Teutonic Knights from a tax that was recently imposed.

5. This is the heading consistent with the *Spinelli Codex*. In Codex Vaticanus 5256 the wording is translated "Book of John of Procida and Palaeologue."

6. In the original the generic toponym *Rumania* is used in referring to the Balkan region of the Byzantine Empire. The reference is to Michael VIII Palaeologue.

7. The greater part of the armada was being assembled at Messina, but additional ships were being constructed in Apulia, where Brindisi was the principal naval base.

8. John of Procida had been the personal physician to Frederick II, and also to John Orsini, who was Pope Nicholas III from 1277 until 1280.

9. Here the narrator alludes to the fact that John of Procida, having been in the service of a Holy Roman Emperor, was more than familiar with protocol.

10. Baldwin II (Baldwin of Courtenay), the last Latin Emperor of Constantinople, died in exile in Naples in 1273, having been deposed by Michael's supporters. The Latin pretender until December 1283 was Baldwin's son, Philip I (see Personages), yet the text refers to the late Baldwin as if he were still alive. Perhaps the narrator meant to refer to Philip, who was married to Beatrice, the daughter of King Charles.

11. "King of Spain" refers to the King of Castile, Alfonso X, mentioned in Personages.

12. "King Charles of France" refers to King Charles I *of Anjou* of Naples, his house being a "cadet" branch of the French dynasty.

13. The Sicilian wording, taken literally, suggests that each man wrote such a letter. It is more likely that there would have been a single letter to which each baron present appended his seal, along the lines of petitions such as England's *Magna Carta.* Often such "seals" were drawn in ink on the document (accompanied by a name) rather than impressed in wax with a signet. Diplomatic correspondence was usually in Latin, of which the Sicilian text in Chapter 14 is probably a translation.

14. Not every phrase in the barons' letter can be taken literally, but the reference to the consort (wife) of King Peter of Aragon as *Lady* of Sicily is indeed literal; Constance Hohenstaufen was the daughter and heiress of King Manfred of Sicily, himself the son of Frederick II.

15. Soriano nel Cimino, as it is known today, is still dominated by the imposing, squarish castle built by Pope Nicholas. The town is located north of Rome near Viterbo.

16. Despite the use of the plural, it is clear that the Pope would have issued a single letter. When referring to formal, sealed correspondence, the plural was not unheard of. In Britain, for example, one still refers to *letters patent* issued by the sovereign. Of course, the Papal letter itself, if it were indeed written, would have been composed in Latin, which remained the language of European diplomacy and learning for several more centuries.

17. In the manuscript the first two characters in the word *xpranissimu* (literally "most Christian") come from the traditional XP monogram of Christ, the first two letters of the Greek *Cristos.* For another use of the Christogram see *Ihu Xpu* (Jesus Christ) in the very first line of Chapter 1.

18. The Kingdom of Aragon, of which the historical capital since 1118 was Zaragoza (where King Peter III was crowned in 1276), was at this time governed largely from Barcelona, the traditional capital of neighboring Catalonia. As Catalonia was a *county* (rather than a kingdom), the monarch was styled simply *King of Aragon* but he was also Count of Barcelona. As King of Aragon, Peter's official residence was the splendid Aljaferia Palace, famous for its Mudéjar architecture (see the photograph), but he spent more time in coastal Barcelona, which facilitated the expansion of his overseas dominions. In Sicilian historiography the term *Aragonese* is used to refer to the dynasty that ruled Catalonia and Aragon, and later Sicily, Sardinia and territories in Greece, an empire known as the "Crown of Aragon." The demonym *Catalan* is used to refer to the people, art and architecture of Catalonia but in common Sicilian parlance it sometimes embraced ethnic Aragonese culture as well.

19. In 1213, Peter II of Aragon (grandfather of Peter III) was killed at the Battle of Muret by French forces under the zealous crusader Simon de Montfort; Peter II was supporting his brother-in-law, Raymond VI of Toulouse. This decisive defeat led to the loss of Peter's lands in the Occitan regions (Languedoc). These were claimed by Montfort, but after he died at the siege of Toulouse in 1218 they were ceded to France, and formally annexed by treaty eleven years later. Significantly, this annexation in the wake of the infamous Albigensian Crusades formed the basis for what became the united France.

20. Pope Nicholas III died on 22 August 1280 at Soriano. See note 15.

21. The rather ambiguous wording might be construed to indicate the present year (1281) or the successive one. It is clear that the conversation recounted in Chapter 38 took place in 1281, most likely in March. See note 22.

22. The pontificate of Simon de Brion "of Touraine" began in late February 1281. When elected, he was referred to as "Martin III" (and this ordinal has been retained for consistency with the original text), but to modern historians he is Martin IV.

23. In Sicilian historiography the Muslim Arabs of northern Africa (now Tunisia, Libya, Algeria) are usually referred to as *Saracens,* while the *Moors* are usually identified specifically with Morocco. However, in medieval Italy these ethnonyms were used rather loosely.

24. Isabella of Aragon, sister of King Peter III, was married to Philip III of France until her death in 1271, caused by a fall from a horse while fording a stream near Cosenza, in Calabria, while returning to France via an overland route following the Tunisian Crusade (which saw the death of Louis IX). When she died she was about six months pregnant with her fifth child.

25. The *tornesel* was a silver coin, and therefore larger than the gold *ounce.* Although the original text states that King Peter clearly refused the financial help of the King of France (see Chapter 40), some later texts indicate that he accepted it. In either case, the text reported here is that of the *Spinelli Codex.*

26. Charles was still entitled by treaty to collect taxes (tribute) from a few coastal territories in northern Africa, but for some

years the Aragonese had dominated the region, which recently saw infighting among the local Muslim leaders in the wake of the death of Sultan al Mustansir (see Personages) in 1277. When he lost Sicily, Charles effectively lost his claim to these taxes, which with the Treaty of Panissar (1285) found their way into Aragonese coffers. See also note 30.

27. In the Middle Ages, the term *Apulia* was sometimes used rather loosely, referring not only to modern Puglia, which includes Bari, Brindisi and Lecce, but to a coastal region running southward from the southern Marches through Abruzzi and Molise to the Apulian Peninsula. This included territories due east of Viterbo.

28. The *Spinelli Codex* uses the word *follunj* (a disloyal person). Filippo Evola notes that this word appears several times in the text, and is not to be confused with *filluni* (fool). *Follunj* is comparable to the Middle English cognate *felon* and the Italian *fellone,* from the Old French *felun.* It seems clear from chapters 42, 45 and other sections that King Charles is characterizing King Peter of Aragon as potentially treacherous, or at least unpredictable, and not to be trusted.

29. Despite its wording, which may seem strange to modern ears (even those of some Roman Catholics), the phrase "earthly punishment" refers to the authority reflected in such Papal acts as excommunication, whereas "divine punishment" would be a reference to eternal damnation, the exclusive prerogative of God Himself. Charles' concern was the welfare of Christians of the Church of Rome, including himself and his allies; he was less distressed by the suffering of Eastern Christians, as shown by his bloody (yet ultimately unsuccessful) campaigns in Albania and Greece in 1280.

30. The Berber lands, later called the "Barbary Coast," were what are now Morocco, Algeria, Tunisia and Libya, historically referred to as *Ifriqiya.* See note 26.

31. The town of Montefiascone is near Viterbo and Orvieto. Continuing unrest in Rome discouraged the presence of the Papal court in that capital city at this point in Martin's pontificate, as in the time of Pope Nicholas.

32. Here again the use of the forceful word *fullunj* (felon) in the original text. See note 28.

33. The Spinelli and Catania manuscripts do not include the phrase *et iunsiru in Trapani,* "and they arrived in Trapani," of the other texts; it is included here for clarity.

34. This assembly of barons is referred to in the original text as a *parlamentu.* Misinterpretation of this word, which in Middle Sicilian often alluded to nothing more than a meeting of barons (or even a simple conversation), has given rise to the widespread, but unsupported, claim among Sicilianist historians that Sicily's earliest legislative parliament antedates England's. The first Sicilian parliament, leading to the barons' election of Frederick of Aragon as King of Sicily, took place in 1295 and 1296. Aside from prefatorial developments like the *Magna Carta* (in 1215), the inception of an effective parliament in England is generally dated to 1258; interestingly, it was prompted by baronial opposition to the support of a proposed Papal-sponsored invasion of Sicily by King Henry III. More generally, see *A History of the House of Lords* (1988) by Frank Pakenham, Earl of Longford.

35. By most accounts the Vespers revolt actually began on Easter Monday, 30 March 1282, not the first day of April, al-

though the insurrection may have lasted several days. However, the manuscript refers to Tuesday (actually 31 March in 1282) as the day the uprising began, and here it is noteworthy that in Sicilian monasteries in the thirteenth century vespers (the time when the revolt is traditionally said to have begun although the narrator does not mention a specific hour) sometimes signalled the beginning of the *following* day, hence April. Another simple explanation, which applies the scientific principle of "parsimony" to this question, is that the correct (traditional) date may not yet have been part of the historical canon by circa 1288 when the narrator probably began writing his chronicle. Such errors are fairly commonplace in medieval records, for example the ordinal of Pope Martin (see note 22 above) ascribed inaccurately by the Papal chancery during his pontificate.

36. The *steri* referred to in the original text was not the existing edifice in Piazza Marina, the "Steri," erected during the fourteenth century by the Chiaramonte family, but rather one of the fortified buildings in the city, most likely one of the many guard towers which, according to the text, was normally the captain's keep. The word derives from the same root as the Italian *osterio,* for which see note 48.

37. The death toll reported by the chronicler is probably overstated and the figure has been the subject of much debate over the centuries, but in 1282 the population of Palermo and its environs may well have been close to a hundred thousand, so it is altogether possible that there were several thousand French in and around the largest city of the Kingdom of Sicily. What is not known with certainty is whether only the French present in Palermo were killed, or whether this figure includes *all* the French killed in Sicily. Other accounts, such as that of Malaspina, give further details of the event; very few of those particulars are included in this volume so as to focus on the present chronicle.

38. The archbishop of Monreale, one of the most important episcopal sees in Sicily, was John Boccamazza, an aristocrat related to the Savelli family and sympathetic to the Angevins. See Personages.

39. James Savelli was the future Pope Honorius IV and related to the archbishop of Monreale. See Personages.

40. Gerard Bianchi, often referred to simply as "Gerard of Parma," was an experienced diplomat. See Personages.

41. Rocca Amatori, now Contrada Roccamatore, near Tremestieri overlooking the Ionian coast south of Messina, was the site of a Cistercian monastery founded in the twelfth century. The monastery's neutrality and its distance from Messina both argued for its security. King Charles' military advisors probably knew that in the invasion of 1061 the Normans had landed south of the city, though perhaps not quite so far away as Tremestieri. Indeed, the army led by Charles in 1282 was probably the largest attacking expeditionary force to land in Sicily since that time. The monastery was largely destroyed by the earthquake of 1908. (In the later manuscripts of the *Rebellion* composed in peninsular Italy the phrase *Rocca Amatori* is corrupted; only the text of the *Spinelli Codex* presents it correctly.)

42. Guy of Montfort, whose career found him involved in numerous adventures, had used similar tactics at Augusta, on the Ionian coast, in 1269. See Personages for Guy of Montfort and Hugh of Brienne.

43. Even if the letter's historicity cannot be established, the text clearly reflects the disdain with which Jews were regarded in Italy by this time, the very ethnonym a synecdoche for "trai-

tor." This may be taken to imply how much the social fabric had changed, indeed deteriorated, since the reign of enlightened Frederick II just three decades earlier. Frederick was the monarch through whom Charles, as *de facto* successor to the Hohenstaufens, claimed the Kingdom of Jerusalem; for Charles this was a *title of pretension,* as Frederick II was the last King of Sicily to actually rule Jerusalem, albeit from a distance.

44. King William II of Sicily, who died in 1189. Dante and Boccaccio seem to have taken a cue from John of Procida in advocating a flattering view of William. See Personages.

45. The meaning of the word *Latins* depends greatly on context. Here it refers not only to Sicilians but to Italians in general, be they Neapolitans, Tuscans or Lombards, as opposed to those, such as the French, who did not speak an Italic language. Earlier, in the chronicle's second chapter, set in Constantinople, *Latins* refers generically to western Europeans (sometimes called "Franks"), and particularly to Roman Catholics, as opposed to Greek Orthodox.

46. The intent of this passage has been questioned for centuries. Clearly, the debatable affirmation about royal revenues reflects Charles' belief, according to John of Procida, that William II held too little land directly (crown, "royal" or "demesnial" estates), his kingdom's wealth being mostly manorial (feudal estates held by vassals). Such a perception may be based on the trend (beginning before 1140) of Sicilian feudal holdings becoming *de facto* hereditary, passing from father to son rather than reverting back to the monarch upon a baron's death. Whatever its basis, Charles' assertion is not confirmed by surviving records of the *diwan* (the royal treasury) or extant feudal rolls such as the *Catalogus Baronum* (destroyed during the infamous Bonellus revolt against William I in 1161 but largely reconstructed by

Matthew Aiello around 1166 during the reign of young William II), nor by significant studies conducted by competent scholars since 1950. Moreover, under the Normans certain "crown" cities in the royal demesne were particularly wealthy; at times during the twelfth century the tax revenue generated by the city of Palermo exceeded that of the entire Kingdom of England. Nevertheless, Charles himself was a worthy administrator unafraid to levy heavy taxes on his subjects, and this was one of the causes of the rebellion against him.

47. Counts and barons. In the Kingdom of Sicily during the thirteenth century most counties were larger than most baronies, so the typical count (the rank is comparable to that of an earl in England) was wealthier, and therefore more important, than a baron. A county might consist of numerous baronies, and within each barony were several manors (fiefs). Guy of Montfort and Hugh of Brienne (see note 42) both held counties in Italy, and the original Sicilian text refers to them as *conti.* Here in Chapter 57 the narrator is referring to the nobility, regardless of feudal rank. Also, the Middle Sicilian phrase *barunj,* like the Italian *baroni,* sometimes refers to the *baronage,* the feudal nobility collectively.

48. In the original, the word *osti* (usually a military encampment or army) is used to describe the location of the wall. Here the meaning of the term is akin to the French *oste,* from which the Italian *osterio* (note the *Osterio Magno* tower in Cefalù) and even the English *host* (an army). See also *steri* at note 36.

49. The reference to *Catalonia* is a transcription error; the text should read *Alcoyll.* The Sicilian emissaries went to Alcoyll (now Collo in Algeria), where King Peter's fleet had arrived after the local disturbance was already quelled, thus avoiding a major battle against the Muslims. His army was therefore fully

manned, equipped and ready to do battle in Sicily. Chapter 61 correctly states that King Peter was in Alcoyll, from whence he departed for Trapani, where (according to most accounts) he arrived a few days later on 30 August.

50. The archbishop of Monreale was an Angevin supporter; see note 38. The archbishop of Palermo, Peter, who bore the appropriate surname *Santafede,* literally "holy faith," was not deceased in 1282 but simply absent from the city when Peter arrived on 2 September; he had embarked upon a quasi-diplomatic mission to the Pope to explain the catastrophic events that occurred on Easter Monday. (Steven Runciman and others have propagated the misperception that he was dead.) King Peter was crowned in Palermo Cathedral on 4 September by the bishop of Cefalù, perhaps assisted by other bishops, although a quaint local legend says he was crowned in a tiny chapel nearby. In this chapter the narrator probably intended "the people" to mean the entire populace, but in legal parlance "popular" assent usually meant *baronial* assent, with medieval European kings crowned by bishops. For more on the Sicilian tradition, see Hubert Houben's *Roger II von Sizilien* (1997).

51. The Latin letters between Peter and Charles were somewhat more verbose than the texts reported here, but the Sicilian appellation conforms to the original: *Petrus dei gratia aragonum et siciliae rex.* Protocol aside, a good number of Peter's letters and charters from this period are conserved at archives in Barcelona and in the Vatican (see the Sources). On 20 September 1282, for example, he dispatched from Palermo a letter for Emperor Michael of Constantinople regarding the betrothal mentioned in Chapter 32 of the *Rebellion.* The *corpus* of Peter's various letters and decrees transcribed in *De Rebus Regni Siciliae* indicates that until May 1283 the monarch issued orders from Palermo, Randazzo, Messina and Trapani mustering

men-at-arms, appointing justiciars and rendering various juridical decisions. Then he issued directives from Catalonia and Calabria.

52. The name of the speaker, Hugh of Brienne, is partially obscured in the *Spinelli Codex* and poorly transcribed in later manuscripts, but scholars are in general agreement on the attribution.

53. Piedimonte is now Piedimonte Matese. Charles placed this limitation in his appellation out of respect for the Pope, as the town was then under direct Papal jurisdiction; a similar example is Benevento. Capua became a Lombard capital in the ninth century. Charles was Count of Provence and Forcalquier *jure uxoris* through his first wife, Beatrice of Provence, who died in 1267.

54. Margaret of Burgundy, Charles' second wife. See Personages.

55. Such concealment was possible because Messina, which faces the Ionian Sea, is surrounded by a ring of steep mountains.

56. The phrase "those holding feudal tenure" refers to counts, barons, manorial lords and enfeoffed knights who provided military service to the king as a feudal obligation. This was typically forty days per year and might accrue from one year to the next. It was not yet a very common practice (in Italy or France) to pay scutage in lieu of such service. When there was a choice, it was normal to initiate military campaigns in Spring or Summer rather than Winter, and retaining the various mercenaries and archers was costly.

SOURCES AND BIBLIOGRAPHY

Background research for this book was conducted over the course of several years, principally in Naples, Palermo, Catania, Messina, Barcelona, Zaragoza and Vatican City.

There are nine known manuscript copies of the *Rebellion,* of which eight are medieval. The author relied principally on the *Spinelli Codex,* consulted at the National Library of Palermo (manuscript number I.C.21 in the old catalogue, now also 4454), which has held it since 1870. It was rebound in the eighteenth century and restored in 1971.

The former owner, from whose estate the library purchased it, was a Neapolitan nobleman, Domenico San Giorgio Spinelli, who is presumed to have inherited the manuscript through a Messinian family. It is possible that the manuscript was for centuries conserved with other important codices in the archive of the Benedictine monastery at San Nicolò l'Arena outside Nicolosi, where Eleanor of Anjou, daughter of Charles II of Naples and consort of Frederick III of Sicily (son of Peter III of Aragon), died in 1343.

Most likely transcribed at some time before 1330 (scholars debate the date), the *Spinelli Codex* is a copy of the autograph usually dated to circa 1290. That it was recorded on paper rather than parchment is not anomalous; paper was produced in Sicily as early as the Fatimid era, and the Palermo Archive of State preserves what is thought to be the oldest surviving paper document in Europe. Moreover, the proscription on the use of paper by the Constitutions of Melfi of 1231 did not apply to private documents. The paper of the *Spinelli Codex* was probably produced in Amalfi as *carta bambagina.*

The first complete transcription of the *Rebellion* was published by Rosario Gregorio in 1791 (see below) but, alas, it was not based on the Spinelli text.

Filippo Evola published a transcription of the *Spinelli Codex* with commentary in Palermo in 1882 (to mark its sixth centenary several books were published about the Vespers), namely his *Lu Rebellamentu di Sichilia: Codice della Biblioteca Regionale di Palermo.* In addition to the verbatim transcription, his book presents notes. This publication coincided with that of the Catania text (see below).

Published in 1865, Vincenzo Di Giovanni's *Cronache Siciliane dei Secoli XIII, XIV, XV* was also consulted. Its *Rebellion,* like Gregorio's, is based on one of the other known manuscripts and is therefore less reliable than the *Spinelli Codex.* Indeed, Di Giovanni's approach was to "italianize" the Sicilian texts as if "correcting" them.

Pasquale Castorina's *Il Vespro Siciliano: Cronaca Siciliana Anonima Intitolata Le Rebellamentu di Sichilia, Codice Esistente nell'Archivio Municipale di Catania,* published in Catania in 1882, was based on a modern manuscript transcribed around 1633 and discovered in 1870. Castorina was the first to openly advocate for (apocryphal) "Athanasius of Iaci" as the author. This he did in 1883, hence the "anonymous" chronicler referred to in the title of his publication *Il Vespro Siciliano* of 1882. See *Catania e Dante Alighieri, ovvero Uno Sguardo Retrospettivo di Anni Seicento, la Cronica di Frate Atanasio di Aci, ed una Società Catanese di Storia Patria* (1883), page 51 and pages 198-201.

The Catania manuscript is faithful to the text of the *Spinelli Codex,* of which it is a copy. It is noteworthy that during editing immediately prior to publication of the Spinelli and Catania texts in 1882 there was very little correspondence between Filippo Evola and Pasquale Castorina (mostly via Antonio Pennino) regarding their respective publishing projects, yet their linguistic interpretations, like the texts themselves, are almost identical.

In practice, Pasquale Castorina was one of the most objective, scientific historians of the nineteenth century to consider the nuances implied by the *Rebellion.* One regrets, however, that his published transcription of the Catania text altered its orthography substantially, and that he accepted without question the historicity of "Athanasius of Iaci."

Enrico Sicardi's lengthy articles, published under the title "Due Cronache del Vespro in Volgare Siciliano del Secolo XIII" in *Rerum Italicarum Scriptores* (1917), number 34, were consulted. These excellent analyses of the *Rebellion,* among the finest ever published, are accompanied by a glossary and the texts of the three most important medieval manuscripts. No examination of the topic could be said to be complete without considering his commentary. However, it must be noted that Sicardi, like Pasquale Castorina, Michele Amari and others, accepted the historicity of pseudo-Athanasius. (Even the best scholars sometimes forget that in the study of history there are experts but no authorities, and that the only valid conclusions are those resulting from sound epistemology based on scientific reasoning.)

Marcello Barbato's *Lu Rebellamentu di Sichilia* (2010) presents detailed analyses based on comparisons among the texts of the eight surviving medieval manuscripts. Here some parts of the chronicle's narrative in Middle Sicilian consist of amalgamated passages, with phrases drawn from manuscripts written after the *Spinelli Codex,* but these are clearly indicated.

The first published transcription of *La Conquista di Sichilia fatta per manu di lu Conti Rugeri di Normandia* by Simon of Lentini appeared in 1865 in Vincenzo Di Giovanni's book (op. cit. supra). Another transcription was published as *La Conquesta di Sichilia fatta per li Normandi translatata per frati Simuni da Lentini* by Giuseppe Rossi-Taibbi (Palermo 1954). For some useful analysis regarding its language, see La Fauci, Nunzio, "La Lingua e la Mano: Evidenze sintattiche ne 'La Conquesta di Sichilia' di frati Simuni da Lentini" in *Schede Medievali: Atti del convegno internazionale di studio nell'ottavo centenario della nascita di San Francesco d'Assisi, Palermo, 7-12 Marzo 1982,* numbers 12-

13; Officina di Studi Medievali, Palermo; pages 295-302.

Various other works were consulted, including translation dictionaries; one of the more scholarly is *Vocabolario Storico-Etimologico del Siciliano* (2014) by Alberto Varvaro et al. The opinions of several Sicilian philologists were solicited and gratefully accepted, while the work of Panvini (see below) includes a good glossary.

For Ciullo's *Contrasto,* the earliest surviving manuscript was consulted in the Vatican. However, the transcription is drawn principally from that of Bruno Panvini published in 1962 in *Le Rime della Scuola Siciliana,* volume 1 (the work consulted by most scholars who have translated these poems into English), and also in *Poeti della Corte di Federico II,* volume 2 in the series *I Poeti della Scuola Siciliana* published by Mondadori in 2008, where the section on Ciullo of Alcamo was edited by Margherita Spampinato Beretta. The excellent book by Frede Jensen is mentioned below. A fine analysis is Cono Antonio Mangieri's *Il Contrasto di Cielo d'Alcamo: Introduzione, testo manoscritto e diplomatico, testo critico-congetturale, traduzione e note* (2005).

The author's observation about the ready capitulation of certain fortresses (specifically Caltanissetta Castle) during the Vespers is based on his consultation of *De Rebus Regni Siciliae,* register entries 1528 and 1529, being decrees of King Peter issued at Solano in March 1283. (See Appendix 2.) The castellan at "Pietrarossa" Castle, a fortress located outside the village of Caltanissetta, surrendered quite readily to a small company of knights. Little of the structure remained following an earthquake in the sixteenth century, but in 1282 it was quite large. Other manuscripts were consulted, such as those in the *Tabulario della Commenda della Magione* (at the Archive of State in Palermo).

A description of the brief reign of King Peter II of Sicily is to be found in Corrado Mirto's "Petrus Secundus dei Gratia Rex Siciliae, 1337-1342" in *Archivio Storico Siciliano,* Series 4,

Volume 2 (Palermo 1976), pages 53-126.

There are several traditional biographies of John of Procida, of which a classic entry is Niccolò Buscemi's *La Vita di Giovanni di Procida, Privata e Pubblica* (1836).

A work of note is "Historia Conspirationis Johannis Prochytae," pages 249-274 in the first volume of *Bibliotheca Scriptorum qui Res in Sicilia Gestas sub Aragonum Imperio Retulere* by Rosario Gregorio (1791). This transcription of one of the later "Italian" manuscripts of the *Rebellion* is far less accurate than the Spinelli or Catania texts. At all events, it may be considered significant of the importance ascribed to the *Rebellion* that the same volume includes the chronicles of Bartolomeo of Neocastro and Niccolò Speciale.

A fine transcription of the Peace of Caltabellotta, with annotations by Antonino Franchi and Benedetto Rocco, first published in the journal *Quaderni di Ho Theologos* in March 1985, was republished in monograph form as *La Pace di Caltabellotta* in 1987.

Despite its publication during the Fascist era, a good Italian account of the reign of Frederick III is Antonino De Stefano's *Federico III d'Aragona Re di Sicilia 1296-1337* (1937). The classic work is Francesco Testa's *De Vita et Rebus Gestis Federici II* (sic), published in Palermo in 1775. (Note the chronic confusion in the king's ordinal; in Sicilian historiography this younger son of Peter of Aragon is usually referred to as "King Frederick II of Sicily.")

The author made a considerable effort to map Palermo as it existed at the beginning of the War of the Vespers in 1282. Apart from endless perambulations (see the Epilogue), numerous works were consulted, including two recent ones, namely Ferdinando Maurici's *Palermo Araba: Una sintesi dell'evoluzione urbanistica 831-1072* (2015) and Henri Bresc's *Palermo al Tempo dei Normanni* (2012). The classic description is Salvadore Morso's *Descrizione di Palermo Antico* (1827).

The chief genealogical reference consulted was the original (1988) edition of *Heraldry of the Royal Families of Europe* ("Lines of Succession") by Jiri Louda and Michael Maclagan, but its details were confirmed by various sources. The prized first (1958) edition of Runciman's *Sicilian Vespers* includes three concertina fold-out pages of detailed pedigree charts. For heraldry during the Angevin era, see Mendola, Louis, "Italian Chiefs of Allegiance" in *Journal of Heraldic Studies* (Los Angeles 1985).

For the historiography of the War of the Vespers, in addition to the histories and commentaries by Runciman and Amari mentioned in the next section, see *De Rebus Siculis* (1558-1560) by Tommaso Fazello. The passage about John of Procida quoted earlier, along with an account of the war generally, will be found in Chapter 4 of "Book Eight" in the first complete (Latin) edition published in 1560, pages 488-490.

The last few decades have witnessed a sober reconsideration of the perspectives popularized by two or three unificationist curmudgeons during the nineteenth century. A good study is "La Leggenda del Vespro nella Storiografia Siciliana dei Secoli XIII-XV" in *Archivio Storico Messinese,* Volume 77 (Messina 1998), pages 49-76, by Ludovica De Nava. Also informative is *Gli Anni del Vespro: L'immaginario, la cronaca, la storia* (1989) by the late Salvatore Tramontana, who considers at some length the work of Steven Runciman (whose *Sicilian Vespers* was published in Italian translation in 1971) and the political influences of Michele Amari, as well as the theories of Filadelfo Mugnos.

For the recognition of the (modern) Sicilian language as part of the world's heritage by UNESCO, see Jones, Mari, *Policy and Planning for Endangered Languages* (Cambridge 2005), pages 124-127 *passim.*

French historians have shown a certain affinity for the branch of their native dynasty that ended up in Italy. Emile

Léonard's *Les Angevins de Naples* (1954) is highly informative; this was published in Italian translation in 1967. A more recent entry is Georges Jehel's *Les Angevins de Naples: Une Dynastie Européenne* (2014). A good biography of Charles I is Michel Grenon's *Charles d'Anjou: Frère conquérant de Saint Louis* (2012). See also Jean Dunbabin's book (below), available in English.

Jocelyn Hillgarth's paper, "The Problem of a Catalan Mediterranean Empire," in *English Historical Review,* supplement 8 (London 1975), brings perspective to its subject.

A good description of Sicily after 1282 is Vincenzo D'Alessandro's *Politica e Società nella Sicilia Aragonese* (1963). For contemporary developments in northern and central Italy, a fine introduction is John Larner's *Italy in the Age of Dante and Petrarch 1216-1380* (1983).

For a discussion and details on the rapport between Rome, Constantinople and Barcelona, see Richard Sternfeld's studies "Das Konklave von 1280 und die Wahl Martins IV" in *Mitteilungen für Österreichische Geschichtsforschung* number 31 (1910) and "Der Vertrag zwischen dem Paläologen Michael VIII und Peter von Aragon in Jahre 1281" in *Archiv für Urkundenforschung* number 6 (1918). A more generalist work, with an interesting narrative, is volume 1 of Kenneth M. Setton's *The Papacy and the Levant 1204-1571* (1976); see specifically pages 124-158. For a critical review of sources, including the *Rebellion,* see Antonino Franchi's "I Vespri Siciliani e le Relazioni tra Roma e Bisanzio: Studio Critico sulle Fonti" in *Quaderni di Ho Theologos* (Palermo 1984), published as a book in 1997.

A History of the Maghrib in the Islamic Period (1987) by Jamil Abun-Nasr very clearly explains the complexities in Tunisia and Algeria during the Vespers era.

The violent life of Guy de Montfort is outlined in John Maddicott's *Simon de Montfort* (1996). See also Louise Wilkinson's *Eleanor de Montfort: A Rebel Countess in Medieval England* (2012).

For information on coinage, see *Le Monete Siciliane dai Bizantini a Carlo I d'Angio 582-1282* and *Le Monete Siciliane dagli Aragonesi ai Borboni 1282-1836* (1959) by Rodolfo Spahr. A general survey of the coinage minted in Palermo from the Phoenician era until 1836, accompanied by numerous photographs, is Francesco Sapio Vitrano's "La Zecca di Palermo dai Primi Insediamenti Fenici al 1836" in *Archivio Storico Siciliano,* Series 3, Volume 20 (Palermo 1970), pages 107-202.

In addition to the aforementioned works, the books mentioned in the following section, "Suggested Reading," were useful. See Appendix 2 (Concordance) for information drawn from the registry of decrees of King Peter in 1282 and 1283, and other important sources for records from the thirteenth century.

A good architectural examination of Sicilian manorial castles (such as those of Caccamo and Mussomeli) is Rodolfo Santoro's "Architettura Castellana della Feudalità Siciliana" in *Archivio Storico Siciliano,* Series 4, Volume 7 (Palermo 1981), pages 59-113.

For notes on the origins of Sicilian heraldry, and the thesis that the art was not introduced in Sicily before 1175, see Mendola, Louis, "English and Italian Legacy of the Norman Knight Figures of Monreale" in *The Coat of Arms,* journal of The Heraldry Society, London, edited by John P. Brooke-Little, Norroy and Ulster King of Arms; NS Volume X, Number 166, Summer 1994 (ISSN 0010-003X), pages 245-254, extracted in *Sicilian Genealogy and Heraldry.*

For the statute on rape in the Constitutions of Melfi, see Powell, James, *The Liber Augustalis or Constitutions of Melfi* (1971), pages 23-26. For an insightful legal analysis on current rape law in the Italian Republic see Van Cleave, Rachel, "Rape and Querela Law in Italy: False Protection of Victim Agency" in *Michigan Journal of Gender and Law,* volume 13, number 273 (January 2007).

See Suggested Reading (following) for additional works, and appendices 2 and 4 (above) for further details.

For the record, the author wishes to state that he does not represent, nor has he ever been employed by, the Italian government or any of the governments, universities, agencies, institutions, organizations or persons mentioned in this book. He has never been affiliated with any political party (or movement) in Italy.

SUGGESTED READING

The following works will be useful to the reader seeking further information and context regarding the events leading up to the War of the Vespers and developments in its wake. These are listed here in order of their relevance.

For the convenience of an international readership the focus is placed on works in English. Medieval manuscripts, academic papers and non-English publications are mentioned in the Sources and appendices (above).

Varying views are expressed in the following works; for example, Runciman and Abulafia entertain slightly differing perspectives regarding Frederick II, whereas the bibliographies in their books reflect an unbiased choice of sources.

The listing of any book here, or in the preceding sections, does not necessarily imply your author's agreement with its general view or entire contents.

The Sicilian Vespers: A History of the Mediterranean World in the Later Thirteenth Century. (1958) Steven Runciman. The classic work on this period of Sicilian history and its impact on Europe and the Mediterranean for centuries to come. Highly recommended is the first edition, which includes three fold-out charts of detailed pedigrees between pages 338 and 339. Early paperback printings, beginning in 1982, have the same pagination and text but without the pedigrees and the third map (Greece and southern Italy).

Charles I of Anjou: Power, Kingship and State-Making in Thirteenth-Century Europe. (1998) Jean Dunbabin. A departure from the usual demonization of King Charles.

History of the War of the Sicilian Vespers. (1850) Michele Amari, translated by Anne Percy with commentary by the Earl of Ellesmere. Good English translation in three volumes; its commentary, based on Amari's Risorgimentalist political views, is highly biased.

The Kingdom of Sicily 1130-1860. (2015) Louis Mendola. The only general overview of the *Regnum* covering the entirety of its existence; note that the preceding chapters on the Normans and Swabians in *this* volume were extracted largely from this work.

Vanished Kingdoms. (2012) Norman Davies. The chapter on the Aragonese Empire is especially relevant to Sicily, though the one dedicated to Byzantium is also important.

A History of Aragon and Catalonia. (1933) Henry Chaytor. A very useful background work.

Emperor Michael Palaeologus and the West 1258-1282: A Study in Byzantine-Latin Relations. (1959) Deno John Geanakoplos. This book covers the background of an area of history rarely considered in detail by historians in western Europe or the Americas. By the same author are several other excellent books dedicated to allied studies, some with a focus on the Muslim world.

Sea Power in the Medieval Mediterranean: The Catalan-Aragonese Fleet in the war of the Sicilian Vespers. (2003) Lawrence Mott. A detailed analysis of the fleet, the ships and the battles.

The Eastern Schism: A Study of the Papacy and the Eastern Churches during the XIth and XIIth Centuries. (1955) Steven Runciman. A fine work that sets forth the background of the conflicts between Rome and Constantinople which shaped Mediterranean politics by 1282.

Frederick II: A Medieval Emperor. (1992) David Abulafia. Perhaps the definitive biography of Frederick II, King of Sicily, King of the Germans, King of Jerusalem, Holy Roman Emperor.

The Emperor Frederick II of Hohenstaufen, Immutator Mundi. (1972) Thomas Curtis van Cleve. A fine biography, different in tone from Abulafia's.

Muslims in Medieval Italy: The Colony at Lucera. (2003) Julie Anne Taylor. A good study of this subject, relevant as the Muslim community in Apulia survived into the Vespers period.

A History of the Maghrib in the Islamic Period. (1987) Jamil Abun-Nasr. A fine general work that provides background for the history of Tunisia and Algeria during the thirteenth century.

Germany in the High Middle Ages 1050-1200. (1986) Horst Fuhrmann. A very good background history for those interested in Frederick II and the Hohenstaufen dynasty.

A Short History of Byzantium. (1998) John Julius Norwich. This is the condensed version of a highly recommended three-volume edition: *The Early Centuries* followed by *The Apogee* and *The Decline and Fall.*

The Normans in the South. (1967) **The Kingdom in the Sun.** (1970) John Julius Norwich. Originally published in two volumes, this is the best generalist's history of Norman Sicily. A good introduction to the following two books dealing with the *Regnum.*

Roger II of Sicily: A Ruler between East and West. (2002) Hubert Houben. First published in German in 1997, this is an informative biography and a long glance into Roger's reign.

The Norman Kingdom of Sicily. (1992) Donald Matthew. A superb, scholarly overview of the Normans' multicultural Italian kingdom and its polyglot institutions.

Four Queens: The Provençal Sisters Who Ruled Europe. (2008) Nancy Goldstone. The captivating narrative concentrates on the period considered by Runciman in his *Sicilian Vespers.*

The Peoples of Sicily: A Multicultural Legacy. (2013) Louis Mendola and Jacqueline Alio. Sicily from the earliest times through the Middle Ages, with an emphasis on the island's pluralistic society from 1000 to 1300.

Women of Sicily: Saints, Queens and Rebels. (2014) Jacqueline Alio. Succinct profiles of, among others, Isabella of Aragon, sister of Peter III of Aragon and consort of Philip III of France, and Constance of Hohenstaufen, Peter's wife.

An Island for Itself: Economic Development and Social Change in Late Medieval Sicily. (2003) Stephan Epstein. A fine analysis with a focus on the period following the War of the Vespers.

The Decline and Fall of Medieval Sicily: Politics, Religion and Economy in the Reign of Frederick III, 1296-1337. (1995) Clifford Backman. Another fine analysis of what came after the Vespers.

The Middle Sea: A History of the Mediterranean. (2007) John Julius Norwich. Great context for understanding the role of the island at the center of this Sea.

The Great Sea: A Human History of the Mediterranean. (2011) David Abulafia. With Norwich's book (above), unsurpassed for placing Sicily into its Mediterranean and global context.

The Poetry of the Sicilian School. (1986) Frede Jensen. Translations of some important poems, with some original Middle Sicilian texts included.

The Kingdom of Sicily 1100-1250: A Literary History. (2005) Karla Mallette. One of the few surveys published thus far in English on this subject.

The Liber Augustalis or Constitutions of Melfi. (1971) James Powell. An excellent translation and analysis of the Constitutions of Melfi, the legal code of the *Regnum* until 1266.

Between Scylla and Charybdis: The Jews in Sicily. (2011) Shlomo Simonsohn. A fine reference. Professor Simonsohn's extensive research is reported at greater length in a highly detailed multi-volume opus, *The Jews in Sicily.*

Sicilian Genealogy and Heraldry. (2013) Louis Mendola. This guide for researchers presents information on the nobility and tracing the lineages of Sicilian families, some to the Vespers era.

INDEX

The focus of the following entries is the chronicle and the period immediately preceding it, as well as some general references. Persons are listed by given name or surname according to that by which they are best known, therefore *Dante* but *Boccaccio*, and *Simon of Lentini* rather than *Lentini, Simon of.* References in the Sicilian text of the *Rebellion* are not indexed here; for these, see the corresponding entry in English.

www.ingramcontent.com/pod-product-compliance
Lightning Source LLC
Chambersburg PA
CBHW032100180726
48284CB00002B/370

9781943639038